THE FIRST THEOLOGIANS

by

Charles W. Lowry

Gateway Editions
Chicago

Gateway Editions is an imprint of Regnery Gateway, Inc.
All inquiries should be directed to Regnery Gateway, Inc.,
950 North Shore Drive, Lake Bluff, IL 60044

Library of Congress Cataloging-in-Publication Data

Lowry, Charles Wesley.
    The first theologians.

    Includes bibliographical references.
    1. Bible. N.T.—Theology. 2. Theology, Doctrinal—
History—Early church, ca. 30-600. 3. Church history—
Primitive and early church, ca. 30-600.
4. Christianity—Origin. 5. Rome—Religion. 6. Rome—
Intellectual life. I. Title.
BS2397.L69 1986   230'.12   85-14866
ISBN 0-89526-804-3 (pbk.)

Contents

**Other books by
Charles W. Lowry**

William Temple: An Archbishop for All Seasons

To Pray or not to Pray! A Church-State Handbook

Communism and Christ
    (A Collier Books Paperback)

Christianity and Materialism

The Kingdom of Influence

The Trinity and Christian Devotion
    (Joint Lent Selection of
        The Archbishop of Canterbury
           and
        The Presiding Bishop, The Episcopal
    Church)

Anglican Evangelicalism
    (with others)

Encyclopedia of Religion (V.Ferm, Editor)
    18 articles

Preface

The late Professor C.H. Dodd, dean for a long generation of New Testament scholars, spoke provocatively
and prophetically of the Gospel of John in his inaugural
lecture at Cambridge University in 1935:

> I am disposed to think that the understanding of
> this Gospel is not only one of the outstanding tasks
> of our time, but the crucial test of our success or
> failure in solving the problem of the New Testa-
> ment as a whole. The Fourth Gospel may well
> prove to be the keystone of an arch which at pres-
> ent fails to hold together. If we can understand it,
> understand how it came to be and what it means,
> we shall know what early Christianity really was
> and not until in some measure we comprehend the
> New Testament as a whole shall we be in a posi-
> tion to solve the Johannine problem.[1]

It was only recently, in the library of St. Edward's
House, London, in the shadow of Westminster Abbey,
that I came across this statement. It excited me intensely. For in the present work, by an unusual and significant coincidence, I have been led as a theologian to
center on St. John's Gospel as the crux of doctrinal
development in the apostolic-subapostolic period and

[1] C.H. Dodd, *The Present Task in New Testament Studies,*
1936, p. 29.

7

as a major determining influence on all subsequent preoccupation with Christian doctrine. At the same time, the genius of this theologian-evangelist decreed that the relation of history and faith should remain at the center of attention for all generations.

I, of course, could not and do not claim to have made any substantial contribution to "solving the Johannine problem." It is probable that, strictly speaking, this problem is insoluble. It is like the question of the historical Socrates—not of who he was historically but of what his ideas and philosophical position were. Plato has adroitly, though no doubt unintentionally, arranged things in such a way as to render precise knowledge of the mind of the historical Socrates impossible.

But if we must be content with uncertainty from the standpoint of history literally understood, conceived of as facts devoid of interpretation, there is clear light on the figure of the Christ as the early Church was grasped by him and progressively visualized him. It is here that I may claim to have brought clarity and some order into an area that has become more and more confused with the avalanche of diverse Johannine literature poured forth during the past two generations.

The present work pivots, from a final point of view, on the Christology and theology of St. John. (For us the Fourth Evangelist, whoever he was, will always be St. John.) But it sets out from the problem, placed in intense focus by the great historian of dogma, Adolf von Harnack, of the genesis of Christian doctrine and the role played in this by Gnosticism and the great Gnostic mystagogues, Basilides and Valentinus, along with their disciples.

It was the position of Harnack that these Gnostics were the "first Christian theologians" and that they were pioneers in a process—that of Hellenization of the Gospel—which would ultimately produce in a milder form the system of classical Christian dogmas or doctrines. There is a theology behind everything, and Harnack's theology—his understanding ultimately of the Bible and of Jesus Christ—was set forth clearly in the book *What Is Christianity?* (the English translation of lectures delivered in German at the University of Berlin in 1899-1900). This was regarded, correctly, by the Roman Catholic Modernists—Loisy, Tyrrell, and von Hugel—as the classical manifesto of Liberal Protestantism.

From seminary days I have been intrigued by the extraordinary phenomenon of Gnosticism and Marcionism and the obscurity of church history during the first three quarters of the second century. The discovery at Nag Hammadi, in Egypt, in 1945 of some fifty Gnostic writings has intensified interest in this transitional period. Without illuminating the response of the Church to this titanic challenge, which was no less than the discarding of the Old Testament and the expulsion of the mother-faith of Judaism, the Nag Hammadi documents do throw light on the complexity of the second-century Church. They indicate the existence of a sweeping ferment in the experience and thinking of Graeco-Gentile Christians in the period immediately following what has been called "The Parting of the Ways" as between Jews and Christians, the Synagogue and the Church, which is reflected in John's Gospel and the Epistles of Ignatius of Antioch (martyred according to Eusebius in A.D. 108).

I have mentioned in the body of this book meeting Bishop John A.T. Robinson at Cambridge, England. I did not say that he had been stricken with cancer, and that the doctors had given him only six months to live. In fact he breathed his last just over six months after our June meeting, in December 1983.

After we parted, we corresponded, our first letters crossing. I sent him postcards from France and from London before flying home. After I got home I received a most unexpected letter from John (a very ill man, mind you), enclosing a Foreword he had written for an English edition of my Life of Archbishop Temple and a copy of a letter to his publisher urging its publication. This gracious act moved me deeply.

I have accordingly felt a bit guilty about disagreeing so flatly with John on his "Redating the New Testament." I am certain though that he knew he was sending up a trial balloon in that venturesome volume and would expect me to speak out with candor. I take this opportunity to pay an affectionate tribute to a gallant fellow pilgrim of "The Way" and an instant Friend. In his death I died more than a little.

It remains for me to express, however inadequately, my very large debt to a loving wife, Kate, who has borne much and given much in producing a flawless typescript from my crabbed handwriting. It seemed, I fear, as she labored away, an endless task.

By the time this book is out I shall have had my

80th birthday. In an adventurous life in which I have
dared to tread at times an uncharted path, a kind Lord
has never forsaken me or withdrawn his beautiful grace.
I see him ever more clearly as the Trinitarian Being who
from seminary days has commanded of me a fascinated
worship and an ardent devotion. It is my prayer that
this book will redound to his glory and the increase of
his Sovereignty—which is and must be the Sovereignty
of Love.

Charles W. Lowry

I have attempted in the work that follows to deline-
ate the situation in which the Church found itself during this period; then I have asked what were the
theological resources available for meeting this most
acute of all the crises known to Christian history. This
led me not forward, in the usual manner, to the so-called
Old Catholic Fathers such as Irenaeus, Tertullian, and
Hippolytus, but backward to the writings eventually
put together as our New Testament and, in particular,
to the theological geniuses Paul, Apollos (who has the
best claim to be the author of Hebrews), and John (the
Evangelist). Here, it seems to me, we encounter the first
and most seminal Christian theologians. We also confront and must reckon with the anchorage of Christian
thought in Christian history from the earliest time. This
is of crucial and decisive significance.

Finally, I make no apology for setting all this in
an exposition of the historical background of the advent of Jesus Christ and the eruption of the stubborn
and powerful movement we know as the Christian

Church. It is a truism to say that Christianity is above all an historical religion, and that the living God of the Bible is the Providential Determiner of history in its broad outcomes as well as the Creator and Ruler of all nature. It is no accident that modern science arose as a child of medieval Christendom. Here Professor A.N. Whitehead, under whom I was privileged to sit at Harvard, is the great authority. Steeped in the classics, and especially in Plato, Whitehead held that it was the rationalism of the theologians of the great Middle Age which tutored the mind of Europe in a transcendence of all dualisms and imparted to it the faith in reason without which science as we know it could not have come into being. (In a curious way this bears on and is clearly relevant to the great rescue of the Church from the threat of Gnostic dualism in the second century.)

I am under particular obligation to a distinguished divine and theologian of the great Lutheran Communion, the Rev. Dr. Wallace E. Fisher. He read this work in manuscript and encouraged me in the confidence that I was onto something of relevance and importance.

Two other friends who read the manuscript of this book in large part and encouraged me to persevere were the Rev. Nicholson B. White, now rector of St. Paul's Church, Cleveland Heights, Ohio, and Mr. Jack M. Goodwin, able librarian of the Virginia Theological Seminary, Alexandria.

Chapter One

The Romance of
Early Christian Literature

The body of literature that has come down to us as
the New Testament, or New Covenant, is the most
influential written work in the history of the world.
This is a fact that can hardly be challenged, even by
skeptics or agnostics or apostles of "scientism" or
converts to the superiority of some species of Eastern religion such as Zen Buddhism. Western civilization is the heir of Christianity; it came into being
as the successor of Graeco-Roman civilization, renewed, fertilized, and inspired by the teaching of
Christ and the organized movement called the Holy
Catholic and Orthodox Church.

The late Arnold Toynbee is the most distinguished and comprehensive historian of civilization
of this century, perhaps of all time. In his great
12-volume opus *A Study of History*, he lays out and dis-
sects the 21 civilizations that have left clear traces in
history. Of these he considers seven still to exist. The
names of these seven distinct, existing societies are
arresting from the point of view of religion. They are
Western Christian Society, Orthodox Christian So-

ciety (mainstream), Orthodox Christian Society (Russian), Islamic Society, Hindu Society, Far Eastern Society (Chinese), and Far Eastern Society (Japanese and Korean).

In his discussion of the relation of universal churches to civilizations, Toynbee writes: "If we cast our eye over the civilizations that were still alive in A.D. 1952, we shall see that every one of them had in its background some universal church through which it is affiliated to a civilization of an older generation. The Western and Orthodox Christian civilizations were affiliated through the Christian Church to the Hellenic civilization; the Far Eastern civilization was affiliated through the Mahayana to the Sinic civilization; the Hindu civilization through Hinduism to the Indic; the Iranic and Arabic through Islam to the Syriac."[1]

Earlier, in treating the disintegration of civilizations, Toynbee had written: "In contrast to the Hellenic Society our Western Society is one of those more generously endowed civilizations which have grown up under the aegis of a 'higher religion' and within the chrysalis of a universal church."[2]

The New Testament is the glory of the Christian Church. It is the Church's guide and compass, recalling her from time to time to her first love and setting forth a changeless pattern on which to model her life.

In this sense the Church is founded on Scripture, on the Old Testament as well as the New, it being clear that the Old is fulfilled in the New and that truth lies in the harmonization of the two. But the Church is a living organism that exists to worship and serve the living God. Her charter is not merely the New Covenant in the blood of Christ, founded on his death and resurrection. It is also the promise of the presence of the Spirit of Truth, God in an eternal form of being, proceeding from the Father, and reproceeding, as it were, from the Son in virtue of his redemptive life and work.

The greatest instance of this present power of the Spirit is the New Testament itself. This select, short library of spiritual literature did not come into existence as sheer miracle, constituting an exception to the laws of experience, thought, inspiration, and composition. The apostles, prophets, and evangelists who produced the New Testament Scriptures were not stenographers taking dictation from the Holy Spirit, as so many believers have thought and still think.

Our Protestant forefathers tended to think this way for a long time. Perhaps their Catholic forerunners did, too, though their way was eased by the old, old tradition of allegorization, which in practice meant the ability to find in a passage pretty much what you wanted to find. My favorite example of this delightful method of exegesis and exposition is the case of Savonarola, who was nothing if not an earnest and eloquent preacher. In Lent 1492 (the date is an easy one to remember), in Florence, he preached every day on the planks of Noah's Ark.

Then there came a revolutionary development. It was a child of the Enlightenment, a fruit of the Age of Reason. Men were led, especially in Germany, to study and examine critically the sacred Scriptures of the Old and New Testaments. They applied to these writings the accepted principles of historical and literary criticism.

The New Testament was produced in the Church, as the Old Testament had been within the nation-church of Israel. It was written by men who, under the inspiration of the Spirit, did not cease to be human. This stunning development, which we call the Higher Criticism, began approximately 200 years ago. This phrase came to be used in contrast to a form of critical study that was older, more self-evident, and less controversial. In consequence, it acquired the name of the Lower Criticism.

The latter discipline is concerned with texts: the comparison of manuscripts and the effort, through the application of common sense and scientific criteria, to reach textual correctness. Textual criticism is necessary because of all the centuries before the discovery of movable type and what we know as printing. The laborious copying out of books by hand as the basis of publication multiplied the incidence of errors. It also afforded opportunity on a wide scale for the injection by scribes of subjective preferences, in the interest of orthodoxy or even of heresy.

Textual criticism is older than the Higher Criticism. Translation required it, for some text had to be used when Jerome prepared his Vulgate Bible. Even before Jerome, an Origen had had his Hexapla or six-columned Bible. This was an attempt to provide a revised text of the Septuagint translation of the Old Testament. Origen is said to have labored for 28 years of his life on this monumental task and to have learned Hebrew in order to qualify himself for it. Each page of this work consisted of six columns, beginning with the current Hebrew text.

The overture or prologue in the drama of the Higher Criticism was a book published in 1771 by the Prussian Lutheran, Johann Salomo Semler. It was entitled *Abhandlung von freier Untersuchung des Kanon (Treatise on the Free Investigation of the Canon.)* In this seminal work Semler, a professor at Halle, showed that the Canon was not an edifice erected miraculously at a single stroke. On the contrary, it issued out of a human and historical process that took centuries.

The Church had not even been of one mind regarding this pivotal matter. The churches of Alexandria, Antioch, and Jerusalem had differences regarding certain books. Rome at one time seems to have frowned on the Apocalypse, as had other churches. It was a controversial work, as was 2 Peter. Hebrews, James, and 3 John were also slow to win universal acceptance.

Moreover, writings finally rejected for the Canon were accounted as canonical in some church circles. These were principally 1 Clement, The Epistle of Barnabas, and The Shepherd of Hermas. The epistle ascribed to Barnabas, probably in reaching for apostolic authority, is quoted as scriptural by Clement of Alexandria and is referred to as a Catholic Epistle[3] by Origen, also of Alexandria.

It is noteworthy that in the Codex Sinaiticus the Epistle of Barnabas is included with the New Testament, following the Apocalypse. There is no indication that it is not in the Canon. Codex Alexandrinus contains the text of 1 and 2 Clement[4] at the end of the New Testament.

The Canon of the New Testament was the result of a growing consensus, not of any single act or edict. The impetus to an authoritative rule in the matter came from the confusion and peril of the second century. The idea of a body of sacred Christian writings forming a second or New Covenant originated by analogy from the Old Testament, the accepted, first Bible of the Church, but called in question by the Gnostics and the Marcionites.

Just as right authorship—Mosaic or prophetic—was crucial in attaining canonical status in the Old Testament for a given book, so in the New Testament the demand was for apostolic authority. This, as we shall see, was fundamental as a motive in the writing of much of the literature of the New Testament. It was all-determinative in the selection of the canonical books.

We have still to trace the creation of this unique body of literature. It is a thrilling, an amazing, and a fascinating story. Not all the standards accepted and employed comply with the code of the literary world we know. But the result—the New Testament as it came to be recognized with the Canon chosen and closed—was magnificent.

If we compare the books that did not make it with those that did, we can hardly doubt or criticize the leading of the Holy Spirit. There is not a canonical writing that is unworthy or unexciting. The mark of inspiration is intrinsic to each one.

The late Professor Thomas Kinloch Nelson of the Virginia Theological Seminary was wont to talk of vital inspiration in contrast to the verbal inspiration of Scripture. It is a sound distinction. The poet Samuel Taylor Coleridge, who was a philosopher-theologian as well of great parts, had a not dissimilar way of interpreting biblical inspiration. "In short, whatever *finds* me bears witness that it has proceeded from a Holy Spirit . . . . in the Bible there is more that *finds* me than I have experienced in all other books put together . . . . the words of the Bible find me at greater depths of my being."[5]

Clearly the human factor is not eclipsed by divine inspiration either in the reading of Scripture or in the minds and hearts of the writers of the book brought together in the Bible. We are concerned here with the literature of the New Testament. How did it come to be written? What was the process of its gradual formation?

If we examine early Christianity phenomenologically, that is, as it appears and is manifest in its totality, what we see is a living movement, the nascent Christian Church, called into being by the Spirit of the God of Israel and of the whole universe, as a result of the life, death, and resurrection of Jesus the Messiah long foretold in the Hebrew or Old Testament Scriptures. The purpose of the Church is (a) to witness by preaching and in worship to the good news of the saving acts of God; (b) to extend in this way the effectual reign of a loving God, not only to all Israel but to the nations of the Gentiles; and (c) to build up in the power of the Spirit and in faith, hope, and love the community of believers who are the called of God in Christ.

In the course of time, in response to its needs and the serving of its divine purpose, this Church threw off literature of diverse sorts, some of which it eventually adopted as scriptures forming the New Testament or New Covenant. The Canon of the New Testament was not finally settled until the fourth century, but this is misleading from an existential standpoint.

The letters of Paul were influential from an early time, but probably not on a wide scale until nearly a generation after his death as a martyr. Edgar J. Goodspeed of Chicago has made out a very strong case for the publication of the corpus of Pauline Letters somewhere around A.D. 90.[6] Goodspeed is influenced by the lack of Pauline influence on the Synoptic evangelists and by the sudden eruption of this influence in various epistles and letters (a useful distinction, epistles being tracts or sermons dressed up as letters but not real letters in the manner of Paul's). It is also noteworthy that collections of epistles or letters became a vogue: Revelation, with seven churches corresponding to the seven in Paul's correspondence; the Pastoral Epistles; the Johannine Epistle and Letters; and early in the second century the Epistolary Letters of Ignatius.

It is not necessary to bear down quite as heavily as Goodspeed does on the role of collections and publication, though it seems to me indubitable that the early Church coming under Greek influence took advantage of publication and culture, and that this had a lot to do with the extraordinary success of the Christian enterprise. Goodspeed speculates that it was the publication of Luke-Acts, with the prominence and heroic stature of Paul in the second volume of this work, which led to the collecting and publishing of Paul's letters, introduced by a kind of Pauline Encyclical, our Ephesians, worked up by the collector-editor.

It is possible that Hebrews, for example, which is anonymous not apostolic in a claimed authorship, was written under the influence of Paul by someone (I believe Apollos) who knew him and also differed with him or at least emphasized other aspects of Christian truth. Also, 1 Peter and James might well have reflected knowledge of specific Pauline Letters as distinct from the published collection. But Paul's new prominence through the Acts could well have been a stimulative factor. Certainly the revival and surge of the epistolary form in early Christian literature is most striking.

The Gospel as a literary form will have a run of popularity in the second century, but there will be a strong motive at the same time for limiting those that are authentic and canonical to four. This comes out in Irenaeus' quaint contention that there can be only four Gospels because there are only four directions.

Undoubtedly there was a Fourfold Gospel Corpus—a collection into a single document— published and circulated at some point in the second century. It was later than the Pauline collection but may have been comparatively early. Harnack thought that it took place in Asia Minor in the reign of Hadrian (A.D. 117-138);[7] Goodspeed dates it 117-125. Justin Martyr (c. 150) probably knew all four Gospels and states it as an established custom that they were read at the Eucharist. His pupil Tatian produced, c. 170, his *Diatessaron*, or Harmony of the Four Gospels.

What we have, then, in the literature that became the New Testament is a body of letters, 21 in number, written by or under the names of Apostles between A.D. 50 and 130 (the latest of these, 2 Peter, may be a few years later); four Gospels written between A.D. 65 and 100; a church history that deals with the early years of the Church in Jerusalem and after that is basically a chronicle of the activities of Peter and Paul, published in the 80s;[8] and the Apocalypse or Revelation, produced in Asia in the early 90s by the fierceness of persecution in the reign of Domitian.

This is our New Testament, winnowed competitively in an age of Greek culture but Roman order and communications, and chosen by the Church under the guidance of the Spirit of Truth to be the Book of the New Covenant. There is nothing in history comparable to this body of literature; it is *sui generis* and its composition and preservation constitute a thrilling romance. Further, for 200 years now the white heat of fierce literary and historical criticism has beat upon it. Some of this is conjectural and speculative, inevitably; but there are tested, firm results that are very enlightening and that strengthen the essential foundations of the Christian faith.

The Christian Church produced the literature, but in turn we see the Church through the literature, as if we were gazing in through windows. We see three strata or stages in the gripping story of early Christianity:

1. Jesus and His Ministry
2. The Era of the Apostles: 30 to 70
3. The Subapostolic Age: 70-120

The crux of the situation historically, in the light of the Higher Criticism, is the first of these strata: Jesus and His Ministry. It comes as a surprise to the

uninitiated lay person that the earliest Christian literature is not the Gospels but the epistles of Paul. Yet
such is the case. Paul wrote his remarkable letters to
churches and individuals over a ten- or twelve-year
period beginning in A.D. 50. No Gospel as such was
then in existence. But this does not mean that the
materials that were going to be put into the compi-
lations and compositions called Gospels were nonex-
istent. These materials—in the form of sayings and
teachings of Jesus and reminiscences of his ministry,
particularly its last phase of suffering, death, and
resurrection appearances—were handed down orally
through careful and perhaps systematic memori-
zation.

This was the first phase of Christian tradition.
There were several reasons for this. The first is that
Christianity began in a period of considerable ferment and apocalyptic expectation in Palestine. Not
all Jews were caught up in it, but large numbers were
and the plain people were highly suggestible. The
Church began as a movement—a messianic movement—within Judaism. There was neither time nor
mood for writing.

A second reason is the prevalence among the
Jewish people at that time of ear-memory.[9] We are
people who read and are dependent on our eyes.
When we want to remember something, we say,
"Let me see that." We need to see it to be sure of
retaining it. With the Jews in the time of Jesus and
after, this was not the case. Ear-memory was highly

developed. Memory in general was better than with us. Minds were not cluttered up with miscellaneous trifles as they are in our culture, and the tempo of life was very different. There was time for reflection and remembering.

As the disciples of Jesus recovered from the trauma of his shattering death and became convinced that he was alive and had commissioned them to be authoritative witnesses, or apostles, they would naturally dwell on the things he had said during the times of their intimate association. His method of teaching by parables made recollection easier and more vivid. The great focus of the parables and the heart of his teaching, the Kingdom of God, also without doubt assisted and stimulated the memories of his followers.

At some point—we do not know how early but it could have been in the great decade of the 50s when Paul was so brilliantly active—the motive of accurate preservation of the Lord's teaching came into play. Someone, very probably Matthew the Apostle, drew up in writing a collection of the sayings of Jesus. Papias, bishop of Hierapolis in Phrygia (Asia Minor), writing about A.D. 130, says: "So then Matthew composed the oracles (*logia*) in Hebrew, and everyone interpreted them as he could."

The same authority singles out Mark, also, and associates him with Peter. This is the famous quotation. "This also the elder John said: Mark having become the interpreter of Peter wrote accurately everything that he remembered of the things that were either said or done by Christ; but however not in order.''

Mark we now know was the first Gospel to be written. Both Matthew and Luke based the narrative portion of their account on Mark, inserting large blocks of sayings and teachings at various points. Any person can see this for himself if he will look at the three Gospels arranged in parallel columns. He will find that almost the whole of Mark (90 percent) is incorporated into Matthew and more than one-half of Mark into Luke (60 percent).

The student of Matthew and Luke, arranged for ready comparison, will find there are numerous sayings of Jesus that are common to both works. This led to the theory of a second common source, Q from the German word *Quelle*, or source. Today, many scholars are discarding this hypothesis as unnecessary and unhelpful. There are so many sayings that are peculiar to each of these Gospels that other sources in any case must be predicated. There is also no reason why both writers should not have tapped the common oral tradition or various collections based on it.

Current scholarship stresses the importance of the point of view from which each Gospel is developed, using materials at hand or at least those favored. Of critical moment is the role of the final writer, or redactor. This person, in the view of the criticism known as *redactionsgesdchichte*, or redaction-history, puts upon the Gospel its decisive thrust and impress. He is the arbiter of its particular purpose.

Thus Mark, produced in Rome, likely reflecting reminiscences of Peter, is the Book of the Hidden Messiah. It answers questions the mixed, Jewish and Gentile, Christian congregation of the world's capital were asking, such as (1) How could the career of one whom we know was the Messiah have ended in disgraceful ignominy and a criminal's death? (2) Why did the Messiah not claim the title earlier and secure fuller recognition during his earthly life, at least among his disciples? (3) What was the attitude of the Messiah toward the Jewish Law? and (4) Why is it necessary for the sake of Christ, the Messiah, to suffer unpopularity, persecution, and even death?

The answer to such questions is given in our earliest Gospel by an author who was most probably the founder of this unique literary genre. In his bracing work he gives his answer not abstractly but in dramatic terms, in the kingly example of a majestic figure who first assails the powers of evil, putting them to flight, and then accepts with grace as from the Father suffering, contempt, disgrace, and even—as the climax of the narrative of the Passion—the sense of dereliction, of awful separation from God. No other word from the Cross is given in this Gospel and the sense of tragedy is truly dreadful.

This dominating and surprising aspect of Mark's Gospel, which Matthew will retain but Luke and John will abandon, is one of the pillar or foundation reasons for trust in the integrity of the essential Gospel tradition. It is inconceivable that the Church, the community of faith, would have instinctively constructed the narrative of the Passion in this manner.

This consideration, together with the incomparable style and character of the parabolic teaching of Jesus, to say nothing of his exalted ethic, constitutes the bridge connecting the Jesus of history with the Christ of the Church's faith and worship. The latter, admittedly, is dominant in the letters of Paul, and the normal layman, again, is bound to be surprised when he comes up against this fact, remembering that these letters are the *earliest* Christian literature.

The Gospels, it is clear, are at once biographical and theological. They partake both of history and of faith. They are not biographies in our sense of lives. The early Christians, and indeed the ancients, did not generally have our interest in personal behavior or our psychological curiosity. They were more practical and moralistic. They sought instruction and examples. The Christians were concerned with who Jesus was, what his relation was to God the Father, and why he was sent into the world.

Herein—along with the need, always present, of conduct, guidance, and example—we have the motivation of the Evangelists, the final redactors or author-editors of the Gospels, whatever their actual names and identities. The Gospels are not primarily biographical but are written, as Johannes Weiss said, "from faith to faith."

Mark is a theological pamphlet. Matthew is a churchman's handbook—a guide to faith and conduct. Luke is a history with a humanistic tinge and an apologetic design. It is the first installment of the first Christian *apologia*—a writing structured and calculated to meet doubts and difficulties in the way of accepting the *fides bona et veritas* (the good faith and truth) of Christianity.

Thus Luke, no doubt the Syrian or Greek physician who was the companion of Paul, had an ambitious design. In his Gospel, followed by the Acts of the Apostles, he undertook to relate with vigor and liveliness as well as truth the story of the Christian movement from the births of John the Baptist and Jesus, to Paul the Roman citizen's appeal to Ceasar and adventurous journey to Rome. Of notable importance, not only for his work but from the angle of understanding the general literary situation in the church and the world around A.D. 80, are Luke's two prefaces. In line with Roman custom, they honor an important person, his Excellency, Theophilus. In addition, the first preface posits the existence of numerous written sources based on traditions handed down from eyewitnesses and servants of the Word. Luke accordingly is in a position, he is saying, to give an authentic and reliable account of the things that have happened.

There remains the Fourth Gospel, John's Gos-

Gospel of John

pel as it was known to the church fathers and will
always be known to the Christian faithful. Here we
have, as the Higher Criticism has recognized from
the beginning, a horse of a different color. It is a
Gospel. It could not have been written had the form
and type of writing known as the Gospel not been
familiar to its author. It is likely that he knew the
earlier related Gospels which we call collectively the
Synoptic Gospels. Many scholars think he knew
Mark and Luke but not Matthew. He is bound to
have known not only the form but the general content of the tradition. Otherwise, we cannot account
for conspicuous omissions such as the institution of
the Eucharist.

John's Gospel is both like and different from
its predecessors. It both continues trends, christological and theological, which we can discern in them
and strikes out in a new, qualitatively unique direction. The attitude toward history and the humanity
of Christ is different; yet both are asserted with vigor
and surely a major design of the Evangelist is to refute and confound Gnostic error.

The Christ of John's Gospel is a figure at once
mystical and metaphysical. At the same time he is
firmly rooted in the world of matter and society, of
friendship and love, of teaching and controversy, of
the reality but also the glory of sacrifice.

This Gospel has the lineaments of a profound
portrait, rooted in a human and historical being but
interpreted with a firm independence so as to bring

out the ultimate truth and meaning of his life and personhood. The Christ of John is a person conscious from the beginning of being the Messiah of Israel, the true and only Son of God, and an absolute, divine teacher, descended from the heavenly sphere, who speaks and acts always in this character, as such a being must have spoken and acted in the fulfillment of his universal, yet specialized mission.

It will forever be significant to the point of miracle that John's Gospel begins where Genesis begins and with the same inevitable words, ''In the beginning ....'' This suggests something of extreme importance, that the Evangelist who was the final redactor-author of this Gospel was a great artist as well as quite probably a Christian prophet. The Gospel of John is a supreme work of art—in this respect above everything else in the New Testament and possibly, unless we except the Book of Job, in the entire Bible.

John the Evangelist is also a brilliant, creative theologian. He builds on the thought of Paul and the unknown author of the Epistle to the Hebrews, whom I like to think was Apollos of Alexandria. But he soars above them both, not only in height and sheer brilliance of conception, but in universal outreach. This is the thinker—no doubt essentially intuitive, always the prophet-artist—who had the wit to marry Hebraism to Hellenism by introducing the Logos doctrine of Philo and Stoic Platonism, reaching back to Heraclitus, most luminous of philosophers prior to Plato. His predecessors had reached out in this direction, Paul notably in Colossians and "Apollos" at the beginning of his original epistle, but it was John of Ephesus who brought about the consummation of the marriage and set the new religion, Christianity, firmly on the path of drawing upon Greek philosophy as well as the Hebrew Scriptures. It is perhaps not too much to say, altering the figure, that Christianity marched over the bridge that John erected to conquer the world and become the paramount influence on human history.

There is much we have not touched on except in the most general way in the literature of the New Testament. We have, however, said enough to make a main point clear, that in this literature we are to gaze as through various windows at the life and thought and people of the early Church.

This is perhaps most vivid and immediately apparent in the epistles of Paul—the ones certainly written by him and excluding 1 and 2 Timothy, Titus, and possibly Ephesians, though I lean toward the view that the last was by the apostle and was his climactic work. But all the books of the New Testament have this function of being windows on the living Church. This is the wonder and romance of this literature. It is unique in all the world. One cannot doubt that its writers were in a special manner inspired by the Holy Spirit.

The Church also, which was responsible for the ultimate Canon, was led by the Spirit of Truth in the slow and tedious business of settling what writings were, and were not, to be regarded as Holy Scripture, joining the Jewish or Old Testament Scriptures.

It remains to note and pay my respects to a trend in the continuing Higher Criticism of the New Testament. There is much movement and much ferment just now in this area. The discovery of the Gnostic Gospels and other writings at Nag Hammadi in Upper Egypt, hard upon the find of the Dead Sea Scrolls, has intensified this critical current.

Basically, this is all to the good. Out of contention and stimulus to new theories and hypotheses, truth comes in the end. The whole amazing, at times diverting, story of the Higher Criticisim validates this view. But it is necessary for the churchman to keep his shirt on—figuratively, of course. He must keep to the tested course and view, and avoid jumping at every novelty of outlook and suggested theory.

A prime example is the recent revolutionary redating of virtually the entire New Testament by Bishop John A. T. Robinson, author of *Honest to God* and currently chaplain and fellow of prestigious Trinity College, Cambridge. Bishop Robinson sets out his extreme conclusions in a book published in 1976 entitled *Redating the New Testament*.

In this audacious volume Bishop Robinson has confronted a curious fact, certainly not new. This is the silence, overtly and generally, of New Testament writers respecting the fall of Jerusalem and destruction of the Temple in the A.D. 70. Actually,

it is far from certain that all the Evangelists were
unaffected by this catastrophic occurrence. I was
taught in seminary 55 years ago that Mark showed
no awareness of the apocalyptic desolation of the
Holy City, but that Matthew did. I am aware, of
course, of the tenuous character of all the evidence
bearing on this issue.

At all events Bishop Robinson is convinced that
there is no clear reflection in the New Testament of
the fall of Jerusalem and of the Temple. It is this
silence that has led him to the view that very probably—he realizes at times how temerarious is his
grand sweep backwards of all the writings—the entire
New Testament was written and in place prior to
the year 70. Robinson even includes 2 Peter and Jude
in the spring of 65. The Pastoral Epistles are restored
to Paul as author and *mirabile!* the earliest of these
is seen as 1 Timothy and dated 55, before 2
Corinthians, Galatians, and Romans.
is seen as 1 Timothy and dated 55, before 2 Corinthians, Galatians, and Romans.

The Gospel of John is estimated at c.-40-65 +
and 2, 3, and 1 John are placed between 60 and 65.
Robinson believes that all, though not Revelation,
are by John the son of Zebedee who is the beloved
disciple. His specific dating in this (page 307 *Redating
the New Testament*):

      30-50 formation of the Johannine tradi-
              tion and proto-Gospel in Jerusalem;

50-50 first edition of our present Gospel
in Asia Minor;

60-65 2, 3, and 1 John; and

65 + the final form of the Gospel, with
prologue and epilogue.

Bishop Robinson makes this extraordinary statement: "I believe that John represents in date, as in theology, not only the *omega* but the *alpha* of the New Testament development. He bestrides the period like a colossus and marks out its span" (page 311). This span he locates as the period between two dramatic moments in Jerusalem "which boldly we may date with unusual precision," namely, 9 April 30 when "early on the Sunday morning, while it was still dark," one man "saw and believed" (John 20: 1-9) and 26 September 70, when in "the dawn of the eighth day of the month Gorpiaeus broke upon Jerusalem in flames" (quoting Josephus, B J 6. 407).

The other Gospels Robinson sees as coming into being over about the same stretch of years as John's, though apparently he would grant the genesis of John a slight priority over the other and put its final form with Prologue and Epilogue. He would put the Johannine tradition on all fours with the Synoptic and think of the two as harmoniously complementary. The earliest New Testament book on Robinson's redating is the Epistle of James. He places it ahead of Paul's Epistles in c. 47-48 and opts for James of Jerusalem, the brother of Jesus, as its author. The date suggested for Hebrews is c. 67.

My first reaction on coming across Bishop Robinson's brainstorm regarding the fall of Jerusalem and consequent scheme of radical redating of the New Testament was one of being intrigued, though skeptical. I have now reread his book carefully, in connection with writing this chapter; and I am convinced that it is a flash in the pan, inherently unlikely and open to objections that are overwhelming in cogency.

My basic feeling is that the bishop's reaction to tempo and time necessary for development is all wrong. Development is written deeply into the corpus of the New Testament. Admittedly, it is clearer and more certain in some areas than in others, and there may be points where it is uncertain. But if we look at the Pastorals (1 and 2 Timothy and Titus) and at the Catholic epistles, especially Jude and 2 Peter, and at Revelation, we cannot escape the feeling that atmosphere has changed, and we are in an age that is very different from the period before 70. And such changes take time; they do not happen all at once.

There is also the question of style of writing, of vocabulary, and of ideas. Robinson sweeps these all too neatly under the rug. In compressing so much in so short a space, alike in accomplishment and in environmental change, he overloads the period before 70. It will not bear the weight he puts upon it. And the cupboard of the decades following 70 is left too bare. This, I believe, was a time of flowering and maturing in the Church. There was a certain settling down after the first generation of enthusiasm. No doubt a time of decline was also in preparation, the kind of hardening and falling away reflected in the Pastorals and some, at least, of the Catholic Epistles.

There is, in addition, the problem of the rising tide of Gentile influence and the fading out of Jewish adherence in the Church. This was an inexorable but surely not a rapid current. The Gospel of John reflects the basic shift here more clearly than does any other New Testament document. Matthew, on the one side, and Mark and Luke, on the other, reflect interim stages related to geographical areas. Matthew is directed, apologetically, to the Jews; it is concerned, as Hebrews is, with the relations of Christianity and Judaism. Mark and still more Luke show the effect of Gentile presence and pressure. The Jesus of Mark is freer in what he says about the Law. Luke is concerned with what the Romans think and with emphasis on the responsibility of the Jews for the condemnation and crucifixion of Christ.

In John, the sharpest controversy is the one between Jesus and the Jews, regarded apparently as an opposing collective entity. It is difficult not to see this as reflecting the period of the parting of Church and Synagogue and ensuing bitterness between the two. And it is tied up specifically with the person of Christ—with his divinity and deity. To the Jews this is blasphemy, and they are pictured as wanting to kill Jesus in consequence of his claims about himself.

There was a period when it was felt that John was close to Paul. Harnack wrote that the Christ of the Fourth Gospel was "a speaking, acting Pauline Christ." While there are elements of agreement and affinity between the two theologians, the differences are great. Paul is early and is a pioneer. As a thinker, he remains very much the rabbi even though he sees the dispensation of the Law as over and is absolute in his conviction that God has acted decisively in Jesus, Messiah and Lord.

It is easier to feel the contrast between St. John and St. Paul than it is to bring it down to concrete terms. The late Archbishop William Temple felt this. In the preface to his *Readings in St. John's Gospel,* he confesses his love for this Gospel above all other books. He adds: "Bishop Gore once said to me that he paid visits to St. John as to a fascinating foreign country, but he came home to St. Paul. With me the precise opposite is true. St. Paul is the exciting, and also rather bewildering, adventure; with St. John I am at home."

I believe we can say objectively that John is at the apex of the New Testament and of early Christianity. He is the end of the line, the omega of this book. But he is not the alpha, either chronologically or theologically. On this I am compelled to differ with Bishop Robinson.

If one wishes to stick as close to history as possible, if his concern is the Jesus of history, he must go to the Synoptic tradition, to Matthew, Mark, and Luke. John will raise far more questions than he can answer. This is true irrespective of the knowledge of Jerusalem shown in the Fourth Gospel and of the distinct possibility that John the Evangelist, who must have known other Gospels (presumably at the least Mark and Luke), was able to correct the Synoptists at certain points, principally the length of our Lord's ministry and the day of the Crucifixion—on the eve of the Passover rather than on the Passover itself.

If, however, we ask, Who was Jesus Christ, and what was his meaning? we are obliged to turn to John and come to rest in the Son and the Father with whom he is one. The greatness of this Gospel is above all, the triune God whom it unveils and, next to that, the artistry and profundity with which this unique literary *genre* is used to portray Christ and the Church by projecting the Word-made-flesh onto the screen of life and action and love and sacrifice.

The man who was used of the Spirit to accomplish this, John the Evangelist, was indeed "a religious genius of the first order" (W.F. Howard) and a very great theologian, supreme in the first century, and "perhaps the greatest theologian in all the history of the Church."[10]

Of these things we shall have a great deal to say further on in this book.

Note on Theology and Theologian

John among the Evangelists became known by the church fathers as *Theologos*. Robert Mackintosh states that this epithet for him may go back as far as Papias (*Encyclopaedia Britannica, 11 ed., s.v. "Theology"*). This, of course, is because of John's Christology, because he declares that Jesus the Christ is the Logos made flesh, and thus is clearly divine as well as human.

The Apologists, according to Harnack, are the first to employ the ideas of *theologein* and *theologia*, but they do so in a narrow sense (*History of Dogma* Vol. II, p. 202, n.1). Both Clement and Origen refer to John's Gospel as "spiritual," and Origen also in his Commentary on John calls it "the eternal Gospel," (I,9). In this Commentary he uses the word *theologia* at least once. In the preface of the Fifth Book, addressed to Ambrose, he complains: "You are not content to fulfill the office, when I am present with you, of a taskmaster to drive me to labor at theology." In his Commentary on Matthew, written later, I have found another rather curious use of the same word. The context is the Transfiguration. "When therefore you see any one not only with a thorough understanding of the theology concerning Jesus . . . do not hesitate to say (his) garments have become white as the light" (XII, 38).

Saints Athanasius and Gregory Nazianzen received the title of *Theologos* and St. John Chrysostom (344-407) used *Theologia* to indicate the divine nature of Christ. It is not until Abelard (1079-1142), who used *Theologia Christiana* and *Introduction ad Theologiam* as book titles, that we encounter the more generalized use which will in time become fixed. St. Thomas Aquinas (1226-74) uses *Summa Theologiae* as the title of his compendious, magisterial work, but according to the new Catholic Encyclopedia (S.V. "Theology") preferred the term "sacred doctrine" for the subject matter covered in the *Summa*. St. Augustine before him had noted the threefold Stoic division of theologies, but preferred "Christian doctrine" as covering the field of Christian teaching (*Civ. Dei* 6.5 Cf. *De Doctrina Christiana*).

Reverting to the period with which we are concerned in this book, it was Philo Judaeus (13 B.C.-A.D. 50) who seems to have introduced the word *theologos* into the Jewish tradition and at that same time very possibly influenced early Christianity. He used this designation for poets, for Moses (the preeminent philosopher, he believed, of all time), and for the Greek philosophers (Mackintosh, op.cit. supra).

Religion with the Greeks was not overdeveloped; they tended to leave theology to the poets and to accept the mythology of Homer and Hesiod without demur. It is here that Plato, not surprisingly, looms large on the horizon of thought. He coins the terms *theologia* in the *Republic*, as Eric Voegelin points out in *The New Science of Politics* (p.70). The context is the rejection of the traditional poets as immoral and unsuitable for the young in the ideal State.

Socrates says, "You and I, Adeimantus, at this moment . . . are founders of a State: now the founders of a State ought to know the general forms (types) of theology in which poets should cast their tales, and the limits which must be observed by them.

"Very true, he said; but what are these *typoi peri theologias* (types of theology) which you mean?

"Something of this kind, I replied:—God is always to be represented as he truly is," (II,379).

In his *Metaphysics* Aristotle builds on Plato. He states clearly that "divine power cannot be jealous," and he adds that there is a divine science which it is appropriate for God to have" (I, 2). Further along (VI, 1), the Stagirite lays it out systematically. "There must then, be three theoretical philosophies, mathematics, physics, and what we may call theology . . . . We answer that if there is no substance other than those which are formed by nature, natural science will be the first science; but if there is an immovable substance, the science of this must be prior and must be first philosophy . . . and it will belong to this to consider being *qua* being—both what it is and the attributes which belong to it *qua* being."

It was this teaching that drew the Angelical Doctor, St. Thomas, to Aristotle. It helps to explain how Harnack, with his German background of systematic theology, could call—we believe erroneously—the great speculative Gnostic thinkers, the first Christian theologians. It explains why a Paul Tillich was so obsessed to spin off an elaborate systematic theology as the crown of his brilliant career. And the whole excursis supplies a background for the thesis that in Paul, Apollos, and John, we have, effectually, *The First Theologians*.

1. *A Study of History*, Abridgement by D.C. Somervell, Vol. II, p. 82.

2. *Ibid*, Vol. I, p. 454

3. Seven books of the New Testament came to be called general or Catholic Epistles: 1 and 2 Peter, James, Jude, and 1, 2, and 3 John.

4. *2 Clement* is universally regarded as later than *1 Clement* (A.D. 96) and as written by someone other than Clement, the fourth Bishop of Rome.

5. *Confessions of an Inquiring Spirit*, Letters I and II.

6. *New Solutions of New Testament Problems*, Chicago, 1927. *The Meaning of Ephesians*, Chicago, 1933. *New Chapters in New Testament Study*, New York, 1937. *An Introduction to the New Testament*, Chicago, 1937 (15th Impression, 1963). See also *Anatomy of the New Testament*, R. A. Spivey and D.M. Smith, Jr., Macmillan, London, 1969, pp. 354, 396.

7. A. Wikenhauser, *New Testament Introduction*, New York, 1958 (6th Impression, 1967), p. 27. He states that John was published in Middle Egypt shortly after A.D. 100 (this is based on the Rylands Papyrus fragment) and that our four canonical Gospels were known to the author of an apocryphal Gospel published in Egypt not later than A.D. 150 (pp. 26-27, cf. p. 86).

8. It should always be kept in mind that Acts was originally published with the Gospel of Luke as a kind of Volume II.

9. cf. the Oxford scholar, O.E. Nineham, *Saint Mark*, pp. 50-51. He speaks of "the wonderfully retentive memory of the Oriental, who, being unable to read and write, had perforce to cultivate accuracy of memory." He adds, "It would be quite in

keeping with Jewish habit if some of the tradition, especially the tradition of our Lord's words, had been formally committed to memory by groups of Christians and later reproduced with remarkable accuracy.''

10. The view of C.K. Barrett (The Gospel according to St. John, p. 114), quoted from R. E. Brown and cited critically by Robinson, page 309.

Chapter Two

The Involved Background: Reason Gives Way to Faith

The first Age of Reason had its beginning around 600 B.C. It initially took the form of turning from "theologians" with their myths and fables to the "physicians," as Aristotle called them, men who saw the physical world as the real world and sought to make sense of it.

It was thus that philosophy came into being. Philosphy, always and everywhere, is the creation of reason. It represents the mind of man seeking to grasp and understand what is by the faculties of reason and logic. This sweeping effort was the gift of the Greeks to civilization.

It was in Ionia, on the seaboard of Asia Minor, that philosophy had its birth. It is a striking fact, too, that Homer, poet of gods and men, came out of Ionia. The date is not certain, but scholars today believe that this first poet of Europe flourished in Ionia about 700 B.C. and wrote both the *Iliad* and the *Odyssey* in their entirety. One of the great cities of Ionia was Ephesus. Here the philosopher Heraclitus was born. In the first century of the Christian era it was destined to become the foremost center of the new, surging faith—Christianity.

It is in Ephesus that the Johannine literature of the New Testament—the powerful Apocalypse and the stunning Fourth Gospel, together with the three epistles of John—will be written. It is quite possible, as the late Professor Edgar J. Goodspeed contended, that Luke-Acts, in extent one-fourth of the New Testament, was produced and published here. He points out the amount of space given by Luke to Ephesus in Acts; it is more than he gives to any other Greek church. Further, Paul's only extended farewell to any of his churches is the one to the elders of Ephesus (Acts 20:17-38).

Beginning with Thales in 600 B.C., the next 500 years will see a flowering of thought about the world and the life and conduct of man of a brilliance and versatility never again matched. I learned from the late Professor Paul Tillich the device of dividing history into 500- or 550-year periods and grasping each one in terms of a problem that constitutes the emergency of that era.

It was my unusual privilege to be Tillich's host for a week in January 1935, when he had just arrived in America and was on tour as an itinerating theological lecturer, under the sponsorship of Reinhold Niebuhr and Union Seminary, New York. I cannot now recall the full scheme of periodization Tillich laid out, but it was a brilliant performance. I do recall that his first period began with the birth of philosophy and his last completed period was that of reason and science ushered in by the Renaissance and ending with World War I.

In fact, I see a striking parallel between these two ages of reason. Philosophy dominates the ancient era, with science in the wings but unable to come to birth. The modern age is the time of modern science, freed from all bonds by the rationalism of medieval theology. This was a favorite thesis of the late Professor A. N. Whitehead. Science is the motor of the modern run, with philosophy its attendant and would-be interpreter, guiding herself increasingly by the results of the sciences.

The respective outcomes of the two eras are strangely parallel. The details are of course different. But in each case reason long regnant wavers and falls, while faith rises. Man feels his insufficiency and human incompetency, and takes refuge in the religion his predecessors had discarded or ridden too lightly.

In my book *Communism and Christ* (first published in 1952), I developed this thesis in relation to contemporary history. I see nothing that has happened in the last three decades that compels any alteration in this thesis. Of course, in speaking of ''a new religious age,'' I used the term in a broad, generic sense —one that embraces false religion as well as true idolatry, mythology, and sheer superstition.

This applies also to the situation at the beginning of the Christian era. Mankind was ready for the

Christ—the time was ripe for the Incarnation— precisely because philosophy had grown old and cold, and the heart of humanity was hot for something more sure that offered healing and peace.

But now we must return to that long and remarkable preparatory period before Christ, indeed back to 600 B.C. and Thales of Miletus in Ionia and his successors in the pursuit of wisdom by reason. This period, however distinct, was not isolated from its past. There are, we must be clear, no hard and fast boundary lines in history. Events, currents, trends, even persons melt into one another; there is constant interpenetration, both horizontally and vertically.

In this connection Father Frederick Copleston, premier contemporary historian of philosophy, has observed that the Ionian period of settled life and rational reflection was early only in relation to subsequent Greek philosophy and the flowering of thought and culture on the Greek mainland. In relation to the past, the first philosophic period was the fruit of a mature civilization, marking the closing period of Ionian greatness while ushering in the splendor of Hellas and, particularly, Athens.[1]

"The glory that was Greece" had many facets. Philosophy and science were coming to birth. Art and letters, history and travel, politics in theory and practice, conduct and social life, the flowering of the *polis* or community of moderate size in all aspects of culture—all were emphasized. Nothing human was rejected or neglected.

The special light of this civilization was reason. The Greek was given the insight that this was man's unique faculty. It lifted him above the rest of creation and made him akin to the gods. He must use this gift and endowment to the fullest, turning it on the world of nature and the nature of man, and using it both to create and to criticize. Philosophy was the special construct of reason. Reason is the organ of knowledge and, as Aristotle says in the opening words of the *Metaphysics*, "all men by nature desire to know." Knowledge leads to "arts and reasonings," the philosopher continues, and it is by these that the human race lives. At this point the gift of wonder supervenes. "It is owing to their wonder that men both now begin and at first began to philosophize." This drive to know in the sense of wisdom and understanding leads to the search for principles and causes (*archai kai aitiai*).

The first philosophers were cosmologists. Their wonder and reason were directed to the external world of nature. The three Ionians of Miletus, Thales, Anaximander, and Anaximenses, all sought for the one common enduring element in nature, the one that was primeval and that persisted through all change. For Thales the ultimate substance was water, and for Anaximenes it was air. In between, Anaximander had a more profound but also a more abstract idea. He posited an infinite and abiding Something, "a nature neither water nor any other of the so-called elements, but a nature different from them and infinite, from which arise all the heavens and worlds within them." It is a substance without limits, an indeterminate infinite. One is reminded of Spinoza's Infinite Substance and Whitehead's Pure Actuality.

The successor of the Milesian Ionians was another Ionian, but from another city. He was Heraclitus, a noble of Ephesus and one of the ablest and most original of all philosophers. It was he who gave the world the concept and term, *Logos*. Perhaps it was for this reason that an early Christian apologist, Justin the Martyr (c. A.D. 150), bracketed him with Socrates and called these two philosophers *"Christians before Christ."*

Heraclitus is commonly grouped with the other Ionians and classified as a thinker who put the weight on *becoming* in contrast to the Eleatic School which stressed *absolute being.* There is some propriety in this, since Heraclitus was an Ionian and since also he came down on another physical element, fire, as the primal element out of which all things come and to which they return. It cannot be denied, moreover, that Heraclitus was impressed with the universality of movement and change. He did say, very acutely, that one cannot step into the same river twice.

Heraclitus had a gift for epigrammatic utterance, and he was both fearless and relentless about saying what he thought. Thus he declared, "Man's character is his fate"; "Most men are bad"; "The

mysteries practiced among men are unholy mysteries''; and ''Nature loves to hide.''

The most sublime and memorable of all the sayings of Heraclitus (and only fragments have come
down to us) is this: ''The sun will not transgress his
measures; were he to do so, the aiders of Justice
would overtake him. He who speaks with understanding must take his foothold on what is common
to all, even more firmly than the city stands on the
foothold of law; for all human laws are nourished by
the divine law. Though this Logos—the fundamental
law—existeth from all time, yet mankind are unaware of it, both ere they hear it and in the moment
that they hear it.''[2]

This fragment suggests both the profundity and
the complexity of the thought of Heraclitus. He was
a major influence on Plato, the great philosophical
synthesizer, and the Stoics drew their basic cosmol-
ogy from his writings. St. John the Evangelist drew
his doctrine of the pre-incarnate Logos from Stoic
Platonism in a time dominated by syncretism, or the
fusion of various strands of thought.

The heart of Heraclitus is not in becoming, as
Hegel thought, simply including him with the other
Ionians in opposition to the Eleatics. No, Heraclitus
says most explicity: ''It is wise to hearken, not to me,
but to my Word, and to confess that all things are
one.'' For Heraclitus the One is fundamental: Reality is One. But it is also and at the same time Many.
Nor is the Many accidental. Both sides are essential

and are in an organic relationship.

Heraclitus' doctrine is unity in diversity, One in Many. The thing, moreover, that explains this paradox, that holds the universe together, is the law of opposites. Strife and tension, turmoil and war, are not accidental but are essential to the unity of the One. "The philosophy of Heraclitus corresponds much more to the concrete universal, the One existing in the Many, Identity in Difference."[3]

The importance of Heraclitus' solution of the One and the Many is underlined when we take note of the school that opposed the Ionian "physicians" and held to the absolute simplicity and unchangeableness of Being. This was the Eleatic School which flourished in Greek Italy. The town of Elea was located near the later Paestum, south of Naples. The leading representatives of this school were Parmenides, Melissus and Zeno. The Eleatics put all their weight on being and permanence. They were the apostles of immutability. Abstract reasoning was given free play. Change was dismissed as illusory, as appearance merely, not reality.

The great name in this school is Parmenides, who flourished around 475 B.C. He is supposed to have reached Athens around 450 at the age of 65 and to have conversed with Socrates. He was a poet and used hexameter verse as the medium of philosphic discourse. He was also a logician, laying down the rules of logical reasoning. In his work the *Way of Truth* he declared that reason is the ultimate judge of truth.

Parmenides is often considered to be an idealist and the founder of idealism. This is very doubtful. He was an absolutist; he was the first exponent of what William James, against the monistic idealists, would call a block universe. But his Being which never becomes, which simply is—ultimate, immutable, impermeable—appears to be thought of as a material substance.

In fact, Parmenides describes the Being which is the world as a solid spherical globe, transparent, homogeneous, without crack or flaw. It has been suggested that in his view of Being, he anticipated vaguely the notion of modern physics that space is not infinite, but curved and finite. The philosophy of Parmenides begins and ends with the assertion of Being: "It is." Any modifications of this give rise to contradictions and therefore must be rejected as untrue. For him Truth was Reality, and Logic, the arbiter of Truth.

If we try to take change seriously and assert becoming, there are two possibilities. That which comes into being must arise either out of being or out of not-being. If it arises out of being, it is the same thing: it already is. If it arises out of not-being, then not-being must be something. Otherwise being could not arise out of it. This is a contradiction. You are back in being. Therefore what is, the "It is," always abides the same. Becoming only seems.

This is the heart of the Eleatic position. The famed paradoxes of Zeno, based on formal mathematics and no doubt suggested by another very complex school of philosophy, the Pythagoreans, are a vivid dialectical way of proving the unreliability of the senses and sense experience. The two examples that are well known are Achilles and the tortoise and the flight of an arrow. Zeno had other illustrative proofs even more ingenious.

Becoming was not eliminated by the logic of Parmenides and his pupils. What was an abiding heritage was the distinction sanctified by Plato between realms of experience controlled respectively by knowledge and opinion, thought and sense. This immensely influential discrimination was solidified by the Platonic doctrine of the ideas, which are the objects of knowledge. Opinion deals with the lower, passing world of creation through the instrumentality of the senses.

Here is a current of thought that is very powerful. It will turn up in Gnosticism, in the Logos theology of the Ante-Nicene church fathers, and in Neo-Platonism. It seems to us to be a strange situation, but the pre-Socratic philosophers had not formulated any clear disjunction between mind and body, spirit and matter. For them the paramount problem for thought was being and not-being, permanence and change. In applying reason to the solution of this question, they were oriented toward the external world, not the inner sphere of subjectivity.

For the pre-Socratic thinkers the world is a unity. There is no question of the bifurcation of nature, against which Alfred North Whitehead in our time launched his philosophy of organism as a giant protest. The first apostles of reason labored before the fall of the mind into the dichotomy of subject and object.

It is not clear whether this dichotomy or division was ever a snare for the ancient mind. We are, however, when we leave the Eleatic monists, on the threshold of the discovery in their uniqueness of the mind and soul. It is to Socrates and his pupil, Plato, that we owe the first mighty agitation of this theme in the West.

Socrates was influenced by an interesting and very modern movement in Athens. It occurred during the Golden Age of that remarkable city-state, usually identified with the rule and leadership of Pericles. This is possibly the greatest age in human history.

I have often meditated on the different past periods that allure and attract. What period, if you could choose to go back in the past and spend a month at a time and in a place of your own choosing, would you chose? Walter Hines Page, Woodrow Wilson's ambassador to the Court of St. James, tells of an English dinner party when this query was put to the assembled guests. A majority, he says, voted for England in the time of Elizabeth, but he opted for Athens in the days of Pericles—and he was not a king. (Athens was a democracy.) Pericles was in power for a much shorter time than Elizabeth I, the most celebrated in all history, and this meant a pure, participatory democracy, for Athens was a city-state. But like the Old South, which during the American Civil War was so much more concerned about constitutional liberty than the North was, Athens was a free society resting on slavery.

The public career of Pericles began in 463 B.C. and lasted 32 years. In 461, he became leader of the democratic party, or faction. The opposing faction was the oligarchic faction. Pericles was an aristocrat but chose the democratic side. Then, as now, the combination of an aristocrat who enjoyed strong popular support was a strong one.

Pericles introduced various reforms extending the authority of the people and affording them tangible benefits. Thus he consolidated his power and was able to increase the sway, the wealth, and the cultural glory of the city. It was under Pericles that the fabulous adornment of the Acropolis, culminating in the Parthenon, was carried out. He was the friend of the sculptor Phaedias and the philosopher Anaxagoras. He was the patron of the theater in the time of Aeschylus, Sophocles, and Euripides.

The culture of the city was reflected in its philosophy. A school known as the Sophists arose and dominated philosophical thinking. This name means ''wise men,'' and when it was first applied was not derogatory but genuine. The first Sophists were thinkers caught up in the spirit of Athens at the high point of artistic ferment, architectural creativity, democratic political activity, commercial enterprise, and economic imperialism.

Not surprisingly, interest shifted away from nature and seeking answers to abstract, ultimate questions. It centered instead on man himself, his nature and significance in the scheme of things. There was also a big demand for practical wisdom—for direction and training in law, rhetoric, and the art of politics.

The Sophists were men in reaction to earlier metaphysical theoreticians. They were humanists; they glorified man. Eventually, they moved toward skepticism and relativism. If we think of the role and temper of public relations practitioners in contemporary American culture, we shall have some idea of the place and outlook of the Sophists.

The first and greatest of the Sophists was Protagoras. His thought has come down to us only in fragments, but it is evident that he was a lively thinker and a pioneer humanist. His most famous saying is one that rings bells in not a few circles today: ''Man is the measure of all things, of those that are that they are, and of those that are not that they are not.'' Protagoras is here expressing skepticism with respect to truth itself. There is no absolute or universal truth; rather, truth is relative to the individual human being. What seems to him true is the only truth he can know. His perception is the only available test of reality. Nor is there any way of deciding as between individuals the truth of one outlook as distinct from another. No higher court of appeal exists.

This is made clear by another fragment that has come down to us from a work entitled *On the Gods*. In it he declared, "With regard to the gods, I cannot feel sure either that they are or that they are not, nor what they are like in figure, for there are many things that hinder sure knowlege, the obscurity of the subject and the shortness of human life."

Such was the outcome of the first century and a half of Greek philosophy. Protagoras clearly reflected a mood and trend in cosmopolitan Athens at the height of her power and creative glory. Problems, however, were looming and a period of decline was at hand. Reaction came as troubles multiplied.

Protagoras was in no way an isolated figure. A whole school and breed of Sophists arose, meeting a practical need in the busy, thriving democracy of Athens and reflecting the thoughtlessness and cynicism of material success. They were typical of "the secular city," but out of their number and influence there arose a moral giant who was to set in motion currents of philosophy of such power as to command the future for many centuries.

The name of this singular figure was Socrates. He was a kind of Sophist. Indeed, it was as a Sophist that he was condemned and executed. Like the Sophists, he was an instructor or teacher. That became his obsession and entire life, but he took no pay and he had no axe to grind save enlightenment and truth.

Socrates agreed with the Sophists that the center of interest was and should be man. He, too, was skeptical and indifferent with reference to speculation about the universe. Where he differed with the Sophists, though he was canny and wary in moving out of agnosticism into ethical Gnosticism, was in affirming that there is something in the universe that can be known, namely, man and the good. Socrates took as his own the injunction inscribed at Delphi on the temple of Apollo: "Know Thyself." The method of such knowledge was self-examination through questioning and reasoning. "The unexamined life," he declared (and I translate literally), "is not livable for man."

Plato was the pupil of Socrates. Born in 427 B.C., he was only 28 when his teacher set the incomparable example of preferring death to intellectual dishonor and moral cowardice. This decision of Socrates to drink the hemlock was a great moment in the history of man; it clinched his reversal of "sophistry" and made an ineffaceable impression on his gifted pupil. "It was the trial, and death of Socrates," says Scott Buchanan, "that stung Plato into the grasping of his life problem and his life work—to save the soul of Greece in Purgatory."

Buchanan, who was dean of St. John's College at the time of the adoption of the Great Books curriculum, stresses the dramatic element in all Plato's writings in his introduction to *The Portable Plato*. In them, "The play is the thing." He charms while he instructs, and the dance of life is in his dialectic.

In Plato, perhaps above all men, we see the beauty of reason and the magnetism of ideas. In him, we see the thinker and the artist combined as they had never been before and never have been since. Socrates had taught informally, by engaging the young and others in conversation. Like Jesus, as far as we know, he never wrote a line. But in Plato's dramatic life-dialogues, in which ideas are batted about like balls in a handball court, Socrates is always the principal character. Plato makes him the mouthpiece of reason overcoming confusion and knowledge triumphing over mere opinion.

The four works that Buchanan chooses for *The Portable Plato* are the *Protagoras*, the *Symposium*, the *Phaedo*, and the *Republic*. Of these, the first that deals with the representative Sophist is not very definitive. Plato chooses to hold his fire. But the heavy artillery is unlimbered in the other three writings. The *Phaedo* deals with the death of the Master and in that context at length with the soul and immortality. The *Symposium*, perhaps the most artistic and sparkling of all Plato's productions, has love as its theme. I have been fond of saying, for many years, that the two ultimate and truly comprehensive treatments of love are the *Symposium* and the *New Testament*. For fullness of truth, they must be taken and held together.

The greatest and most influential of all Plato's writings is the *Republic*. Its subtitle is *Concerning Justice*. It is believed that Plato composed it after his first visit to Syracuse and that it was published around 366 B.C.

It is impossible, really, to describe this fantastic work in a few sentences. It is not easy to isolate its dominating motif or motifs. It is a utopia, the first of this genre in history and the inspirer forever after of this class of works. But it is so much more. Justice has a claim to be the overriding theme, and it is certain that the sentiment of justice burned in the soul of Plato like a consuming but inextinguishable flame. Yet there is nothing as difficult to harness and define as this conception, and the *Republic* is far from satisfactory in this respect. It would be a much lesser work if it did not leave many loose, dangling threads.

The *Republic* is also riven with philosophic and religious motifs. The late Archbishop Temple was fond of pointing out that its tenth and last book has the immortality of the soul as its theme. The sixth book celebrates the Idea of the Good, the sun of the transcendental and eternal universe and the ground of knowledge as distinct from opinion. Plato aims very high in the *Republic* and his intellectual arrows frequently disappear in the stratosphere of philosophy. But this is far from being the sum and substance of the work, even though the notion of philosopher-kings is dear to his heart and remains a superb dream.

The best description I can give of this daring, glittering, baffling, innovative treatise is that in it, Plato turns the light of reason on everything. Nothing is exempted. There are no sacred cows, save reason itself.

He is thoroughly Greek in that he sets out from society, which for him is the city-state, not from the individual. He cannot conceive the good life, or that at which it aims, well-being or happiness, apart from community.

The great problem, therefore, in Plato's view, is how to achieve a good state. His inquiry regarding this takes him on an involved mental journey, but he never flinches. With superb boldness he follows where reason leads, looking at the origin of the State or society, at its composition in basic classes, at the necessity of war and hence of soldiers, trained and disciplined, and of leaders or guardians, chosen for their excellence.

This takes Plato into the subject of education, a subject in which he is deeply interested. The basics are music and gymnastics. Music includes literature, and Plato comes out boldly for the exclusion of the epic poets because of their immorality and especially the false and unworthy picture they give of the gods and the divine. He lays it down that God must be represented as he is, not as the author of all things but of the good only. And God is true: he cannot change, and he never deceives, never lies.

In the name of truth and for the sake, too, of preventing fear, Plato accepts what we would call censorship.

What about women? What is their place? Here

Plato is so modern that he takes one's breath away. He will make little distinction between the male and the female. Their education should be the same. Women should be trained equally with men, even for war. This raises the question of nudity. Plato passes over it casually. Men in Greece exercised without clothes. Gymnasium means "place of the nude." Women are to do the same; everyone, Plato says, will speedily become accustomed to this.

Then comes the assertion of community alike of property and of women—or more correctly, of men and women and family. Plato is actuated by the passion of excellence, with reason the organ of determining what is good. So for the guardians, the elite of the State—not for all—there can be no private property and there can be no family to turn the leaders aside from the path of disinterested virtue and absolute dedication to the State.

Moreover, sexual intercourse and the begetting of children cannot be entered on lightly or carelessly; it is too important an enterprise. The aim must be the production of the finest and noblest offspring. Hence the State must arrange the mating of the sexes and, after children are born, must take them away from the parents and see to their nurture and education. Two motives are present here: the first is eugenic, to breed for the best according to genetic laws; the second is the avoidance of pride in family and the natural desire to advance one's own progeny, regardless of merit or the good of the State.

Finally, the guardians were to have the highest and most specialized training in philosophy. This is the context in which Plato takes off on one of his highest philosophic flights—one that will unveil his Idea of the Good, the first principle of truth and being, yet neither of these, a reality which is to the supersensible world what the sun is to the sensible universe.

Plato introduces and justifies his incursion into the deepest world of philosophy by what might be called his impossible dream. It is the vision of the philosopher-king. "Until philosophers are kings, or the kings and princes of this world have the spirit and power of philosophy, and political greatness and wisdom meet in one, and those commoner natures who pursue either to the exclusion of the other are compelled to stand aside, cities will never have rest from their evils,—no, nor the human race."

Plato's vision of the Idea of the Good is followed by the parable of the cave, which brings out by vivid illustration his uncompromising transcendentalism. This has momentous consequences in what might be called existential application. It means that experience in the ordinary, sensible world is an apprehension of appearance only. Plato calls this apprehension *doxa* or opinion, and differentiates it from *gnosis,* or knowledge, which is always of the ideas or universal forms and involves the world of perfect being. The realm of opinion is in between being, which gives knowledge, and not-being, which generates ignorance. This epistemological scheme is one that persists down to and beyond the coming of Christianity. When Christianity leaves the soil of Judea and turns to the Greeks and Greek culture, it will come into deadly combat with the notion of the superiority of *Gnosis* and will have the fight of its life, with enormous stakes.

There was, in fact, humanly speaking, a real chance that the Christian movement would be swamped and swallowed up by Gnosticism and Marcionism, in tandem or separately. Especially impressive is the swift move of Marcion, who may at one time have been a bishop, to found a rival church similar in organization, and to propagate it with abounding energy and considerable success. Justin tells us as early as 150 that Marcion with the aid of demons has won a following "spread over every race of men."[4] Epiphanius (320-412) names it as infecting by his time Rome and Italy, Egypt, Palestine, Arabia, Syria, Cyprus, and Persia.[5]

It is the thesis of this book that the first theologians of the church, the human trinity of Paul, Apollos, and John, gave Christianity a grounding that enabled it to repel the aggressions of the Gnostic—Marcionite heresy—the most comprehensive and threatening in all church history. At stake was the very being of the religion of Christ, the true Messiah sent of God into the world.

The mainspring of Gnosticism was the rational bias and epistemology of Plato. For him, knowledge was possible and ultimate. True knowldge took one away from the shadows of time and flesh into a transcendental sphere. The difference was that Plato was above all a thinker, a philosopher, and that his existential situation was civic and political in the manner of Greece in its classic period. Religion was relevant to this life of man in its full actuality, but it did not take man out of the setting of psycho-physical or soul-body existence. Rather, in union with philosophy, it inspired him to search for justice and to see this as including and demanding excellence in all things.

By the time of Christ's birth the classic setting had gone forever. The passion for knowledge directed by reason had grown cold, and a new and very different age had dawned. It was an age of belief, of thirst for salvation, of hunger for union with God. This new setting had not come into existence overnight. The process of its gestation and birth was a lengthy one. It had a definite historical background, carrying with it political, geographical, and sociological as well as intellectual factors.

The summary of this is in the transition from Hellenism, or the world of Greece, to the Hellenistic Age. The latter period was ushered in by Alexander the Great (pupil of Aristotle), the genius extraordinary who left the joys of contemplation for the lusts of action and had conquered the world by the age of 30. After Alexander's untimely dealth in 323 B.C., his loose empire was divided among his generals. Out of this, five distinct kingdoms emerged: Macedonia

and Greece (taken over by General Antipater),
Thrace (by Lysimachus), Asia Minor (by Antigo-
nus), Babylon or the Near East (by Seleucus), and
Egypt (by Ptolemy).

The fundamental thrust of the Hellenistic situation was cultural admixture or syncretism. Cosmopolitanism replaced particularism. The outlook of
man had left the city-state far behind. It reached out
to and embraced the cosmos as a whole. Alexander
took Greek culture with him but broke with the teaching of his tutor Aristotle that Greeks are Greeks and
the remainder of mankind are barbarians. Though
already the husband of Roxana, a Bactrian princess,
he took to wife two Persian princesses, the daughter
of Darius III and that of Artaxerxes III. He insisted
that his officers follow suit. Eighty did, and thousands of his soldiers soon afterward married Persian
women. Alexander gave each obedient officer a substantial dowry and paid the debts of the marrying
soldiers. He invited Greek colonists into Mesopota-
mia and Persia, thus originating the Hellenized
Asiatic cities destined to make history as key elements
of the Seleucid Empire. Finally, he drafted 30,000
youths of Persia, educating them in Greek ways and
teaching them the Greek manual of war.

Thus Alexander set in motion, from opposite
directions, two mightly cultural currents, the Hellenic
and the Oriental, or Asiatic. Included in the latter
force and influence was Judea and the idea and tradition of Israel. Greek and Jew were to meet, and

the encounter was destined to shape mightily all subsequent history.

There were other Semites around, as there still
are. This fact was brought home to me in a hotel
in Damascus in 1975. This remarkable city is perhaps the oldest continuously inhabited metropolis in
the world. You can still see and walk down the street
called Straight, to which Saul of Tarsus was directed
after he had met Jesus on the road to the Syrian
capital.

In a three-day period in my hotel I encountered
a delegation of Soviet women. In their own way they
were distinctive enough. They were followed by a
troop of Syrian women, presumably on tour or at
a convention of some sort. I was very struck by their
appearance and remarked that they looked like super-
Jews. The Jews of today are, of course, one of the
most mixed races in the world. Whatever Judaism
is, whatever Israel is, it is not a race. I mention and
use this contemporary illustration to emphasize the
importance in the Hellenistic period and in primitive Christianity of Syria and the Syriac tradition.
The proximity of Antioch to Jerusalem was a fact
of enormous import, inherently and still more because of the destruction of Jerusalem and the Temple
by the Romans in A.D. 70.

To return to the two powerful currents of the
Hellenistic phase of history and their intermingling,
the primary development was the spread of Hellenic
culture eastward, as far as India. In particular, the

New East as a whole accepted and to a considerable extent assimilated Greek civilization. This included Palestine and Judea as well as the Jews of the Dispersion: an amalgamation of Hellenism and Judaism had taken place long before the advent of Christ. Examples are: the Book of Ecclesiastes, the personification and elaboration of Wisdom in *Proverbs* and the *Wisdom of Solomon*, the philosophical theology of Philo in Alexandria (which, though contemporary with Christ, presupposes a long period of syncretic development), and the reign of Herod the Great, who was above all an unabashed Grecophile.

But no cultural advance of this kind can be one-sided. The soul of Greece in reaching out to the Orient became Orientalized: it offered the East philosophy but found itself accepting salvation in diverse modes as a more satisfactory answer to the mystery of life and being.

Will Durant has said that the Greeks offered the East philosophy, the East offered the Greeks religion; and that religion won because philosophy was the luxury of the few while religion was the consolation of the many. Other scholars have emphasized the backwardness and disinterest of Greece in matters of religion. The Hellenic genius, as we have stressed, was rational, with reason extending to and embracing the soul of beauty. The Hebrew stands in contrast to this.

Of Stoicism, a conspicuous phenomenon of the Hellenistic Age, Durant notes that many components of its creed were Asiatic, and some specifically Semitic. "In essentials, Stoicism was one elemental phase of the Oriental triumph over Hellenic civilization. Greece had ceased to be Greece before it was conquered by Rome."[6]

This is a basically accurate assessment of the Stoic essence, and assuredly this creed and ethic will be immensely important to Christianity. But Durant goes too far and proves the peril of dogmatic conclusions drawn by an outsider, when he declares: "From Zeno of Tarsus to Paul of Tarsus was but a step, which would be taken on the road to Damascus."[7]

We can see today very clearly that religion and ideology can coexist in a culture. The degree of blending and/or separation will depend on education and culture. This is the way it was in the Hellenistic and Roman periods. Stoicism was destined to become the characteristic ideology of the emerging one world, conscious of the cosmos as well as of regions, races, and cities. We can see how philosophy takes on a religious cast in Stoicism.

A conspicuous example of this phenomenon, foreshadowing a long and momentous development, can be seen in the moving poem of Cleanthes (fl. 230 B.C.), —his Hymn to Zeus.

Thou, O Zeus, art praised above all gods:
many are thy names and this is all power
for ever.
The beginning of the world was from thee:

and with law thou rulest over all things.
Unto thee may all flesh speak: for we are
thy offspring.[8]
Therefore will I raise a hymn to thee: and
will ever sing of thy power.
The whole order of the heavens obeyeth
thy word: as it Moveth around the earth:
With little and great lights mixed together:
how great thou art, King above all for ever!
Nor is anything done upon the earth apart
from thee: nor in the firmament, nor in
the seas:
Save that which the wicked do: by their
own folly.
But thine is the skill to set even the crooked
straight: what is without fashion is fashioned and the alien akin before thee.
Thou hast fitted together all things in one:
the good with the evil:
That thy word should be one in all things:
abiding for ever.
Let folly be dispersed from our souls: that
we may repay thee the honor wherewith
thou hast honored us:
Singing praise of thy works for ever: as
becometh the sons of men.

One could easily think, as he gets caught up in
this hymn, that he was reciting a "Psalm of David."

It is worth noting also that the founder of Stoicism, Zeno, a native of Cyprus, was accustomed to

say that he owed most, not to Antisthenes (the teacher of Diogenes and founder of the Cynic school) or to the *Republic* of Plato, but to Socrates as example and ideal. In the great martyr-sage we see piety and ethical conduct combined.

Stoicism will become especially important as Rome becomes an empire and the ruler of the world. Marcus Aurelius, one of the few examples of virtue in a monarch, stands out as an instance of Plato's ideal, the philosopher-king. But he was not in practice an innovator or in any degree a utopian. The most he could do was hold the empire together. Plato, of course, had been explicit in saying that only a city of limited size could even attempt to be a just republic.

Important as Stoicism was, and influential as it would be for Christian thought in theology and ethics, it was bound to remain more an ideology for rulers, lawyers, and philosophical spirits than a code or religion for the masses in the Hellenistic-Roman era. The characteristic development of this time was the rise and sweeping invasion of the mystery religions, moving in general from East to West. In a sense, this singular and enormously important development was a continuation, in an expanded and intensified form under characteristic Hellenistic influences, of the celebrated Greek mysteries, notably the Eleusinian mysteries and those of Orpheus and Dionysus.

There is still much that is not known about this

subterranean, secretive, numinous feature of Greek corporate life and culture. Its source was Greek religion when the gods were adhered to in earnest and long before philosophy had emerged to bid for the mind as well as the soul of the Hellenes. Perhaps the mysteries, with their fabled secrets and exciting initiatory rites, persisted in the life of Greece much as the Freemasons and other fraternal societies with secret aspects, elaborate rituals, and fantastic titles have persisted, and still persist in America. But originally, they were connected with purification from sin and the hope of life beyond death; and in their reincarnation prior to and parallel with the rise of Christianity these motifs were renewed and strengthened.

Factors in the rise and spread of the mystery religions were, most importantly, the decline of self-reliance and confidence in reason, the desire for immortality, the syncretistic cosmopolitanism of Hellenistic culture, and the miracle of Roman order with easy facility for various forms of communication, including travel.

Rome was the seat of power, and power always attracts. There was a saying that all roads lead to Rome, and this applied in religious as well as secular ways. Christianity came into the world at a moment of intense spiritual striving and concern. It also found itself up against strong rivals in the mystery cults, all of which originated as Christianity had, along with its mother Judaism, in the Near (or Middle) East.

Thus the cult of Mithras came out of Iran; that of Cybele, the great mother, arose in Asia Minor; those of the various Baals in Syria and of Isis in Egypt. Common myths run through these faiths: in each one there is a divine saviour, a god or lord who has passed through the experience of dying and rising again and who, as lord of a particular cult, offers to the believing initiate union with himself in this experience. The importance of this for the substance and development of Christianity cannot be overestimated.

The figure of the suffering deity in the mystery religions is commonly vague and crudely conceived; it is always bound up with other interests and deities appropriate to them. Nowhere is there a clear-cut figure rooted in history in the manner of Jesus the Christ. Nevertheless, the importance for Christianity of these mystical salvation faiths with their general pattern of a saviour-lord is undoubted and probably incalculable.

This does not depend on the issue of their direct influence on Paul the Apostle and the Gospel which he believed, elaborated, lived, and preached. On this question Albert Schweitzer, great proponent of the eschatological interpretation of Jesus, aligned himself with the conservative scholars, denying that Paul's Christ-mysticism was in any respect affected by the mystery religions. To this matter we shall turn in a moment.

Regardless of this issue, either way, the mystery

religions were the allies as well as the life-and-death rivals of Christianity. One of the oldest and most widely followed of these cults was that of Cybele, the "Great Mother of the Gods." This goddess in all her aspects, we are told—Roman, Greek, and Oriental—reflected the same qualities, and always predominantly universal motherhood. She was the great parent of gods and men, and also of the lower orders of creation, such as the winds, the sea, the mountains, and the earth itself. She was thought of as "the All-begetter, the All-nourisher, the Mother of the Blest."

The affinity of the Great Mother with the wild side of nature found expression in the orgiastic character of her worship. Her attendants were called the Corybantes and were wild, half-demonic beings. Her priests, the Galli, were eunuchs in female garb, with long, anointed hair. Joining with priestesses, also, they celebrated her rites with castanets, tambourines, flutes, horns, and cymbals. These accompanied mad yelling and dancing, the frenzied excitement building up into self-scourging and laceration, and ending in utter exhaustion. Sometimes self-emasculation by candidates for the priesthood would take place as a phase of this delirious worship.

The worship of the Great Mother in some form was very old, but in its fully developed form as known in Rome in the period of the Empire and in the Christian era, it was accompanied by that of Attis, Cybéle's son. The original symbolism here is that of

Mother Earth in relation to her fruits or children. But the rites went much further than this, portraying the birth of Attis, his self-mutilation, death, and immortality. They took place in Rome as an annual spring festival, beginning on April 4.

In literature, apart from the poet Catulbus, Cybele has left slight impression. But in the history of religion, as Grant Showerman has said, her importance is very great. "Together with Isis and Mithras, she was a great enemy, and yet a great aid to Christianity. The gorgeous rites of her worship, its mystic doctrine of communion with the divine through enthusiasm, its promise of regeneration through baptism of blood in the taurobolium, were features which attracted the masses of the people and made it a strong rival of Christianity; and its resemblance to the new religion, however superficial, made it, in spite of the scandalous practices which grew up around it, a stepping-stone to Christianity when the tide set in against paganism."[9]

What was the relation of the mystery religions to the development of Christian faith, experience, and theology? This is a subject that has exercised many European and American scholars. I sat at Harvard under one, Professor Kirsopp Lake, who was deeply affected by the assumption that the central formation of historic Christianity as a religion was due to the example and magnetic attraction of the mystery cults.

It was, and is, most interesting that Albert

Schweitzer, the principal factor in demolishing the
liberal Christian dream of a religion of Jesus as
opposed to the traditional Christological construct,
set himself like flint to oppose any Hellenization of the
Gospel by Paul or any influence on the Apostle to
the Gentiles from contact with or unconscious ab-
sorption from the mysteries in their early Roman
period. Schweitzer's targets are Reitzenstein, Bousset, and even Adolf Deissmann. These scholars
differed considerably in their account of the Hellenistic influences playing upon Paul and manifest in his
Christ-centered mysticism. Thus Reitzenstein assumes that the Christology of Paul results from an
original synthesis of Jewish and Hellenistic mystery-
religion concepts. Bousset posits a prior Hellenization
in the church at Antioch, which Paul will encounter
when he arrives on the scene. Bousset emphasizes
the *kyrios* figure in the mystery cults and sees this
worship and identification transferred to the worship
of Jesus as Lord alongside the idea of the Messiah.
It was out of this worship of Jesus as Lord that Paul
discovered and developed his mysticism.

Deissmann does not go this far, but he assumes
a moulding influence from the religious ideas familiar
to Paul as a youth in the Hellenistic world of Tarsus. Paul in his pre-Christian period knew Hellenism
as well as Judaism. It was, however, his experience
of meeting Jesus on the Damascus Road that sparked
the Apostle's Christ-mysticism. Ideas already in his
consciousness helped him fill out his thoroughgoing

christocentric impulse and experience.

Schweitzer argues that had Paulinism been a Hellenized Christianity, it would have been much more influential as such in the period immediately following. He cites also the fact that primitive Christianity did not reject Paul's teaching as foreign to it. Either way, we have a phenomenon that is inexplicable on the Hellenistic hypothesis.

It is from and by eschatology that Schweitzer would explain the mysticism of Paul. He fits Paul on to the radical, apocalyptic, eschatological view of Jesus which he considers the only interpretation consonant with the facts filtered to us through the Gospels. In order to make his Pauline argument airtight, he is compelled to limit rigorously the number of unquestionably authentic letters of the Apostles. These, he holds, are Romans, 1 and 2 Corinthians, Galatians, Philippians, 1 Thessalonians, and Philemon.

Schweitzer lists them simply in the order that is traditional. This is for him without chronological significance. He rejects not only the Pastorals (1 and 2 Timothy and Titus) but 2 Thessalonians. The problem of Colossians and Ephesians he sees as complex. They differ greatly from the clearly genuine epistles, but there is too much that is Pauline in them to allow their dismissal as simply spurious. "Whatever solution may be given, however, to the complicated literary problem of the Colossian and Ephesian Epistles it is not of primary importance for the exposition of Paul's teaching."[10]

It is not our purpose to evaluate Schweitzer's view of Paul in any systematic way. He is stimulating and has many incisive and suggestive insights. For example, he brings out clearly that Paul is both a mystic and a non-mystic, linking this with his Jewishness. There is in this "Pharisee of the Pharisees" no God-mysticism, but only a Christ-mysticism.

The contrast here with a later theologian, the Evangelist we know as John, is arresting and illuminating. The union of the disciple with the Son, in this Gospel, is at the same time union with the Father.

> "In that day you will know that I am in my Father, and you in me, and I in you." (14:20)
> "Jesus answered him, 'If a man loves me, he will keep my word, and my Father will love him and we will come to him and make our home with him.'" (14:23)
> "I do not pray for these only, but also for those who are to believe in me through their word, that they may all be one; even as thou, Father, art in me, and I in thee, that they also may be in us, so that the world may believe that thou has sent me." (17:20-21)

Schweitzer delineates with helpful clarity the border separating the Hebraic and the Hebraic-

Christian from the Hellenized Christian outlook. The key figure here is Ignatius of Antioch. He sees Ignatius and Polycarp as standing in between Paul and John. "The Hellenistic conception of redemption through union with Christ is set forth with remarkable completeness in the Gospel of John."[11]

Ignatius is full of Paul's phrases and concepts, yet he has moved over into another realm in basic assumption and understanding. His Christianity is Hellenized, where Paul's is not. But, Schweitzer concedes, by inserting into the un-Hellenizable belief in Christ as the bringer of the Messianic Kingdom the derivative belief in the Messiash as the bringer of the resurrection through the being-in-Christ and in the sacraments as guaranteeing the being-in-Christ, Paul brought into being *a Christianity susceptible* of Hellenization.

The crux is the very un-Jewish idea of divinization. Through the redemption wrought by the God-man, the Logos-made-flesh, and through the mediation of this redemption in the Sacraments, flesh and Spirit are united and the human person in his fulness receives the gift of immortality.

The crossover is very clear in Ignatius. He was the man "to whom it fell to renew the mystical doctrine of the being-in-Christ in a thought-form appropriate to the time."[12] Ignatius knew Paul's Epistles and quotes many Pauline phrases, especially variations of "in Christ." But he is unable to fill these phrases with Pauline content. Dying and rising with

Christ cannot have for him the vivid, eschatological
meaning it had for Paul. For the apostle the union
of flesh and Spirit is unthinkable; for Ignatius it is
a necessity of Christian thinking.

Gnosticism plays a role here. The Gnostic
turned away from both body and flesh. For him
redemption and immortality are here in a return of
spirit to Spirit. Against this, Ignatius is bound to de-
fend a bodily resurrection, but he can do so only by
developing the idea that the flesh is transformed by
the working of the Spirit and made capable of immortality. Thus: "Even what you do in the flesh is
spiritual, for you do all in Christ Jesus" (Eph. 8:2).
"Abide in Christ, both fleshly and spiritually" (Eph
10:3). In this conception of "fleshly and spiritual union" (*Magn.* 8:2), Ignatius is enabled to explain not
only redemption in Christ, but its presupposition,
the Incarnation, and its mediation through the sacraments. In writing to the Romans, Ignatius says: "It
is God's bread which I desire, that is the flesh (sarx)
of Jesus Christ, who is of the seed of David; and as
drink I will have his blood which is imperishable
love" (7:3). To the Philadelphians he says: "Give
heed to celebrate only one Eucharist; for there is only
one flesh of our Lord Jesus Christ and only one cup
for uniting with his blood" (4). To the Ephesians
he addressed perhaps his most famous phrase:
"Breaking one bread that is a medicine of immortality, an antidote not to die, but to live in Jesus
Christ evermore" (x).

These statements on the Eucharist in Hellenistic rather than Hebraic and Pauline vein prepare us for the realism of the Johannine Christ in chapter 6 (though this Gospel may well be older than Ignatius' Epistles).[13] Our Lord's disquisition on the Eucharist following the miracle of the Feeding of the Five Thousand is dramatic and artful, introduced by the contrast between the food that perishes for which men labor and the food that endures to eternal life, which the Son of man on whom the Father has set his seal will give to those who believe. The manna that "our fathers" ate in the wilderness is brought in. But that was not the true bread.

Jesus then leads his fellow Jews and disciples on to the ringing declaration, which could be figurative had he stopped there: "I am the bread of life." But he goes on to make the contrast with the fathers who ate manna in the wilderness and died. But not so with this bread, which a man may eat and not die. "I am the living bread which came down from heaven; if any one eats of this bread, he will live for ever; and the bread which I shall give for the life of the world is my flesh."

The term "flesh," as Schweitzer realized, is crucial. In John's narrative it leads the Jews to dispute among themselves, "How can this man give us his flesh to eat?" This is the cue to the most realistic eucharistic statements, paralleling the words of Ignatius still to be written:

Truly, truly I say to you, unless you eat

the flesh of the Son of man and drink his
blood, you have no life in you; he who eats
my flesh and drinks my blood has eternal
life, and I will raise him up at the last day
. . . . He who eats my flesh and drinks my
blood abides in me, and I in him. As the
living Father sent me, and I live because
of the Father, so he who eats me will live
because of me. (6: 53-57.)

The emphasis on eternal life in the Gospel of
John is deeply significant. It is a great part of the
perennial and universal appeal of this, the spiritual
Gospel, as Clement of Alexandria first called it
around 180. But this John is setting himself, as the
First Epistle of John makes specifically clear, against
incipient Gnostic heresy. There can be no elimination
of the flesh created by God. The Old Testament must
stand as the Scriptures of the Church inspired of old
by the Spirit who spoke through the prophets. "Salvation is of the Jews," as the Lord says bluntly to
the woman of Samaria at the well of Jacob (4:22).

To this tremendous issue we must now turn and
deal with in some detail. We know that the tide toward a pure spirituality was running high in the
Graeco-Roman world where the culture was basically
Greek, though in a syncretic not an exclusive form.
Judaism really won out, despite the crudities with
which the Old Testament seemed to abound. Christianity remained "the most avowedly materialist of

all the great religions,'' in the celebrated and oft-quoted phrase of Archbishop William Temple.[14]

The point of immediate concern is that Christ came when he did, because the world was ready for a great salvation-faith. Reason for the moment had run its course, had shot its bolt, as a sufficient answer. It had aimed high in the sixth to the third centuries B.C. It was not enough, even though it had produced a Socrates and a Plato and though in Stoicism, in spirit lineally descended from Socrates, we have a system incarnating *logos* from top to bottom and avoiding every manner of mystical ecstasy or spiritual ascent.

It is noteworthy that this philosophy, which was both a philosophy of life and a metaphysic or world-view, managed to remain materialistic and to fashion an impressively worshipful Pantheism at the same time. For the Stoic God is mind-fire, a reason-stuff that fills the world and perfectly and providentially orders all things. In some ways, this philosophy represents more an act of will, a determination to control, than the voice of reason.

In an Epictetus, the slave-Stoic, and a Marcus Aurelius, the Emperor-Stoic, we see an attitude of mind and an outreach of spirit that go beyond the premises and logical allowances of the Stoic system. We see how powerful the need and will to worship are. This will is like a potent coiled mainspring. It is not in man to hold it in for long. And worship is the expression of love. It is devotion to the highest in act.

Neoplatonism did not have the problem that afflicted the Stoics, for the essence of Plato is transcendentalism. Reason and imagination are wedded in this tradition as they were in Plato himself. But in Neoplatonism we witness the thirst for eternal life in individual experience.

For Plotinus the *summum bonum* (the supreme good) is ''the flight of the alone to the Alone.'' This remarkable, seemingly sunny and optimistic philosopher lived and worked at the lowest period politically in the history of Rome. His dates are 205-270, and this was the time when the imperial throne was in effect up to the highest bidder and assassinations were rife as never before.

The contrast with the age when Plato lived and wrote is striking. Athenian democracy was on the toboggan, unable to stand up to Sparta or to find remedies for its inherent weaknesses. During his productive life Plato was in reaction against the corruption of democratic Athens. But he was in reaction. He was in his own way a civic activist. He called for political and social reform. This is the mainspring both of his *Republic* (written in the prime of his life) and of the *Laws* (the more chastened utopia of his old age).

Plotinus by contrast is totally apolitical. He has no hope at all or interest in the social civil order. Meaning is found in turning one's back on this world and rising to realms and worlds unknown where the

Divine is all.

At this point Neoplatonism is on all fours with Gnosticism, even though Plotinus is more favorable to Nature and her beauty and rebukes the Gnostics for their overweening dualism. This was the background of Christianity, and there was danger that the new faith would confine the good news of the Gospel to a heavenly salvation, following the deep impulse of the age.

In the Christian East this happened to a certain extent. But this situation was altered by the Church's rejection of the Gnostic and Marcionite attempt to jettison the Old Testament and the whole Jewish tradition. The idea and reality of the Kingdom of God was not lost.

A second factor of enormous moment was the persistence of the Church as an organism with a definite hierarchical structure that in time fell heir in the West to social and civil responsibility. It was this which made possible the rise and progress of civilization under Christian auspices. The great Middle Age was able to come into being.

Professor Elaine Pagels, in her brilliant book *The Gnostic Gospels* based on the exciting Nag Hammadi discoveries, explores the political and sociological implications of the Gnostic controversy. Taking the least heretical and dualistic of the Gnostic sects, the Valentinians,[15] as a primary example, she shows their threat to biblical monotheism and the authority of the emerging Catholic hierarchy centering in the monarchical bishop who represents the one God, Creator and Redeemer.

Professor Pagels disclaims advocacy of return to Gnosticism, despite her fascination with this outlook as revealed in the new treasury of its original documents.[16] This is her mature, overall conclusion:

> We can see, then, how conflicts arose in the formation of Christianity between those restless, inquiring people who marked out a solitary path of self-discovery and the institutional framework that gave to the great majority of people religious sanction and ethical direction for their daily lives. Adapting for its own purposes the model of Roman political and military organization, and gaining, in the fourth century, imperial support, orthodox Christianity grew increasingly stable and enduring.[17]

I forget who it was who said, "The natural man is a Catholic." Professor Pagels, citing A.D. Nock's view of the Orthodox church's "perfect because unconscious correspondence to the needs and aspirations of ordinary humanity," acquiesces in the general verdict of history. However, she sees in the new perspective light on the manner in which certain creative persons throughout the ages, from Valentinus and Heracleon to Blake, Rembrandt, Dostoevsky, Tolstoy, and Nietzsche, have found themselves at the edges of orthodoxy, gripped by the figure of Christ and compelled to use Christian symbols.[18]

Previously, scholars as disparate as the Germans, von Harnack and Bousset, and F. C. Burkitt of Cambridge have taken a more somber and severe view of the Gnostic heresy. Thus Harnack saw the Gnostic systems as representing "the acute secularizing or Hellenizing of Christianity, with the rejection of the Old Testament." The Gnostics "are therefore those Christians who, in a swift advance, attempted to capture Christianity for Hellenic culture, and Hellenic culture for Christianity, and who gave up the Old Testament in order to facilitate the conclusion of the covenant between the two powers, and make it possible to assert the absoluteness of Christianity."[19]

Wilhelm Bousset represents the most drastic view taken of Gnosticism. For him, it was "a spiritual movement existing side by side with genuine Christianity;" it is to be defined as "a distinct religious syncretism bearing the strong impress of Christian influences." "In short, Gnosticism, in all its various sections, its form and its character, falls under the great category of mystic religions which were so characteristic of the religious life of decadent antiquity." Its "ultimate object is individual salvation, the assurance of a fortunate destiny for the soul after death." And finally, "it must be considered an uniqualified advantage for the further development of

Christianity, as a universal religion, that at its very outset it prevailed against the great movement of Gnosticism."[20] It is half a century now since I came across the verdict on Gnosticism in relation to the Christian Church of Professor F. C. Burkitt of Cambridge University. It has remained steadily in my mind as the most perceptive grasp of practical historical realities in the Gnostic connection so far articulated. I set it down as what remains for me a final word.

> In the conception of the Church—that is, the organized body of believers,—as a thing in itself to be worked for and fostered, lies, I think, the point of difference between Catholicism and Gnosticism, between Aphraates and the *Acts of Thomas*. To the convert of Judas Thomas there was literally nothing left on this earth to live for. "Would that the days passed swiftly over me, and that all the hours were one," says Mygdonia, "that I might go forth from this world, and go and see that Beautiful One with whose impress I have been sealed, that Living One and Giver of Life to those who have believed in Him, where there is neither day nor night, and no darkness but light, and neither good nor bad, nor rich nor poor, neither male nor female, nor slaves nor freemen, nor any proud and uplifted over those who are humble."

The old civilization was doomed, but this religious Nihilism puts nothing in its place. To the orthodox Christian, on the other hand, the Church stood as a middle term between the things of the next world and of this. It was the body of Christ and therefore eternal, something worth living for and working for. Yet it was in the world as much as the Empire itself. The idea of the Church thus formed an invaluable fixed point, round which a new civilization could slowly crystallize.[21]

1. A History of Philosophy, Vol. I, Part I, p. 30.
2. This translation is the one used by Archbishop William Temple in his *Readings in St. John's Gospel*, Vol. I, pp. 3-4. It is likely that this is Temple's own translation of the original Greek.
3. Copleston, op.cit., pp.56-7.
4. *Apol.* I, 26.
5. *Haer.* xlviii.
6. *The Story of Civilization*, Vol. II (*The Life of Greece*), p. 658. These sentences embody a most arresting insight. Remember the cosmopolitan bent and thrust of Stoicism. This cannot immediately be Jewish; it must be the legacy jointly of Alexander and Rome.
7. Ibid.
8. This is the quotation attributed by Luke in Acts 17:28 to Paul speaking in Athens.
9. *Ency. Brit.*, 11th Ed., Art. *Great Mother of the Gods.*
10. *The Mysticism of Paul the Apostle*, Seabury PB, pp. 42-3.
11. Ibid., p. 349.
12. Schweitzer, Ibid., p. 339.
13. On Schweitzer's view.

14. *Nature, Man and God*, p. 478. cf. *Readings in Saint John's Gospel*, I, p.xx.
15. There is a tempting apparent parallel between Valentinus, the most brillant and attractive of the Gnostic theologians, and Plotinus in their views, both of the nature of ultimate Deity and the need to restrict dualism. It would be interesting to see this seeming parallel investigated. The two men are approximate contemporaries.
16. *The Gnostic Gospels*, p. 151.
17. *Ibid.*, p. 149.
18. *Ibid*, pp. 149-150.
19. *History of Dogma*, E.T., I, pp. 226, 227.
20. *Ency. Brit.* 11th ed., art. *Gnosticism*.
21. F.C. Burkitt, *Early Christianity Outside the Roman Empire*, pp. 84-6.

Chapter Three

The Attempted Explusion Of Judaism

Looking back over nearly 2000 years of Christian history, it is instructive to note and to evaluate the crises that the Christian movement has experienced. Life in all its forms is subject to peril. It must fight off enemies and find the strength to overcome foes both from within and from without. This is true of individual organisms. It is true of human beings. It is true of states and of civilizations. Arnold Toynbee has popularized the formula of challenge and response in his epochal study of societies viewed as civilizations in his multivolumed, but modestly entitled work, *A Study of History*. There is no history more instructive or fascinating from the angle of challenge and response, or crises faced and overcome, than that of the Christian Church. Of all the challenges that have come upon the Church, the greatest perhaps came in an obscure period—the second century.

We know a great deal about the Church in the first century. We have, as we have seen earlier, a copious literature that covers the origins of Christianity and the first creative advance, radiating out from

Palestine in all directions. This is a selective literature, to some extent occasional and even atypical.
There are gaps in the drama that it chronicles, and
there are many events about which we wish we knew
more. Nevertheless, we do have in the New Testament a marvelous mirror that enables us to see vividly
the sweep of the Gospel of Christ for two generations
—on down to A.D. 100-110.

In particular, and this is a paramount blessing,
we have the story, as it were, on film. And it is a film
of power. We see the action, the energy, the enthusiasm, the powerful thrust of the breath of God. We
know that something tremendous and awe-inspiring
took place. The mighty works of the Lord in an age
of the Spirit are there for us to contemplate for all
time and to recur to, particularly as need arises. We
cannot be too thankful for the inspired records thrown
up in unconscious imitation of the Hebrew Scriptures, which the first Christians revered and to which
they constantly appealed as they were meeting
challenges and crises and finding what proved indeed
to be the way of vitality and abundant life for themselves and the world.

The Christian Scriptures, as we now view them,
making up the New Covenant or Testament, were
instrumental in the overcoming of destructive forces
in the second century. These forces were very strong.
They threatened to drag the Church out of the developmental path indicated and laid down for her by her
brief past and to force her into a new, a strange, and

a wildly innovative orbit.

The Christian crisis of the second century was an identity crisis. It was the most serious and the most dangerous period that the Church has known. What was proposed was nothing less than the rejection and expulsion of the whole Jewish background of Christianity.

Where Paul, in writing to the church in Rome in the middle 50s, had lauded the Jews as the source of all that was precious and distinctive in the Christian inheritance, the Gnostic intellectuals of the second century, whom Harnack calls "the first theologians," wanted to free Christianity from the inferior impediments of the Old Testament, including the burden of a bungling Demiurge or Maker and Shaper of matter, the Creator according to Genesis of the heavens and the earth with all that is in them.

Paul grieves for his brethren who have turned away from the love of God in Christ Jesus, which is so great that nothing in the whole universe can separate those who believe from it. Immediately following this lyric outburst at the end of Romans 8 he speaks of the "great sorrow and unceasing anguish in his heart." He even wishes that he were accursed and cut off from Christ for the sake of his brethren, his kinsmen by race. "They are Israelites, and to them belong the sonship, the glory, the covenants, the giving of the law, the worship, and the promises; to them belong the patriarchs and of their race, according to the flesh, is the Messiah. God who is over all be blessed forever. Amen.''[1]

The Gospel of John, which must have been produced just a generation after Romans, reflects a situation of climax in Jewish-Christian relations. Sadly, the Synagogue is not only closed to envoys or apostles of Christ; it is bitterly hostile to the messianic sect that has now advanced to the worship of Christ as Lord and God, perfectly one with the Father.

The Christians unfortunately but not unnaturally return the compliment. They see the Jews as willfully blind in their unbelief and turned away from the God of Abraham and Moses and the prophets. This is the explanation of the central polemic in the Gospel of John. The criticism of the author and of the Christ is directed against the Jews collectively, and not, as in Matthew and the Synoptic tradition, generally against the scribes and Pharisees.

The climax of the polemic is reached in John 8 where the argument revolves around Abraham and his true children. Jesus suggests that from their actions they are not truly Abraham's children. Rather, ''you are of your father the devil, and your will is to do your father's desires. He was a murderer from the beginning, and has nothing to do with the truth, because there is no truth in him . . . . But, because I tell the truth, you do not believe me. Which of you convicts me of sin?''

The Jews then accuse Jesus of being a Samaritan and having a demon. He brings the subject round to death and his power over it. He says, ''Your father

Abraham rejoiced that he was to see my day; he saw it and was glad." "The Jews then said to him, 'You are not yet fifty years old, and have you seen Abraham?' Jesus said to them, 'Truly, truly, I say to you, before Abraham was, I am.' So they took up stones to throw at him, but Jesus hid himself, and went out of the temple.'"[2]

It would, however, be easy to get a misleading impression from the fourth Evangelist's portrayal of the Jews in relation to the Christ and the Church at the end of the first century. Tragically, this has happened as a matter of history and contributed unquestionably to the anti-Semitism that became endemic in Europe and to some extent in the whole world of the continuing diaspora.

It does not excuse the role of Christians in this tragedy to note that the Jews through their rabbis contributed to the polemic and the mutual *odium theologicum*. Truth nevertheless compels us to balance the books on the outlook of John the Evangelist and Theologian. Scholars are nearly unanimous that he was a Jew, not a Greek. He is explicit in having the Messiah say to the Samaritan woman at the well of Jacob, "Salvation is of the Jews."

In this Gospel it is understood from the beginning that Jesus is the Messiah. It is thus that John the Baptist acclaims him and that disciples follow him. When Philip finds Nathaniel, he says to him, "We have found him of whom Moses in the law and also the prophets wrote." And when Jesus sees

Nathaniel coming toward him, he says, "Behold, an Israelite indeed, in whom is no guile!" And Nathaniel, who had been skeptical at first, especially about Nazareth as the hometown of Jesus, exclaims: "Rabbi, you are the Son of God! You are the King of Israel!"

John the Evangelist plays up Nicodemus, "a ruler of the Jews," and later Joseph of Arimathea, according to St. Mark "a respected member of the council, who was also himself looking for the Kingdom of God" (Mark 15:43). Matthew says simply: "There came a rich man from Arimathea, named Joseph, who also was a disciple of Jesus" (27:57).

John both abbreviates and elaborates the Synoptic material on Joseph. Joseph is "a disciple of Jesus, but secretly, for fear of the Jews." He asks Pilate for the body and his request is granted. Joseph takes away the body of Jesus, but is joined by Nicodemus, "who had at first come to him by night," and who now brings "a mixture of myrrh and aloes, about a hundred pounds weight. They took the body of Jesus, and bound it in linen cloths with the spices, as is the burial custom of the Jews." John adds the information that in the place where Jesus was crucified, "there was a garden, and in the garden a new tomb where no one had ever been laid." He goes on to suggest that because of the Jewish day of Preparation and because "the tomb was close at hand, they laid Jesus there" (19:38-42).

The Fourth Gospel is more Jewish also than the

other three in its emphasis on the Jewish feasts and Jesus' participation in them. The unique chronology of the Lord's ministry is closely united with the various feasts and with trips to Jerusalem to observe them. The Evangelist possessed a very accurate knowledge of Jerusalem as well as of Jewish customs. He tells us, too, that on the night of the betrayal and arrest, "another disciple" accompanied Simon Peter to the residence of the high priest and that "this disciple was known to the high priest." It was thus that Peter was able to get into the court of the high priest's house and deny in Jesus' presence that he even knew the Master. It seems clear that this is the disciple "whom Jesus loved," who at the Supper "was lying close to the breast of Jesus" (13:23).

It is noteworthy also that in the dialogue with Pilate as written up in John's Gospel, the discussion hinges on the accusation that Jesus had made himself king of the Jews and on the nature of that kingship. And it is in this Gospel that Pilate refuses to alter the inscription placed over the cross: "Jesus of Nazareth, the King of the Jews."

Moreover, in John's version of the Palm Sunday entry into Jerusalem, there is a great crowd of the Jews who go out to meet him, crying, "Hosanna! Blessed be he who comes in the name of the Lord, even the King of Israel!" (12:9,12,13)

Clearly the Gospel of John is a bridge document. It is steeped in Judaism as far as background is concerned. It accepts the Old Covenant—Moses and the Law—and the Prophets as authentic and as preparatory for a new and universal development, directed to the whole created world. It is aware at the same time of the surrounding Graeco-Roman order and of the hospitality of this environment to the religion of Christ.

A strong bid is made in this Gospel to Greek-dominated culture. This is the significance of the immortal prologue to John's Gospel and the bold introduction of the concept of Logos, going back 500 years to Heraclitus, as the key to both the order of creation and to the miracle of redemption. At the same time the Evangelist is aware of Philo's domestication of the Logos in advanced Judaism and of the element of syncretism that it typifies. Nor should it be forgotten that twice in John's Gospel, proper bids are made directly to the Greeks. (See 7:33-36 and 12:20 ff.) And, of course, in chapter 4 Jesus claims for his own the Samaritans, breaking with the strong tabu of the Jews.

I have paused to survey at length the relation of John's Gospel to Judaism because of its contemporary as well as its historical importance. Let the last word be that of my great mentor, Archbishop William Temple, who was one of the supreme Christians of this century. In his *Readings in St. John's Gospel*, which has been called by his biographer, Dean F. A. Iremonger, the greatest devotional treatise written by an English churchman since William Law's *A Serious Call to a Devout and Holy Life*, Temple has a short section entitled "The Lord in Controversy."

The key to rightly grasping the chapters studded with controversy, in the archbishop's view, is to remember that this Gospel is "the interpretative expression of a memory." He instances the Rabbinical type of dialectic employed, which "is regarded by eminent Jewish scholars as evidence for the substantial authenticity of the account."

Now, memory tends to harden an antagonism. This is typical where the rememberer is, as Temple believed, an intimate disciple, John, one of the sons of Thunder who wished to call down fire from heaven (Luke 9:54). "But though the relationship is depicted as one of sheer antagonism, with consequent hardness in the outlines of the opposing persons, there is not in the picture here given of the Lord any petulant irritation, such as some have thought that they found there. Our moral antagonism to the spirit of those who oppose us is so much mixed up with the emotional reaction of our offended self-concern that we are almost incapable of impersonal anger—the dreadful anger of perfect love at hate or selfishness. So we read the Lord's stern words as though they were contemptuous or ferocious. But there is no necessity to do that. The dramatic quality of the narrative requires that the ferocity should be all on one side, and confronted with unruffled calm on the other. That such calm is provoking to the irritated cannot be denied; but the fault is not with the calm."[3]

This is an attractive interpretation that reconciles any seeming contradiction to the central love-motif of the Johannine writings. It may well be a final word. But in any event, on our view of John's Gospel as primarily a theological drama setting forth the Church's ultimate understanding of the Divine Word and Son in relation to the Father, it is permissible to allow for the intrusion of a human, all-too-human, element that does not reflect the mind of Christ. To the redactor of the Gospel, the hatred of the Jews was a fearful reality, directed against one who was himself divine.

To sum up, Paul saw the Jewish people as a whole rejecting the Messiah-Saviour who had come. This was before the fall of Jerusalem. Also, from the beginning he had felt a special vocation to take the Gospel to the Gentile-Greek world and had done so. This had been his mission, approved by Peter and the Twelve, and later sanctioned formally at a special council in Jerusalem presided over by Jesus, the brother of the Lord.

At this time, too, Paul's far-reaching innovation with respect to the Law as it pertained to non-Jewish believers received categorical acceptance. The judgment as pronounced by James went this way: "Therefore my judgment is that we should not trouble those of the Gentiles who turn to God, but should write to them to abstain from the pollutions of idols and from unchastity and from what is strangled and from blood."[4]

Paul's deepest thinking, however, was more

revolutionary. We can trace it in his letters, especially in Galatians. Here he claims a direct revelation of his gospel; he tells of opposing Peter to his face at Antioch; and he philosophizes that the law was provisional and temporary: it was our tutor or custodian until Christ came with the good news of a divine love that justifies us by faith, and not of works at all.[5]

By the time John wrote, the breach between the Synagogue and the Church is complete. And the quarrel has taken on harsh and bitter overtones. One of the great tragedies of history has begun. Henceforth, the field of expansion for Christianity is the Graeco-Roman, Gentile world. Judaism is basically closed off. But the Church still has as her official Scriptures the Old Testament. And, of course, there were descendants a plenty of Jewish Christians.[6]

Every vital religious faith merges with a culture. It cannot exist without putting down roots. The Hellenistic world now becomes the environment in which the Christian Church is grounded and must make its way. This cultural world was syncretic, but the basic thrust was Greek with Oriental motifs and overtones. Greek intellectualism was a strong continuing factor. But, as we have seen, the dominating drive was to find an assured salvation, a meaningful and transforming union with the divine.

From the Greek tradition, with Plato an ever-present influence, came the idea of *Gnosis*—knowledge as participation. From the Oriental mysteries came the idea of revelation embodied in a vivid and

powerful myth. Thus the stage was set for the rise
within the new, dynamic, appealing mystery, with
its majestic figure of Christ, of the ferment and the
sectarianism we knew as Gnosticism. The church
fathers regarded this movement as a Christian heresy,
and the new evidence from the recently discovered
Gnostic writings confirms this view. A great many
histories of Christian thought and doctrine must, in
consequence, be revised, for the German *religionsgeschichte* school of Reitzenstein, Bousset, and Bultmann (who succeeded Bousset at the University of
Giessen) carried enormous weight for half a century.

The ''history of religion'' scholars not only
amalgamated Gnosticism and the mystery religions.
They pushed Gnosticism back historically, giving it
an existence before Christianity and independent of
it. Thus they were able to visualize an intersection
of two definitive spiritual currents, with each
profoundly influencing the other.

Accordingly, a Reitzenstein could say that Paul
was ''the first and greatest of the Gnostics.'' A Bultmann could seriously hold up the Johannine Christ
as assimilated to the image of a pre-existent Gnostic
redeemer myth and regard the Fourth Gospel as
basically a Gnostic document.[7]

What shall we say of the overall Gnostic phe-
nomenon in the light of our copious Christian sources
(Irenaeus, Tertullian, Hippolytus, and Clement of
Alexanderis) and present scholarship based on the
Nag Hammadi discoveries? Writing not as a tech-

nical specialist but as a teacher of the history of doctrine with a particular fascination for the Gnostics and the obscurities of the Church in the second century, I see this kind of a picture.

The early Church, save at Jerusalem up to A.D. 70, was not an organized body. It had no clear structure. There was an element of connectional authority, even of loose hierarchy, rooted in the office and role of Apostle. But it was fluid. There was also an unofficial but recognized order of prophets, by definition spontaneous and individual, but at the same time wielding a peculiar authority. And there were teachers, necessary at first to interpret the prophets but sure to develop as key figures in local churches. Paul singles out these three: "God has appointed in the church first apostles, second prophets, third teachers."[8]

The Christianity of the apostolic and subapostolic age (30 to 90 or 95) was a movement of the Spirit. It was veritably a fulfillment of the prophecy of Joel and the infant Church was acutely conscious of this. It was from the start a matter of local groups and assemblies (*ecclesiae*), characterized by spontaneity, enthusiasm, and freedom. Paul's Letters following on the first chapters of the Acts give us records, as it were, on film. We see living, breathing local churches.

We are made witnesses also of the exercise of apostolic authority. But the authority in question is hardly institutionalized. It is rooted in spiritual instinct and moral force. Paul's appeal is to the memories, hearts, and better selves of his converts—and to the position he has occupied.

We see also in Paul's Epistles the pneumatic character of the primitive Christian movement. The classic example or expression of this is 1 Corinthians, especially chapters 12-13. With this Galatians 5 and Ephesians 4 should be compared. The magisterial role and power of the Spirit is preeminent in the Christianity of the churches to which these letters are addressed.

Nor are we restricted to the Pauline literature and its dynamic witness to the Spirit, an element not confined to any number of special passages but permeating all Paul's thought and consciousness. The Gospels of Mark and Matthew present a figure who moves continually in the power of the Spirit.

The prophetic mission of John the Baptizer is continued and amplified in Jesus of Nazareth. The accounts of the baptism are an important link in this understanding, and Mark's phrasing in introducing the follow-up of the Temptation is particularly striking. He says, after the descent of the Spirit on Jesus at his baptism, that "immediately the Spirit drove him into the wilderness."[9] Mark, who is in a great hurry here as elsewhere, files by title, as it were, the Temptation, noting only that it was of 40 days duration among the wild beasts, and that the angels ministered unto him.

Both Matthew and Luke are in full accord with

the role of the Spirit in the life and work and direction of Jesus the Christ, but it is Luke who in Acts provides the definitive pneumatic interpretation of the Church in its founding and pristine calling through the miracle of the first Pentecost. In the Gospel of John we encounter a revision of divine roles, necessitated by his exalted Christology.

In the Acts Luke presents the classic account of the first Pentecost and of the stirring events of that day that bound together in the strongest possible manner the assembly or gathered body of disciples who looked to and believed in Jesus as the Messiah, crucified but risen and reigning at the right hand of the Father. Clearly Luke sees also and presents the primitive Church as definitively apostolic.

> There were added to them in that day about three thousand souls. And they continued stedfastly in the apostles' teaching, and fellowship, in the breaking of bread and the prayers.[10]
> And with great power gave the Apostles their witness of the resurrection of the Lord Jesus: and great grace was upon them all.[11]

Matthew does not use the word ''apostles,'' but his outlook coheres with Luke. At the end of his Gospel the Lord Jesus appears in Galilee to the eleven disciples and imparts to them his Great Commission: ''Go . . . make disciples of all the nations, baptizing them into the name of the Father and of the Son and of the Holy Ghost.''[12]

Father Raymond E. Brown in his brilliant study of Johannine Christians and Christianity in *The Community of the Beloved Disciple* holds that this school, or individuated church, was distinct from the mainline Apostolic Churches, a term he prefers to the Great Church. The latter he would reserve for the Church of the second century, which had a more highly developed authoritative ministry and which repelled Gnosticism and the Marcionite schism. Brown is very convincing in his presentation of what he calls the one-upmanship of the Johannine Christians centering in their Christology and in the role of the Beloved Disciple in comparison with the Twelve and even with Peter, the hero of Matthew, especially, and of the Acts, secondarily. In relation to the ministry and ecclesiology, he finds a reverse situation from that of Christology. The Apostolic Churches are more advanced here and normative than John and his followers.

Brown's position is integral to what he appears to regard as a series of layers, laid down more or less like geological strata, in the formation of the Fourth Gospel. I am more impressed by its essential unity and consummate artistry. Also, the high sacramentalism of John must not be overlooked, and assuredly in both chapter 20, where the Lord breathes on his disciples in imparting the Holy Spirit with the power to forgive sins, and chapter 21, with the very special threefold commission to Peter as shepherd, the Evangelist goes about as far as it was possible to go in making common ground with the Apostolic Churches.

In the First Epistle of John there is, as indeed Brown recognizes, an almost Lucan note in appealing to the witness of direct, firsthand apostolic knowledge. This could represent a definite intent of rapprochement with the other churches. And, of course, 2 and 3 John are explicitly written by a presbyter, or elder. This must be a link with what we must now look at, the development in local churches—as time went on and the demand for authority became more pressing—of the presbyterate and episcopate.

This is a vexed question over which learned men have labored for centuries and in which the only certain thing is that the development was variable, not uniform. And this, given the situation of the founding and expansion of Christianity in the first two generations as we have seen it to be, was inevitable.

Elder, or presbyter, denoted persons of importance in ancient society who were given respect because of their age and experience. They would naturally come to the fore in local churches, and with an increasing need for order and authority elders would become official leaders. We can tell from the New Testament that this was happening. There are a number of passages in the Acts indicating this,[13] with corroboration from James, 1 Peter, and at least two passages from Pastorals attributed to Paul.[14]

The word "bishop" (*Episcopos*) occurs five times in the New Testament, the cognate term Episcope once. The instance in Philippians 1:1 is probably simply a matter of nomenclature. Paul's greeting is to the saints, "with the bishops and the deacons." In Acts 20 it is clear that elders and bishops are different terms for the same officials of the church at Ephesus. In 1 Timothy and Titus the situation is not entirely clear, but there is a strong indication that the office of bishop or overseer is emerging as the creation of the local presbytery. It may be that we are seeing a step in the direction of the emergence at Antioch by A.D. 110 of the local monarchical bishop who functions along with the presbyters and the deacons.

The letters of Ignatius leave no doubt as to this development. An earlier work, the diffuse but attractive Epistle of Clement in the name of the Roman church to the Corinthians, seems to fit into the stage suggested by the Pastoral Epistles. Clement speaks first of the bishops and deacons and links them with the idea of authoritative succession from the apostles. "The Apostles received the Gospel from the Lord Jesus Christ, Jesus the Christ was sent from God." The apostles, who seem to be identified with the twelve sent out by Jesus in the Gospels on a preaching mission, "appointed their first converts, testing them by the Spirit, to be the bishops and deacons of the future believers."[15]

In an arresting statement Clement, who is viewed by tradition as the fourth bishop of Rome, declares, "Our Apostles also knew through our Lord Jesus Christ that there would be strife for the title of bishop."[16] But it appears, when he gets down to brass tacks in rebuking the still unruly and fractious Corinthian Christians, that this church is ruled by presbyters.[17]

Williston Walker, of Yale, after noting that for all his stress on Episcopal authority Ignatius knows nothing of an apostolical succession, writes:

> It was the union of these two principles, a monarchical bishop in apostolical succession, which occurred before the middle of the second century, that immensely enhanced the dignity and power of the bishopric. By the sixth decade of the second century monarchical bishops had become well-nigh universal. The institution was to gain further strength in the Gnostic and Montanist struggles; but it may be doubted whether anything less rigid could have carried the Church through the crises of the second century.[18]

Now we must enter as far as we can the obscure but vital world of second-century Christianity. We must try to picture it in a general way.

First of all, the Christian movement is in process of growth. It has a wide appeal; it is spreading rapidly; and it is reaching out in all directions. Primarily, it is attracting Greek-speaking Gentiles of

many backgrounds all around the Mediterranean Ba-
sin. It is penetrating more deeply into the hinterland
of Palestine, Syria, Persia, Asia Minor, Cyprus,
Greece, Italy, Gaul, Spain, North Africa, and Egypt.
In innumerable cities and towns there were churches.
Among the most important Christian centers were
Antioch, Damascus, Caesarea, Ephesus, Smyrna,
Laodicea, Colossae, Hierapolis, Ancyra, Byzantium,
Philippi, Corinth, Thessalonica, Rome, Carthage,
and Alexandria.

Life in the ancient world was basically urban;
cities were the seat of civilization. Travel was ordered
and relatively easy; there was much moving about
in the Roman Empire by land and sea. Many people
were well-educated and widely read. Publication and
book trade, curious as it seems to us given no printing, were well-established institutions. The importance of this for the Christian movement could hardly
be exaggerated. The Gentile Graeco-Roman world
was a reading world; the Palestinian Jewish world
was not.

We can get a good idea of the sociology of the
Christian movement as it moves into the second
century by bearing in mind the Corinthian church
as revealed in Paul's Letters, especially 1 Corinthians. The people were curious, independent, intelligent, diverse, given to factionalism. They were
very much of their world.

More than a hundred years later, Clement of
Alexandria gives us a detailed, very fascinating ac-

count of the culture and social life of a great city, Alexandria. He relates the Christian in his faith and ethical outlook to this life. There is another excellent mirror of life and problems as they appeared to Christian leaders in the New Testament—in the Pastoral Epistles to Timothy and Titus and 2 Peter. One can assume that in point of date, they come well in between Paul's Corinthian Epistles and the writings of Clement of Alexandria. They reflect the Church in the 90 to 120 generation.

The atmosphere that comes through in the late New Testament writings is very different from that of works written in the 50s and 60s. The fire is burning low; enthusiasm has declined. The ecstatic, spirit-filled congregations reflecting closeness and brotherly affection seem to have grown cold, formal, worldly, immoral, and disobedient.

No doubt the descriptions are one-sided and must be discounted from an overall standpoint, but here are some samples.

Honor widows who are real widows . . . .
But refuse to enroll younger widows; for when they grow wanton against Christ they desire to marry, and so they incur condemnation for having violated their first pledge. Besides that, they learn to be idlers, gadding about from house to house, and not only idlers but gossips and busy-bodies, saying what they should not . . . .
For some have already strayed after

Satan.[19]

Teach and urge these duties. If anyone teaches otherwise and does not agree with the sound words of our Lord Jesus Christ and the teaching which accords with godliness, he is puffed up with conceit, he knows nothing; he has a morbid craving for controversy and for disputes about words, which produce envy, dissension, slander, base suspicions, and wrangling among men who are depraved in mind and bereft of the truth, imagining that godliness is a means of gain . . . . For the love of money is the root of all evils.[20]

But understand this, that in the last days there will come times of stress. For men will be lovers of self, lovers of money, proud, arrogant, abusive, disobedient to their parents, ungrateful, unholy, inhuman, implacable, slanderers, profligates, fierce, haters of good, treacherous, reckless, swollen with conceit, lovers of pleasure rather than lovers of God, holding the form of religion but denying the power of it.[21]

They count it pleasure to revel in the daytime. They are blots and blemishes, reveling in their dissipation, carousing with you. They have eyes full of adultery, insatiable for sin. They entice unsteady souls.

> They have hearts trained in greed. Ac-
> cursed children![22]

I have often thought, reading the Pastorals, that they
might have been written in our time and about our
urban, sensate, free-wheeling, anarchic American
culture. At least if it is not reflective of the moral
majority, nor yet exactly of the counter-culture still
with us, it seems akin to the world reflected in typical novels and soap operas that have become the
opium of American women of all classes—upper,
lower, middle, and upper-middle—even of the idle
rich.

Now, remembering the wide distribution of
churches and the lack of a strongly coordinated connectional organization, and bearing in mind the large
number of literate, serious, reading folk able to follow after this or that wandering philosopher (Justin
always wore the philosopher's cloak) or to sample one
or another of the surging mystery religions, we can
see how people of the type of Gnostics as exemplified in the Nag Hammadi writings could have arisen
in the Christian churches.

First, let us look at the earliest references or
allusions to Gnostic thinking that we have in Christian literature; then we can note the distinctively
Gnostic material from whatever source that bears on
its origin and early grounding. Lastly, we can see
how it (including Marcionism) became a powerful
movement and a dangerous heresy, with the Apostolic Churches (later, the Great Church) narrowly es-

caping being engulfed by a doctrine that was aristocratic, philosophical, Hellenistic, cosmopolitan —and anti-Jewish, antibiblical, anticlerical, and antisacramental. It was also anti- and nontraditional, even though it claimed to have an older and more authentic tradition, just as by allegorization it was able to utilize and manipulate to a degree Hebrew and Christian Scriptures.

The oldest allusion to Gnosticism in the New Testament, and possibly anywhere, seems to be in Paul's Letter to the church at Colossae. I cannot doubt for a minute that this is by Paul and gives us the crown of his developing Christology.

It is in the great summary Christological passage in chapter 1, which may have been evoked by a combination of a Judaizing element equipped with an elaborate angelology and an incipient or rising Gnostic strain. The key word from the point of view of Gnostic philosophical theology is *pleroma*. The verse in which this pregnant word is first used is a striking one. "For in him (Christ) the whole *pleroma* was pleased to dwell,[23] and through him to reconcile to himself all things, whether on earth or in heaven, making peace through the blood of his cross."

Paul then goes on a little further to repeat this startling assertion in an even sharper manner. "For in him dwells the entire *pleroma* of Godhead in a bodily form."[24] This statement is preceded by a warning against "philosophy and empty deceit, according to the tradition of men, according to elemental spirits of the universe and not according to Christ."[25]

After this strong statement about the pleroma of Godhead (note that with the Gnostics the pleroma or hierarchy of divine entities serves a mediatorial function connecting the ultimate, indescribable One or depth of all and the created material world), Paul launches into a distancing of Christianity from circumcision and the law. He then speaks out sharply on rules of eating or drinking:

> So let no one take you to task on questions of eating and drinking or in connection with observance of festivals or new moons or sabbaths. All that is mere shadow of what is to be; the substance belongs to Christ. Let no one lay down rules for you as he pleases, with regard to fasting and any cult of angels, presuming on his visions and inflated by his sensuous notions, instead of keeping in touch with the Head under whom the entire Body, supplied with joints and sinews and thus compacted, grows with growth divine.[26]

It looks very much as if the apostle is striking out at extremes both on the Gentile and on the Jewish front. Quite possibly, there is in Colossae a syncretistic merging of the two. As is well known, the church fathers believed that Gnosticism originated with Simon Magus (the magician) whom Philip the

Apostle encountered when he took the gospel to Samaria, following the severe persecution in Jerusalem typified by the stoning of Stephen.[27]

According to Irenaeus,[28] the three oldest Gnostic systems were from Simon, Menander, also of Samaria and likewise a magician, and Saturninus of Antioch, in Syria. For Simon and Menander the world was created by angels, who had been generated by an *Ennoea*, or first inward thought, which had gone forth from the ultimate Power. Angels were produced by *Ennoea* and it was by them that the world had been created. "Saturninus, like Menander, set forth one father unknown to all, who made angels, archangels, powers, and potentates." The world, according to Saturninus, "was made by a certain company of seven angels," of whom one was the God of the Jews.

All three of these primal Gnostics agree in retaining the idea of a created world but by angels, not the highest God. The first two have the notion of generation or emanation in the spiritual realm. This will become a foundation concept of the great Gnostics. Saturninus seems to have kept the Jewish view that all angels and heavenly beings were created, not generated or begotten.

Thus it is entirely possible that the genesis of Gnosticism is to be found in ex-Jews disillusioned by the final failure of orthodox Davidic messianism and the apocalyptic hope. Their speculative angelology was merged with Greek intellectualism, ontological dualism, poetic mythological mysticism, and a superiority complex to spawn the great fantastic Gnostic systems, elaborated by Basilides, Valentinus, and their disciples.

Distinct from this all-out, surging heresy are the Christian Platonists of Alexandria—Clement and Origen. These thinkers, however, were halfway Gnostics who retained both the Old Testament and the normative Christian Scriptures already becoming an embryonic canon, but were able by allegorization to eliminate the Hebrew crudities and to go far in the direction of Hellenization. Origen especially was deeply Christian in his Christology and in the compelling influence of the four Gospels, on two of which, Matthew and John, he produced elaborate commentaries.

In a class by himself, a sort of theological "sport," is Marcion, born around A.D. 100 and very possibly the son of a bishop. He was a wealthy shipowner who came to Rome about 140 and undertook to take over the Church in the interest of of the most audacious and astonishing heresies of history.

Marcion was a kind of Paulinist. Paul the Apostle was his hero and avowed prototype. Harnack is fascinated by this bold sectarian adventurer, regards him a religious genius of the first order, and wittily characterizes him as the only person to understand Paul, but adds, "and he misunderstood him."

Scholars are unable to decide whether Marcion belongs to the Gnostic movement or must be classi-

fied as *sui generis*, an authentic original. I lean to the
latter position, principally because Marcion is one
of the terrible simplifiers, whereas the main thrust
of Gnosticism theologically was toward complexity
and infinite elaboration. But Marcion was anti-
Semitic in the deepest sense; he viewed the Old
Testament and Jewish exclusivity with horror. He
proposed to throw out the entire Jewish legacy and
tradition, denying flatly the Johannine affirmation
that "salvation is of the Jews."

Marcion is harsher here and more uncompromising than the great Gnostics, partly because
he rejects or at least declines to use the allegorical
route in exegesis and interpretation. This requires
him to do what Thomas Jefferson did in the White
House during his presidency, take scissors and use
them on the canonical Gospels in order to separate
the authentic Jesus from the evangelical misunder-
standings and distortions that had crept in and spoiled
the purity and beauty of the original Gospel. Of
course, the normative standpoint and guiding criteria
of the two rationalists, separated by over sixteen
centuries, were very different.

It is unnecessary to go into the proposals of
Marcion at this point. Later on, we shall do so and
shall point out an arresting affinity between Marcion
and the modern Christian mind. Now we must return to our review of the New Testament in the
search for the impact of Gnostic beginnings. We have
noted Colossians and the Acts. We must turn now

to the Pastoral Epistles attributed to St. Paul, the Johannine literature, and 2 Peter. No long tarrying at any point will be required.

It is in 1 Timothy that we really strike pay dirt. At the very end of this Epistle, critically important as to time and evidence that the Gnostic leaven was internal to the Church, is a warning against what is to become a swelling heresy.

> O Timothy, guard the deposit, avoiding the profane, worthless utterances and contradictions[29] of what is falsely called knowledge (*gnosis*). For some by professing this missed the mark as regards the faith. Grace be with you.[30]

There is reason for associating this letter with the Gospel of John. In 6:13 the reference to a good or noble confession before Pontius Pilate suggests John's account of Jesus before Pilate.

> You say that I am a king. For this I was born, and for this I have come into the world, to bear witness to the truth.[31]

John repeatedly quotes the statement, "No one has ever seen God"; and in 1 Timothy 6:16 we read: "who alone has immortality and dwells in unapproachable light, whom no one has ever seen or can see."

This is very helpful from the point of view of dating 1 Timothy and suggests a date around A.D.

100. The view taken of faith and doctrine and the mirror it presents of church life and problems are corroborative of this subapostolic period. There is also a link between 1 John and 1 Timothy, as we shall see momentarily, in the intrusion of problems reflecting the presence of Gnostic views and Gnostic Christians.

The other Pastoral Epistles, 2 Timothy and Titus, are of a piece with the first letter to Timothy in concepts and emphasis. They do not add anything to the reflection of a Gnostic presence unless it be the emphasis on all scripture as inspired in 2 Timothy 3:16. The denial of this would be a chief tenet of both Marcion and the principal Gnostic theologians.

Two passages in 1 John are pertinent. The first one, in chapter 2, develops the antichrist motif. "Who is the liar but he who denies that Jesus is the Christ? This is the antichrist, he who denies the Father and the Son. No one who denies the Son has the Father."

So far, the kind of denial is not pinned down. But in chapter 4 we read that the test of the Spirit of God, as distinct from other spirits, is the confession that "Jesus Christ has come in the flesh." Every spirit that does not so confess Jesus is not of God and "is the spirit of antichrist." Further along, the author equates this anti-Docetic and anti-Gnostic confession with believing that Jesus is the Christ and is the Son of God.

This construction of the Christological polemic

in 1 John and its anti-Gnostic import are confirmed in the shorter and blunter Second Epistle of John. Here the Elder addresses "the elect Lady and her children" and pulls no punches. "For many deceivers have gone out into the world, men who will not acknowledge the coming of Jesus Christ in the flesh; such a one is the deceiver and the antichrist."

One of the most interesting of the New Testament library of letters is 2 Peter. First of all, there can be no doubt of its being a pseudonymous writing. The purposes of the author in writing are crystal-clear, and there is no possibility of the letter being taken for an apostolic work. There are clear references to other New Testament writings: to 1 Peter, to one or more of the Synoptic Gospels, and to the epistles of Paul. One must assume that he has the collected editions of Paul before him. It seems likely, too, that he uses Jude rather than the reverse.

The tone and vocabulary of the epistle are very Greek. The author stresses knowledge but desires to undergird it as trustworthy. Through the precious promises of God in Christ, he tells the Christians to whom he writes, they "may escape from the corruption of the world because of passion, and become partakers of the divine nature."[32] This very un-Hebraic idea of divinization will in time become a commonplace, but this is the only place in the New Testament where it is explicit. The Johannine writings are perhaps on the edge of such a concept, but they never plunge in.

The writer is concerned to invoke eyewitnesses of the majesty and supernal glory of Christ, as against "cleverly devised myths."[33] He also speaks of "destructive heresies" that deny Christ, brought in secretly by false teachers and of their licentiousness. These are fiercely denounced.[34] He maintains against scoffers "following their own passions" the reality of a coming day of the Lord and of Divine judgment.[35]

This letter could be directed against incipient Gnostics and types that in time will go in that direction. It is tempting to see this confirmed in what he says about Paul. He refers to "all his letters" and singles out the fact that "there are some things in them hard to understand, which the ignorant and unstable twist to their own destruction."[36] We know that Paul was the anointed of Marcion and that the Gnostics were stimulated by certain sayings of Paul and were led to try to base their teachings on him. This could be the explanation of 2 Peter's emphatic reference to Paul.

It remains to note relevant data in the body of early Christian literature known as the Apostolic Fathers. To this should be added, finally, certain indispensable information derived from Justin Martyr, datable around A.D. 150.

In dates the Apostolic Fathers are evidently correlative as a whole with the late New Testament books just noted, the Pastorals, 1 and 2 John, Jude, and 2 Peter. Of these the last is the latest New Testament writing. The editors of the Oxford Study Edition of the New English Bible go so far as to propose the date of "perhaps about A.D. 150" for 2 Peter. On the other hand, they think Jude was written in the "late first or early second century."

In summary, it is safe to say that in this part of the "mirror" provided by the New Testament, we are dealing with a fifty- or sixty-year period running from A.D. 90 to 140 or 150.

Turning to the Apostolic Fathers, the earliest is 1 Clement, probably written in A.D. 96. Next, probably, is the Didache or Teaching of the Twelve Apostles, usually dated about 110, but containing earlier material. Closely parallel with the Didache in time are the Epistles of Ignatius, third bishop of Syrian and Antioch, who was condemned to be sent to Rome to be killed by the beasts in the amphitheatre. According to Eusebius, the date of Ignatius' martyrdom was the tenth year of Trajan's reign, or A.D. 108. It is possible that it was later than that, say 115. Trajan was emperor from 98 to 117. Ignatius en route to Rome to die wrote seven letters, which are among the most important documents of early Christianity.

Next comes 2 Clement, in some circles at some point closely associated with 1 Clement and called a second epistle. It is in reality a letter only in name and in chapter 19 the author states clearly that he is reading aloud an exhortation to assembled "brothers and sisters."

Therefore 2 Clement is an ancient homily or sermon. The object of the writer is threefold. He wishes to inculcate a high Christology, a life of purity, and belief in the resurrection of the flesh.

The preacher does not appear to have any polemical purpose. His aim is to edify, to build up his hearer in faith and life with a view to an abundant life in the world to come. The opening sentence is as memorable as any sermon on record. He begins:

> Brethren, we must think of Jesus Christ
> as of God, as of the Judge of the living and
> the dead, ''and we must not think little of
> our salvation.''

It is to be noted that this is an inversion of the Johannine outlook; we are exhorted not to see God the Father in the Son, but the Son in the light of the God whom we know. There is no certainty about the dating of 2 Clement. It was almost certainly produced between 120 and 170, and 150 is a good intermediate guess.

The Epistle of Barnabas is a letter in form whose author sought to gain currency for his writing by attributing it to Barnabas, the companion of Paul. It may have been a general treatise, or it could have been intended for a church or group imbued with Alexandrian ideas. The writer wishes to warn Christians against a Judaistic conception of the Old Testament. He uses allegorical exegesis, carrying it even further than Philo. He appears to deny literal value to any commands of the Law and teaches that an evil angel misled the Jews into thinking that the ceremonial part of the Law had to be literally observed.

This epistle may have been written in the first century, or after 132. There is internal evidence either way. The ten kings of chapter 4 are thought to refer to the Roman Emperors; and, alternatively, in chapter 16 he refers to the hope of rebuilding the Temple, its destruction by the enemy owing to the war, and the true spiritual temple of the Lord's creation in man. The second reference is presumed to be to the second Roman war.

The Shepherd of Hermas, a western Roman apocalypse, is the longest of the writings labelled Apostolic Fathers. It was apparently written around 148, since at the time of the Muratorian canon some accepted it as canonical on the ground that Hermas was a brother of Pius, a Pope at that time. It may be that it was written serially, over a period of twenty to thirty years preceding 148. It is divided into Visions, Commandments, and Parables. Anyone reading it will understand its omission from the Muratorian Canon.[37]

Two other writings are included in the group bearing the name Apostolic Fathers, one properly and one improperly.

The Martyrdom of Polycarp is the earliest known account of a Christian martyrdom. It is in the form of a letter from the church of Smyrna to

the church of Philomelium. The date of the martyrdom is believed by modern scholars, correcting
the earlier date given by Eusebius, to be either February 23, 155, or February 22, 156.

The Epistle to Diognetus, an anonymous apologia for Christianity, is of uncertain date but certainly
belongs with the Apologies. It has been thought that
it was written by Hippolytus (c. 160-235). In any
event, it is a treatise of rare beauty, rising to a great
height in laying out the essence of Christianity. More
than any other single book, outside the New Testament in the first three centuries of the Christian era,
this anonymous apologia addressed to someone with
the same name as a teacher of Emperor Marcus
Aurelius explains what made the new religion of
Christ irresistible.

This epistle suggests the most notable apologist
of the century for the new religion, St. Justin the
Martyr, more generally known as Justin Martyr.
Justin stands out for several things. To begin with,
he apparently wrote the first full work directed against
Marcion. It has not survived, but Irenaeus cites it[38]
and Justin in his *Apology* denounces Marcion repeatedly and in uncompromising terms.[39]

Justin started out as a philosopher, and in a
sense never ceased to be one. Even after his conversion, he continued to wear his philosopher's cloak.
Furthermore, he saw no sharp dichotomy between
Christianity and philosophy. The new religion was
rather the fulfillment of philosophy. Of the latter he

said in discussion with the Jew, Trypho: "Philosophy is a knowledge of that which is and an understanding of the truth; and happiness is the reward of this knowledge and wisdom."[40]

Despite his philosophical inclinations, Justin is remarkably comprehensive and orthodox in his grasp of Christianity. He shows himself to be well acquainted with the Synoptic Gospels and holds to them fully. He affirms a new and more perfect, eternal law of God. He calls for repentance as the ground of forgiveness of sins and lays weight on Christ's law of love as set forth in the Sermon on the Mount. He believes strongly in demons, really devils, for they inspire wickedness. He is a millennialist of the "pre" variety and believes in heaven and hell.

He expounds the truth of the Dominical Sacraments and provides a precious, detailed account of Baptism and the Eucharist, our first such after the New Testament. In short, Justin is a stout witness to a flourishing, expanding centrist Christianity on Gentile soil the middle of the second century, contemporary with Marcion and the great Gnostic heresiarchs and well before Irenaeus and Tertullian.

This fits well with the picture of the Church in the *saeculum obscurum* (obscure age) or second century as it discloses itself in the later writings of the New Testament and in the Apostolic Fathers. It remains for us to note further the latter and attempt some generalizations.

This body of writings divides itself basically into

the Ignatian Epistles and the rest. Ignatius (as indeed we saw earlier) is in the line of Paul and John. He is a strong Christologist and comes out swinging against Docetism and incipient Gnosticism.

McGiffert possibly puts this a shade too strongly, but he is basically right when he says: "The letters naturally contain no systematic statement of Ignatius' Christian beliefs, and yet there runs through them a very definite conception of Christianity, a genuinely mystical conception, which allies him to Paul and John and distinguishes him sharply from all the other so-called Apostolic Fathers."[41]

McGiffert sees these Fathers as representing a type of Christianity very different from Paul's or anything like a mystery religion of salvation. Rather to them Christianity appeared "as a moral system similar to the Judaism of the dispersion but stripped of all racial and national features." He adds that they chiefly thought of Christianity as a law, but a divine law, eternal and universal. It is also a revealed law, and Jesus Christ is its revealer and the revealer of the sanctions attached to it.[42]

The Christology of the Apostolic Fathers is a high Christology. Jesus Christ is the Son of God and is himself God. As we have seen, 2 Clement states this explicitly. How this can be is little inquired into. Nor is there any thought of surrendering or compromising monotheism.

Thus Mandate I of the Shepherd of Hermas declares, "First of all believe that God is one, 'who made all things and perfected them, and made all things to be out of that which was not' . . . Believe then in him, and fear him, and in your fear be continent.''

In general, we can say that the Apostolic Fathers represent a kind of republication of Judaism, stripped of particularistic features, and with a divine Christ added on as teacher, revealer, and saviour. There is a slight tendency to anti-Jewish sentiment, but nothing suggesting the outlook of Marcion. Nor is one made aware of the existence of Gnostic sophistication, save in the case of Ignatius. The latter knows of Gnosticism in connection with Christology and resurrection, and strikes out strongly for orthodoxy.

> Be deaf therefore when anyone speaks to you apart from Jesus Christ who was of the lineage of David and Mary, who was truly born and ate and drank, was truly brought to trial before Pontius Pilate, was truly crucified and died while those in heaven and earth and under the earth looked on; who also was truly raised from the dead.[43]

> There is one Physician, who is both flesh and spirit, born and yet not born, who is God in man, true life in death, both of Mary and of God, first passible and then impassible, Jesus Christ our Lord.[44]

He warns the Magnesians ''not to fall into the

snare of vain doctrine, but to be convinced of the
birth and passion and resurrection which took place
at the time of the procuratorship of Pontius Pilate.''[45]
Clearly Ignatius is aware of what Gnostics do and
will do with the person of the Lord. He is also out-
spoken in condemnation of Judaism. And, of course,
he is the great pioneer proponent of the monarchical
bishop.

It is monstrous, Ignatius says, ''to talk of Jesus
Christ and to practice Judaism.''[46] And here he
wraps up a great deal: ''Be subject to the bishop and
to one another, even as Jesus Christ was subject to
the Father, and the Apostles were subject to Christ
and to the Father, in order that there may be a union
of both flesh and spirit.''[47]

This looks down the line directly to Irenaeus,
Tertullian, and Hippolytus. But there was not yet
a Great Church or even a clear central line of development. It took a resounding crisis, and a threatened crash, to bring this into being. As things were,
there was great variety, abounding vitality, largely
unchecked freedom in the churches that rimmed the
Mediterranean and were expanding all around into
the interior hinterland. There is a passage in Origen's
Contra Celsum that indicates the inevitable development, not now slow in coming:

> As men, not only the laboring and serving
> classes, but also many from the cultured
> classes of Greece, came to see something
> honorable in Christianity, sects could not

fail to arise, not simply from the desire for controversy and contradiction, but because several scholars endeavoured to penetrate deeper into the truth of Christianity. In this way sects arose, which received their names from men who indeed admired Christianity in its essence, but from many different causes had arrived at different conceptions of it.[48]

We are now in a position to sum up the situation in the first and middle decades of the second century and to see how the strong currents that emerged in the middle third of the century came about.

The Christian Church in this period was decentralized, more than in the compact apostolic age. It was growing rapidly. The Graeco-Gentile world was large and exceedingly varied. It was attracted to a Christ who had come down from heaven and was known and worshipped as Lord and Saviour. The separation of the Church from Judaism and the restrictions and peculiarities of the Jewish Law increased its appeal to Gentiles of all sorts and conditions. This was particularly true after the catastrophic Second Jewish War of 132-135.

This whole development eased the scandal and burden of Jewish apocalyptic and the eschatology derived from it. It also made it possible to think of liberation from the crudities and barbarities in which the interminably lengthy and complicated Old Testament abounded. Finally, it was not impossible to think of a more credible and creditable view of deity, of creation, and of rescue or salvation.

This, it would seem, is exactly what happened. There was nothing to prevent the outcropping of marked individualism and extreme variety. But religion is a social and corporate affair. There is a limit to the allowing of anarchy. It is only within the bosom of a specific background faith and worship that persons can arise of whom it may be said, "Religion is what the individual does with his solitariness."[49]

What seems to have happened is that strong trends developed in which knowledge (both inward and external) as opposed to faith was emphasized, and individuals of spiritual talent and even precocity arose and expressed themselves freely. Eventually, powerful minds in combination with charismatic personalities appeared and, as is inevitable in religion, attracted followers. In this way the great Gnostic schools arose, and the powerful antichurch of Marcion.

As is now well known, a rich find in Gnostic literature was made at Nag Hammadi in Egypt, in December, 1945. It consisted of some fifty books, probably literally a Gnostic library written in Coptic and copied in the fourth century (after Constantine established Christianity) for preservation from likely confiscation. Of all these books the most significant in the view of a distinguished authority, Professor

Robert M. Grant, is the *Gospel of Thomas*. It contains 114 sayings, parables, and dialogues ascribed to Jesus and his disciples. Half or more of these have parallels in the Synoptic Gospels. Others are very different, but where parallels exist the thrust in Thomas is novel and subjective in an existential sense. Here is the second saying from this Gospel:

> If those who draw you on say to you, 'Behold the kingdom is in the heaven,' then the birds of the heaven will be there before you. If they say to you, 'It is in the sea,' then the fishes will be there before you. But the Kingdom is within you[50] and outside you. When you know yourselves, then you will be known.

Other Gnostic sayings that direct the self inward and have a certain existential ring could be quoted. Then there are many free, unconventional, rather daring texts that could be quoted. A number are by, or have to do with, women. Elaine Pagels has assembled a collection of sayings that indicate a recognition of women in churches and the confession of a feminine component in the Godhead, in sharp contrast to the orthodoxy that prevailed.[51]

One sample of the unconventional sort may be given here. It is from the Gospel of Philip.

> . . . the companion of the [Savior is] Mary Magdelene. [But Christ loved] her more than [all] the disciples, and used to kiss her

[often] on her [mouth]. The rest of the disciples were offended. . . .They said to him,
"Why do you love her more than all of
us?" The Savior answered and said to
them, "Why do I not love you as [I love]
her?"[52]

It is clear from the documents now available that
there was a great deal of freedom in some churches,
at least in the early and middle second century. This
is not entirely out of line with the evidence of
subapostolic New Testament sources noticed above.

The most valuable aspect of this revelation of
life and thought in the second century Church, apart
from its intrinsic interest, is the proof it gives of the
Christian genesis of Gnosticism. This is what the
church fathers claimed. To modern scholars and
some theologians it seemed impossible that such a
view could be true. They were so taken up with the
syncretism of the whole period, and with the role of
the prevalent mystery religions antecedent to and
contemporary with Christianity, that they felt obliged to hypothecate a pre-Christian Gnosticism and
a Gnostic redeemer who was the prototype of the
Johannine Christ and, to a lesser extent, the Christ
of Paul.

The *coup de grace* has in all probability now been
administered to this ingenious hypothesis;[53] the result is a new and powerful witness to the impact
of the Christ of the New Testament on the Graeco-
Gentile mind of an era characterized by a belief in

"gods many, and lords many."[54] For many years now I have lived with and brooded upon the Christ of the New Testament in his totality—who is, after all, the Christ of Christian worship and faith—and I am more and more enthralled by this figure, truly unique in beauty, glory, wonder, and at once the Son of man and the Son of God. Long ago, I concluded that this Christ was the primary asset of Christianity and the Christian Church, and that his attractiveness to Graeco-Gentiles in the second and third centuries was irresistible. As much as anything, he explains the astonishing multiplication within Christian ranks of Gnostic types.

This leads me to an important distinction, which I am glad to see has been made by a distinguished French scholar and student of early church history. There were in the Church of the second century Gnostics and Gnostics. Some were thoughtful, aspiring, independent, free-thinking lay folk. They remind us of existentialists, depth-psychologists, psychiatrists, scientific-minded religionists, and graduates of psychoanalysis or psychotherapy today.

Then there were the theologians, who were also philosophically minded and did not make any sharp distinction between metaphysics and thoughtful religion. They were influenced by the long philosophical tradition and the vocation of the peripatetic, practicing philosopher, who went about wearing his professional badge, the philosopher's cloak. These types were very serious, as the Neoplatonists and the

Christian Platonists of Alexandria were. It was an age of mysticism, of hopelessness about the world and of flight from it up to the realms of divinity and Godhead.

What I have in mind and believe to be an important clarification in the problem of grasping the Gnostic phenomenon is stated in this way by His Eminence, Jean Cardinal Danielou:

> The break with Judaism, which is the hall-mark of this period, reveals itself in such writings as the Epistle of Barnabas and the letters of Ignatius of Antioch. In some cases it takes the form of a complete rejection of the Old Testament. This is what we find in the then vigorously developing move-ment of Gnosticism. The essence of Gnos-ticism is the rejection of the God of Israel. He is regarded as an inferior demiurge, and his creation and his Law are rejected with him. Gnosticism is an extreme ver-sion of the Pauline tendency. Its principal exponents are Satornilus and Carpocrates in Syria, Marcion in Asia Minor, and Basilides in Egypt. *One must distinguish the Gnosticism that is a total rejection of the Jewish god and of Judaism, from the gnosis that is sim-ply a search for higher religious knowledge and that is found in this period among Judaeo-Christians as well as among ex-pagan converts.*[55]

In this passage Danielou does not stress as much as I have the systematizers or theologians. But a little further on, he notes the signs of a growing concern to present the truths of the faith coherently.

> This concern is the Christian expression of a desire for synthesis which is one of the characteristics of the spirit of the age. This concern is scarcely noticeable in the Apologists. It makes its appearance with Valentinus and his disciples, particularly Ptolemy and Heraclion. The *Treatise on the Three Natures* which has been discovered at Nag Hammadi, and which is the work of Valentinus' school, is one of the earliest known theological synstheses. The theology of the Valentinian school is related to Gnostic radicalism.[56]

Danielou adds that Clement of Alexandria shows a similar preoccupation, but that "the really great synthesis is Origen's. It amounts to a general effort to explain the whole economy of the creation by starting from the love of God and the freedom of Man."[57]

The Gnostics did indeed set out to explain the creation, rejecting *in toto* the biblical version and outlook. This involved them in an elaborate transcendental rendering of the drama of Godhead. It takes the form of a kind of philosophic poem. It is a little hard to be sure how much is poetry, and how much

metaphysics. Implicit in the burden of theistic speculation is a judgment of the meanness of the world.
The full Gnostic thought little of the created order,
if order it could be called. In fact, the Gnostic went
so far as to present the cause of creation as an abortion of the God-element, Sophia. Yet it would be
wrong to ignore the loftiness of Valentinus when he
comes to deal with the highest or ultimate Godhead.

It has been generally held that Valentinus was
essentially a *Platonizing Gnostic* (a phrase from Hippolytus), as distinct from an adherent of a more drastic Oriental dualism. This very able thinker seems
to have conceived the whole universe as a grand chain
of being, beginning with the ultimate, abysmal
ground of being, moving on through various ema-
nations of divinity and spirit, and descending at last
to the lowest scale, which is matter.

According to Clement of Alexandria, Valentinus laid down the principle that the cosmos is as inferior to the living Aeon as the image is inferior to
the living countenance.[58] The Divine Aeons con-
stituted for this greatest of the Gnostics the pleroma
or fullness of Godhead. At the head of the pleroma
is an unnamable or Ineffable Dyad consisting of the
Unutterable (called also Bythos or Depth and unbegotten Father) and Sige or Silence. From this Dyad
proceeds another Dyad or Pair, Nous or Father and
Truth. Thus we get the highest Tetrad.

The Tetrad produces a second Tetrad: Logos
and Zoe or Life, Man and Church—the First Og-

doad. The Aeons continue the productive flow or emanational current: from Logos and Zoe proceeds a Decad (or Ten); and from Man and Church a Dodecad or Twelve Aeons. The names, about which there is some confusion, are not too important.

The fact of Thirty Aeons making up the pleroma is significant, for believe it or not, the number "thirty" is derived, first, from the fact that the Saviour (a favorite Gnostic term) did no work in public during the space of thirty years (Luke 3:23); and second, from Matthew's parable of the laborers sent at different hours into the vineyard (ch. 20). For some were sent the first hour, others about the third hour, others about the sixth hour, others about the ninth hour, and still others about the eleventh hour. Add these up, and you get the figure of thirty.

These are perfect examples of the fertility of allegorical exegesis, but what is more important, they show the influence on Valentinus of the Gospels and support the patristic view that these were Christian and not alien heretics.

But we have not yet reached creation. It came about in this way. Of the thirty Aeons, the last two were the Desire and Sophia, or Wisdom. Sophia experienced passion apart from her confrere Theletos, or Desired. What drew her was the desire to comprehend the Unutterable or Unbegotten Father. In consequence of this, she gave birth to a shapeless substance (the female issue without the form supplied by the male sperm, in the Greek way of thinking).

This inchoate substance was primal matter.

In another development of the Valentinian system (which may not have been held by Valentinus himself), there is a second, lower Sophia, left behind when her mother returns to the heavenly Aeons. This lower Sophia, called Achanoth after the Hebrew, gave birth to actual matter and to the Demiurge who fashioned the actually existing world with his angels.

It is difficult for us to enter into the spirit and the logic or rationale of this mythology in some way grounded on an ultimate abstraction, but it must be remembered that these details have been filtered to us through orthodox partisans. As an example of the richness of the thought of Valentinus, which such an outline as the above obscures, let me quote from a fragment preserved by Hippolytus.[59]

> The Father, however, was solitary, subsisting, as they say, in a state of quietude, and Himself reposing in isolation within Himself. When, however, he became productive, it seemed to Him expedient at one time to generate and lead forth the most beautiful and perfect [of those germs of existence] which He possessed within Himself, for [the Father] was not fond of solitariness.
>
> For, says he, He was all love, but love is not love except there be some object of affection. The Father Himself, then, as He was solitary, projected and produced Nous

and Aletheia, that is, a dyad which became
mistress, and origin, and mother of all the
Aeons computed by them [as existing]
within the Pleroma.

This is the passage that Archbishop William
Temple refers to in a letter written to me from Cambridge University at a meeting of the doctrinal commission over which he was presiding in September 1937. He says, "As regards the 'social Trinity, of which we spoke—I think 'social' does overemphasize the liberality. But I think those theologians must be right—even if the tradition started in a heretical camp—who have held that self-giving must be an eternal activity within the divine Being—not (of course) as a substitute for self-giving to what is other than God, but as the fount of it."[60]

The archbishop had read the fragment quoted by Hippolytus in my Oxford thesis for the doctorate, and we had discussed the passage and the fact that it is not till Augustine that the nature of love is introduced into discussions of the Trinity.

But Gnosticism is a soteriology, a salvation system, as well as an account of creation, breaking with the Old Testament. Orthodox Christianity from the beginning has seen creation as of God and good, but empirically as fallen away from its essential nature and requiring rescue, redemption, renewal, a second birth, and a new creation. Gnosticism by contrast is dualistic. It sees creation as a grievous mistake, due to accident or stupid bungling. The spiritual or divine element in the creation must be separated out of the amorphous and hopeless mass of matter and drawn back up into the transcendent or heavenly realm where it took its origin.

The question arises, How did the spiritual get drawn down into the hylic or material? The answer broadly is that the abortive offspring of a feminine Aeon, which accounts ultimately for the material and animal world, had elements of divinity in it. The Valentinian mythology at this point gets very complicated as well as fantastic, but the gist of it is that Sophia's enthymesis (or inborn idea) to which she had given birth, though it was shapeless and without form for lack of a male input, was separated off from her and the pleroma to become the matter of this lower, chaotic world. This enthymesis was necessarily a spiritual substance, possessing some of the natural attributes of an Aeon, even though it was amorphous and deficient, indeed "an imbecile and feminine production."[61]

As already indicated, an Achamoth has to come out of this weird abortion and a Demiurge (the God of the Hebrews) with his angels. But there is present in the created result a spiritual element, as well as an animal soul, and a purely material substance. In this way, the basis is laid for the rigidly aristocratic and predestinarian doctrine inhering in three kinds of man—the spiritual, the psychic, and the hylic. Achamoth is the source of the spiritual seed, the Demiurge of the animal nature, and the material is just there, hopelessly corrupt and irredeemable.

We have here the key to the Gnostic eschatology. The spiritual man is destined to return to the pleroma, and nothing can prevent this, for spirit is spirit. Nothing with an animal nature will find admittance to the pleroma, but animal man with the Demiurge may go into an intermediate habitation. Hylic men with all that is material are destined for the everlasting bonfire "which lies hidden in the world."

Gnosticism, unlike the main Christian tradition and the Great Church, is incurably aristocratic and superior. Some Gnostics simply divided the race into those who had it and would be saved, and those who were doomed to perdition. The Valentinians were less drastic and held out a restricted hope to Christians who had faith, even if they had no possibilty of becoming knowers and Gnostics. These would be saved in an appropriate manner. Hylic men were without hope.

There seems to have been a strong predestinarian strain in the Gnostics. This is what led to antinomianism in some cases. The spiritual could not be affected in any decisive way by the fleshly or the material. It is probable that the note of predestination in Paul and in John, limited and checked though I believe it is, is one of the attractions of these writers for the Gnostics.

Two other important points must be made. Gnosis for Plato and his disciples meant "knowledge by participation''; that is, it involved the self of the knower.

It was personal and it mattered, as distinct from impersonal, purely objective knowledge. It involved, too, the forms or universals from the higher, transcendental world of ordered and unchanging perfection. But it was not revealed knowledge. There was nothing hidden or esoteric about it.

The Gnosticism of the Gnostics was religion—and a religion of salvation and revelation. Gnosis involved a content, a saving secret, that had to be disclosed. The revelation was held to have been embodied in a secret tradition, handed down, so all Gnostics claimed, from the apostles.

It was claimed also that there were many gospels and letters of apostolic origin, in addition to those accepted in the main line and by the Great Church. The central revelation, at least for many Gnostics, was communicated and unified by holy consecrations and in mystic rites. But not all Gnostics believed in sacraments or sacramentals. These were the true and logical spirituals. They held that ''the mystery of the ineffable and invisible power cannot be performed by means of visible and perishable created things.''[62]

But—and this is the second and fundamental point—the revelation came through Jesus Christ. The Gnostics regarded themselves as Christians. The heresy, though it owed much to Plato and to more extreme types of Oriental dualism, was a Christian heresy and originated with persons regarding themselves as Christians. The Gnostic Christ was the Christ of the New Testament, of Paul and the Gospels, especially John. But that does not mean they felt bound by these documents and the main line of exoteric Christian tradition.

They considered that they possessed a superior knowledge of the Revealer and Redeemer. They assimilated him to the outlook and system adopted on other grounds and then imputed to him the Gnostic theosophy. In particular, they spiritualized the Christ. They were basically Docetists. These were people who thought that Christ, a divine being, only appeared to die on the cross, or only appeared, for that matter, to be truly man, to have real flesh and blood and bones.

Whether there were Docetists who influenced the Gnostics or Gnostics who invented Docetism, we do not and cannot know. Also, there were degrees of predication of semblance and unreality respecting the human or incarnate Christ among the Gnostic schools. But the thing that is certain is that the Gnostic heresy was directed against the monstrous scandal (to the Greek mind) of a God who became man and truly suffered and was really crucified and actually died.

Here the Gospel of John is pivotal, though whether the Gospel as distinct from the First and Second Johannine Epistles, was affected by the rise of Gnosticism and was directed against it is a question. This Gospel is very polemical—against the dis-

ciples of the Baptist and the Jews. But it does not
seem to be pointed in affirming the Incarnation and
the bodily Resurrection. It merely continues and carries to a final term the tradition of the other evangelists and of Paul and Apollos (Hebrews).

This, of course, if a correct view of John the
Evangelist, strengthens his witness as a theological
interpreter of history. He is not pummeled or pres-
sured at this point by an aggressive adversary. That
is coming up later, though soon.

The Gnostics did produce a very lovely and
beautiful account of the origin of Jesus. It is to their
credit, even if the narrative is highly imaginary and
mythological. And it reenforces what I have emphasized above, that the figure of the New Testament
Christ had a very powerful, universal appeal.

It is Irenaeus who gives us the Gnostic version
of the genesis of Jesus, called also Saviour and Christ
and (patronymically) Logos, and Everything. He is
the production of the entire divine pleroma, the whole
pantheon of Heaven. It happened in this wise.

But the one Holy Spirit taught them [the
Aeons] to give thanks on being all rendered
equal among themselves, and led them to
a state of true repose . . . Next they tell
us that these beings sang praises with great
joy to the Propator [First-Father], who
himself shared in the abounding exaltation.
Then, out of gratitude for the great benefit conferred on them, the whole Pleroma

of the Aeons, with one design and desire, and with the concurrence of Christ and the Holy Spirit, their Father also setting the seal of his approval on their conduct, brought together whatever each one had in himself of the greatest beauty and preciousness; and uniting all these contributions so as skilfully to blend the whole, they produced to the honour and glory of Bythus, a being of most perfect beauty, the very star of the Pleroma, and the perfect fruit of it, namely, Jesus.[63]

This brings us to Marcion. All the Gnostics appreciated Jesus. But Marcion was the most christocentric of all the heretics of this school. This may be because he was so deeply under the spell of Paul: Paul who said, "For me to live is Christ." And for him, the blinding, transforming, ultimate reality was the love of God in Jesus Christ.

This, it seems, is what captivated and captured the shipowner from Pontus, on the Black Sea. He may or may not have been a Gnostic among Gnostics. Harnack gives strong reasons for differentiating him from the authentic Gnostic philosophic theologians. For one thing he was one of the terrible simplifiers. He was grasped with overwhelming power by one idea, the love of God and a God of love.

It was impossible that this God could be the bungling Demiurge or the wrathful Lord of Hosts of the Old Testament. Marcion, it is important to remember, did not deny the existence of this God nor of his works. It was all too evident that an evil, stupid, repulsive world existed. And there had to be an explanation for it, though this does not seem to have interested Marcion. He was not a philosopher. He did hate the world, the flesh, and, presumably, the devil. He despised the fashioner of such a world. He was a thoroughgoing ascetic. He decried marriage, the union of the sexes, the ugly process of parturition. All this must be brought to an end.

But here was this wonderful Jesus who had appeared out of the nowhere proclaiming the love of God. His God had to be the highest God, one far above the Demiurge of the Jews whom Christians had accepted and whom they worshipped as Creator and Father in Heaven.

Marcion so believed and set out to vindicate this incredible God, the Veiled Being unveiled by Jesus. How had it happened that men had been so mistaken and confused? First of all, the Jews had mixed things up dreadfully. Paul had seen this and had broken with their horrid Law. History, too, had reenforced this judgment. The second Roman War, in which it was said 580,000 had been killed, had ended in 135, with Jerusalem once again totally destroyed.

The early Christians had been Jews and had been beguiled into accepting the Old Testament as the true scriptures. This was senseless and clearly wrong. But what then was the source of truth, what was there to put in place of the Old Testament or alleged covenant directed and revealed by the Creator God?

Marcion's answer was to create a canon of Christian scriptures from the apostolic documents he knew and which the churches knew and emphasized. Marcion's Bible—the first Christian Bible, as far as we know—consisted of an expurgated edition of the Gospel of Luke (Marcion interpreted Galatians 1:8 as referring to a written Gospel) and ten epistles of Paul. The Pastorals he omitted, presumably because they were not then published with the Pauline corpus, and he freely revised the ten letters to bring them into accord with Paul's teaching as he understood and wanted to believe it. He also rejected the Acts and the Apocalypse.

Marcion is generally credited with having given the first strong impetus to a canonical New Testament. His effort and the whole Gnostic problem noticeably accelerated the crystallization of the mind of the Church with respect to Christian Scriptures as well as a rule of faith and an authoritative historical ministry.

In addition to his Bible, Marcion wrote an important book called *Antitheses*. In this work he set down different passages side by side with a view to showing the contradictions between the Old and the New Testaments and also within the Old Testament itself. Tertullian puts the matter in this way:

> First it is certain that the whole aim at which he labored even in the drawing up

of his *Antitheses*, centers in this, that he may
establish a diversity between the Old and
the New Testaments, so that his own
Christ may be separate from the Creator,
as belonging to this rival god, and as alien
from the law and the prophets.[64]

Marcion seems to have laid great weight on the
difference between the actual Christ and the Messiah
or Christ predicted and expected by the Jews. Tertullian makes this point and incidentally summarizes
succinctly the heart of Marcion's position in a
magisterial passage:

Marcion has laid down the position that
Christ, who in the days of Tiberius was,
by a previously unknown god, revealed for
the salvation of all nations, is a different
being from him who was ordained by God
the Creator for the restoration of the Jewish
state, and who is yet to come. Between
these he interposes the separation of a great
and absolute difference—as great as lies
between what is just and what is good; as
great as lies between the law and the gospel; as great (in short) as is the difference
between Judaism and Christianity.[65]

This brings out the originality of Marcion: in
opposing the good to the just, he is calling Plato
squarely into question. Indeed, in a number of
respects he differs from the great Gnostics. He does

not seem to be interested in elaborate speculations or ultimate explanations. On the other hand, he is not always consistent. He held on to baptism and the Eucharist, following the church model in his own antichurches, except that he rejected the use of wine. Yet in his view of the Saviour and the flesh, he seems to have been a radical Docetist.

In his Gospel Marcion tells us nothing of Christ's birth. Had the Lord been born he would have been the debtor and subject of the creator of the world, and this Marcion could not admit. Accordingly, his Christ enters the world full-blown, coming down from heaven to Capernaum in Galilee in the fifteenth year of Tiberius Caesar.[66] For this extraordinary teacher that was the beginning of the Gospel.

As the Christ could not have been born, he could not really dwell in a human body, made up of flesh and blood. To the hater of the flesh and of the material universe this was inconceivable. Yet, strange inconsistency! Marcion magnified the apparent sufferings and death of the Lord Christ, seeing them as an exhibition of the redeeming love he came to reveal.

In taking leave of this genius who, like his master Paul, was not afraid to seem a fool for Christ, let me quote the opening sentence of his basic book, the *Antitheses*. The lyric quality of this outburst is almost uncanny, yet not entirely surprising. He was a man truly grasped by Jesus the healer, saviour, and lover of souls. This is the Marcionite paean of praise:

> O miracle upon miracle, ecstasy, power, and wonder it is, that one can say nothing about it, nor think about it, nor compare it with anything.[67]

It is an astonishing story, and highly dramatic. It has fascinated me for years. I can think of nothing in the history of mind, thought, or spirituality more startling, more drastic, or more daring.

It happened within 115 years following the crucifixion of Christ. Within this period—hardly more than three generations in duration—a new religion was born. It started out as a movement within Judaism. It may well have been for some time much more Jewish than we commonly think or find it easy—given our New Testament—to think.

Eusebius, the first Church historian after Luke, writing around A.D. 300, says specifically, "I have learned from written documents that, until the siege of the Jews under Hadrian, there had been in Jerusalem a succession of fifteen bishops, all of whom are said to have been Hebrews of ancient stock. In fact, the entire church of Jerusalem consisted at that time of practising Hebrews."

Within 25 years of the destruction of the Holy City and its Temple enclosing the Holy of Holies by Hadrian, the Church had reached a "Parting of the Ways." The Synagogue had closed its doors and drawn up its drawbridge to the Nazarenes; and the Church, as the Gospel of John shows, had reacted strongly to the stubborn resistance and undisguised hostility of God's ancient people, the Jews.

The Church, however, was left with the Bible, which was also the Holy Book of Israel. The two communities still had much in common with respect to faith. They both continued to look to the living Creator God, who had given the Law to the people of the Covenant and sent to them his prophets.

But here a decisive breach asserted itself. The prophets clearly had foretold the coming of a messiah. The period of the birth and life of Jesus was a time of intense messianic expectation. The Christian community, as its name indicated, was sure that God had acted and had sent into the world, and into history, his anointed Son and representative agent, the king of the Jews.

The Messiah had come, as the prophets had foretold. But though he was of the house of David, and though his followers hailed him as Christ and King and Lord, to many, indeed most, Jews this was incredible. For this man had been condemned by Church and State as an upstart and an agitator, and had been executed as a criminal on a cross.

The Jews said it was incredible, impossible, a mad delusion. The Christians responded that it was all according to the prophecy of Isaiah and many other prophecies. And they hailed and proclaimed his vindication by God the Father through his mighty resurrection from the dead and exaltation in heaven to the right hand of the power and glory of the universe.

There matters rested, in one sense. But in another there was no rest, but rather perpetual activity and ceaseless movement of mind and spirit as Christ was preached and worshipped not only at Jerusalem, but at Antioch and Damascus and Caesarea and in Egypt and Asia and Greece and Italy and Rome.

This expansion had received a potent reenforcement through the miracle of the conversion of a prominent and dynamic Pharisee who had been the leading adversary and persecutor of the Christian sect, Saul of Tarsus. He was also a brilliant intellect and an acute theologian. And his whole being had been engaged by this crucified Jesus, known and adored by Christians as Lord and Christ and Son of God.

Then, soon after his death and Peter's in Rome as martyrs, Jerusalem fell and the Jewish sector of the Church was decimated and scattered. The Jewish people drew in upon themselves, and the refusal to believe in the Christ, noted and analyzed with sorrow by Paul in the Epistle to the Romans, became more marked and decisive. By the time of the writing of a Fourth Gospel, the Gospel of John, the breach was wide and irreparable. The parting of the ways had been reached. At the same time John, even in embracing the Logos doctrine of the Greeks and the Alexandrian Jewish philosopher, Philo, had boldly declared, "Salvation is of the Jews."

Not for John any more than for Paul was the Gospel of Christ conceivable apart from the Old Testament and the living God, the creator of the world, who had entered into covenant with Israel. But the Gentile world, the Graeco-Roman culture ramifying in myriad directions, was not the compact, relatively unified world of Jewry.

The Gentile world was far-flung, cosmopolitan, heterogeneous. There was, fortunately, unity in the sense of the Roman peace, a tranquillity of basic order that made communication and interchange possible and encouraged the march of ideas and faith-cults. This was a world, too, that was in reaction from mental and spiritual aridity. It suffered from "a failure of nerve," culturally and intellectually speaking. It was thirsty for meaning, for a friendly power that galvanized life here and gave the soul hope for a destiny beyond death.

This was the Graeco-Roman world, the pulsating, plural, syncretic cosmopolis, which Christianity took now as its ordained orbit and sphere of expansion. In this relatively free and varied world the dominating ideas were Greek. There was a widespread heritage of philosophy, which tended to be an admixture of many things—Platonism, Stoicism, the ideas of Aristotle, Epicureans, Cynics, and even Skeptics. There was also a swirl of religions, mostly from the East but influenced by the older Greek mysteries: mystery religions of salvation, promising union with the Divine and a blessed immortality.

Such was the world of the second century and the situation of Christianity. The churches found that their gospel and worship had wide appeal. They grew apace, but now were dominantly and often exclusively Gentile. To the Graeco-Gentiles the Old Testament was often more a problem than an asset. Happy with the Christian cults, enthralled with the figure of a dying and rising God who had actually lived among men, and concerning whom memoirs had appeared going back to the time of his appearance and recording his teaching and the events of his life, death, and resurrection, they were less impressed with the book called the Old Testament and viewed as the source of authentic teaching and true knowledge.

In comparison with the literature of the philosophers, past and present, the Old Testament seemed backward and uncultured. Its naivete both morally and intellectually was a scandal and raised questions about the Jews and Judaism. In Rome the terrible war of the late 60s was remembered, and seventy years later war broke out again. It was prolonged and put down with difficulty, but once again the Jews lost with heavy casualties and the destruction again of Jerusalem. This unquestionably had a strong impact in much more numerous, dominantly Gentile churches. It may be that it crystallized the movement to remove the Old Testament and expunge Jewish influence from Christianity.

The theological consequences of this were dramatic. Very able men, notably Valentinus and Marcion, set out to re-ground the faith, replacing the crude and uncertain myths of the Jews with a sure and reliable system in which knowledge, not opinion and not mere faith, is central. It is not clear that Marcion invoked the catchword of gnosis, but he applied logic and reasoning fearlessly in his *Antitheses* and he carried his revised version of the true God and the primacy of love and goodness to the people, founding new churches widely and setting up the most vigorous opposition orthodox Christianity was to know prior to Arius and Arianism.

Mainline Christianity was able to repel the Gnostic craze and the Marcionite offensive. In doing so, it solidified and expanded the base of the Great Church, equipping it for the long centuries ahead and giving it an organic structure that would permit survival as Rome in the West sank into darkness, and provide the basis of a new and glorious renaissance under Christian auspices of human civilization.

There can be no doubt that the repulse of the Gnostics saved Christianity from the quicksands of rudderless theosophy. Had the Jewish background of the new religion been eliminated in favor of total Hellenization or a rootless idealism married to an extreme dualism (the proposal of Marcion), the history of,the Church and of the West would have been gravely altered. It is likely that Christianity would have suffered the fate of the rival mystery religions, which were its principal competitors in the first three centuries.

The question arises, What enabled the mainline Great Church to overcome the tremendous drive to swamp it in the sea of Gnostic speculation? What were the theological resources that gave it the insight and energy to hold to the center and to defeat the drive for the elimination of the Old Testament and all Jewish influence?

To these basic questions we must now turn.

1. Romans ix 2-5. RSV slightly altered. In the AV this is the one passage in which Paul asserts the full and absolute deity of Christ. I agree with the revisers in placing a full stop after the Messiah or Christ.

2. John viii. 48-59 (RSV).

3. *Readings in St.. John's Gospel,* Vol. I, pp. 105-106.

4. Acts 15: 19.

5. Galatians 1: 11-12; 3: 24-26.

6. See infra, pp. for the special significance of *Hebrews* for Jewish-Christian relations.

7. See Hugh Anderson, *Jesus and Christians Origins*, Chapter I to Appendix 257-9, 263-4. I have drawn on this masterly study in summarizing the *religionsgeschichte* position and influence. cf. also Albert Schweitzer, *Mysticism of Paul the Apostle.*

8. 1 Cor. 12 : 28. Cf. *Didache* 11-13, 15. The three "orders" are clearly continuing, but their relationships to one another are not clear.

9. Mark 1 : 12.

10. Acts 2 : 41, 42. RV.

11. 4 : 33.

12. 28 : 19. RV.

13. Acts 11:30, 14:23; 15:4,5,23; 16:4; 20 : 17.

14. James 5:14; I Peter 5:1; 1 Timothy 5 : 17; Titus 1: 5.

15. I Clement 42
16. 44
17. 47:6. 54:2. 57:1
18. *A History of the Christian Church*, p. 48.
19. I Timothy 5 :3, 11-15 (RSV).
20. *Ibid.* 6 : 2b, 3-5, 10a.
21. 2 Timothy 3: 1-5a.
22. 2 Peter 2: 13-14
23. i : 19: My own translation. The word "God" commonly supplied is not in the Greek.
24. ii : 9
25. ii : 8 The word *stoicheia* translated here as "elemental spirits" can mean heavenly bodies or the stars. cf. II Peter iii. 10, 12.
26. ii : 16-19. Moffatt's translation. The exhortation is continued for four more verses.
27. Acts viii : 1-13, 18-24.
28. *Adv. Haer.* I. xxiii, xxiv.
29. Literally, *antitheses*—the name of a work of Marcion designed to show the fallacies of the Old Testament. Some scholars have thought this is a reference to Marcion and have dated I Timothy around A.D. 140. This is almost certainly wrong.
30. vi : 20-21 (translating directly).
31. xviii : 37
32. i.4
33. i : 16
34. ii : 12-21
35. iii : 3ff
36. iii : 15-17
37. A list of New Testament books that could be read in public worship. It probably reflects the use in Rome around A.D. 200. Discovered in the 1730s.
38. op. cit. IV. vi : 2
39. Apol. I : xxvi., 1vii
40. *Dialogue*, Chap. III
41. *op. cit.*, I, p. 37
42. *op. cit.* I, pp. 68, 69, 70

43. *Trall.* 9
44. *Eph.* 7
45. *Mag.* 11
46. *Ibid.*, 10
47. *Ibid.*, 13
48. *c. Celsum* III. 12
49. Whitehead, A.N. *Religion in the Making*, p. 37. cf. p. 6. This philosopher adds: "The great religious conceptions which haunt the imaginations of civilized mankind are scenes of solitariness: Prometheus . . . Mahomet . . . the Buddha . . . the solitary Man on the Cross" (p.9).
50. cf. Luke xvii. 21. See also 1 Cor. xiii. 12 and Gal. iv. 9
51. *Op. cit.* Introduction and ch. III
52. Quoted by Pagels, ibid, p. xv
53. cf. Quispel, G., *Gnostic Studies* (Istanbul, 1974, p.3). This scholar thinks the death sentence may have been administered to Bultmann's hypothesis of a pre-Christian Gnostic redeemer as well as to Harnack's thesis that early Catholicism was the Hellenization of primitive Christianity.
54. I Cor. viii. 5
55. *The Crucible of Christianity*, ed. Arnold Toynbee, p. 296 Italics mine.
56. *Ibid.*
57. *Ibid.*
58. *Stromateis* iv. 13
59. *Refutation*, vi. 24
60. Quoted in full in my book *William Temple: An Archbishop for All Seasons*, page 124
61. Irenaeus, *Haer*, I. ii. 4
62. Quoted by Robert M. Grant in *The Crucible of Christianity*, p. 324.
63. *Haer*. I. ii. 6
64. *Adv. Marc.* iv. 6
65. *Ibid.*
66. cf. Luke iii.1 cf. iv. 31
67. Quoted by Grant, *op. cit.*, p. 326

Chapter Four

Chapter IV The Theological Resources Of The Early Church

I was taught in seminary that doctrine and theology really came after the New Testament. This reflected the idea that the Jewish mind was religious but not truly theological. After all, any "ology" involves *logos* or reasoned expression, something scientific in some measure. All this came in from Greece; the Hebrew genius was not logical or intellectual, but concrete, pictorial, active rather than reflective. It was little given to abstraction and was sublimely untroubled by paradox or contradiction.

In general, it was accepted in the nineteenth century and received in the twentieth that the special genius of the Hebrew people was religious. Theirs was the gift of faith and obedience. The Greek genius was quite different. It was both artistic or aesthetic, and it was intellectual. In particular, it was in Greece that philosophy was born. Philosophy means reason; it is the result of confidence in human rationality and the strong urge to exercise this gift.

The Greek felt that it was reason that made him akin to the Divine. This led not only to philosophy

but also to science. Aristotle, Plato's pupil, was led
to survey all nature and to draw up systematically
all that man knew or could know by reasoning from
observation about it. He is the father of science, as
well as the first encyclopedist.

It is one of the great paradoxes that Aristotle was
so credible and convincing that he helped science to
become fixated and to vegetate for eighteen to nine-
teen centuries. Mankind had to unlearn Aristotle in
a measure and back up, in order to give birth to modern science and begin the brilliant assault on the mysteries of nature typified by such giants as Copernicus,
Galileo, Francis Bacon, Newton, and Einstein.

But, if science seemed to have no further to go,
theology as a systematic enterprise came into being
as a result of the coming of Christ. Whether this could
have occurred if the Jews as a whole had accepted
him, no one can say. One can say that in order to
become universal, the Gospel had to break out of its
Hebraic cocoon and reach out to all nations and
peoples.

This, as we have seen, is what happened. But
this development, coinciding with disaster for the
Jewish people as well as withdrawal by rejection of
the Gospel on their part, brought with it grave danger. This danger was acute Hellenization, wholesale
secularization, involving the rash attempt at throwing
overboard the Old Testament and the entire Jewish
inheritance of Christianity.

This sweeping movement, which we know as

Gnosticism and Marcionism, occurred in the second century. As we can now see very clearly in the light of the Nag Hammadi discoveries, there was a real possibility of a free-wheeling Christian movement becoming dominant and taking over the mainline Great Church as we now trace and visualize this Church.

The impetus for this movement came from the swift influx of Graeco-Gentiles of many races and traditions. It was influenced in its interpretation of the Gospel by Hellenic thought, especially Plato, and by the thirst of the time for revelation and salvation. It had the opportunity to arise and spread as a result of the decline of firm apostolic authority and tradition. The mainline Church was floundering in this period while episcopacy was developing, as we can see from Ignatius, and reaching out for linkage with the Apostles and their authority.

By A.D. 180, Irenaeus and, soon after him, Tertullian and Hippolytus were affirming against the Gnostics a central, mediating theology that embraced the monotheistic God-doctrine of the Old Testament, linked redemption with creation, and advanced a clear and definite doctrine of the Trinity. As fundaments of this theology and over against the Gnostic mythology, three things were claimed: that there was a rule of faith—an authoritative, regulative creed; that in addition to the canonical Old Testament there was a crystallized, canonical New Testament or Covenant; and that there was an authoritative threefold ministry linked in authoritative succession from the Apostles.

This development, which Harnack calls the Old Catholic Theology or theology of the Old Catholic Fathers, is a biblical theology, somewhat more developed and systematized. It is in strong contrast to the free, cosmic, highly imaginative, speculative theology of the Gnostics—and in a more restrained vein, Marcion—and it falls short in systematic reach and logical perfection of the grand scheme of Origen, the first great systematic theologian of the Church.

Origen, fellow pupil with Plotinus, of Ammonius Saccas, overshoots the biblical mark under the influence of Platonic speculation. But at the same time he accepts the whole Bible, and certainly weaves into his system basic elements of the New Testament. Above all, he catches, as the Gnostics do not, the spirit of the New Testament and of the Old as interpreted and understood in the New.

This throws us back on the resources that mainline Christianity had for withstanding and rejecting the Gnostic-Marcionite heresy. These resources had to be theological in a real sense. That is, there had to be doctrines—interpretations of faith and Christian experience and conviction.

Let us look, as an example, at the doctrine of the Trinity. Both at Cambridge, USA, and later at Oxford I was drawn to the special study of this doctrine and did degree theses on it. At Oxford, for the doctorate in philosophy, I produced a mammoth production on this profound and inexhaustible subject. It ran to 550 foolscap pages, with about one-third of the whole given up to single-space footnotes. I was, I fear, unduly influenced by the example of Harnack's *Dogmengeschichte* in English translation, though I used and quoted extensively his one-volume summary *Grundriss der Dogmengeschichte* in German.

Now the doctrine of the Trinity, in fully explicit and developed form, is not found in the New Testament. It is not found in the Apostolic Fathers. It is hardly found in the Apologists, though important spade work is present here. Nor is it found in the Gnostics. They represent a retreat into polytheism and mythology. The word "trinity" (*trinitas*) is first found in Tertullian (fl. 200),[1] but the doctrine is full-blown with Irenaeus and in this form—as a dogma—is to be identified with the Old Catholic Fathers.

Does this mean that there is no Trinity in the New Testament? The answer assuredly is No; and it would be a mistake to assume that the compendium of letters, gospels, history, and apocalypse is without a theology of the Trinity. On the contrary, it is the New Testament in its fullness that necessitates, renders inevitable, a doctrine of the Trinity.

This came home to me with especial force in my early research at Oxford when I undertook, stimulated I believe by some monograph of Harnack, to trace the genesis of the religious formula of the Trinity, viz. the baptismal formula commanded by the risen Lord in Matthew 28:19.

When we remember that baptism in the Acts is in the name of the Lord Jesus only,[2] and when we note that the name in Matthew is singular but is linked with three divine subjects or *personae*, and that these are the Father, the Son, and the Holy Spirit, we are bound to descry the signature of a theologian who is thinking systematically. On careful analysis the Gospel of Matthew bore out this conclusion. In comparison with Mark, 90 percent of which he incorporates with some changes, and with Luke, Matthew has a Christology that stands well in between these two Evanglists and John.

Thus, to get down to specifics, Jesus is presented in Matthew not only as the Messiah of prophecy, but also as, in his teaching, explicitly the fulfiller of the Law and as, in his own person, the divine Son of God. The statistics here are impressive: Mark uses the title "the Son of God" eight times. Seven of these are taken over by Matthew. In addition, the title is introduced into the Marcan material six times. The phrase "My Father," which does not occur in Mark, is introduced into the Marcan material six times, into the non-Marcan material seven times. "Your [thy] Father," which occurs once in Mark and is incorporated by Matthew, occurs fourteen times in non-Marcan material; "our Father" once; "their Father" once.

Most important possibly of all is the fact that Mark's one instance of worshipping Jesus (v. 6—a demoniac and excised in Matthew) has become ten in Matthew. Luke knows nothing of this.[3] His tendency is have the glory given to God. He prefers the simple phrase "Father," and alone among the Evangelists is fond of the phrase "the Lord" (*ho kyrios*), using it fourteen times. This suggests a link with Paul. Nor should it be forgotten that Luke, at the death of Jesus, has the centurion refer to him as "a righteous man" in preference to Mark's "Son of God."

Of particular significance is Matthew's correlation of Holy Spirit with Son and Father in his baptismal formula. It can be said dogmatically, in view of the degree to which the entire New Testament is saturated with the consciousness of the presence and activity of the Spirit, that a third name and *persona* was bound to be added to those of the Father and the Son.

The Spirit of God is also very important in the Old Testament. From the standpoint of action and power, it represents the fact that the God of Abraham, Isaac, and Jacob is the living and personal God. He has a will and purpose, as well as being Mind and the Ground of Being. This is perhaps the ultimate issue that was at stake in the controversy of mainline Christianity with the Gnostics and Marcion. The Trinity as the one all-comprehensive Christian doctrine preserves this precious biblical truth along with a full and sound grasp of the Incarnation and the meaning of Christ.

In the Gospel of John we have the clinching development from a trinitarian standpoint. The basic concern of the work is Christology. We reach in it not only the apex of the New Testament as to the place and meaning of Jesus the Christ, but also the utmost bound of human thought in this regard. In the relations of the Father and the obedient servant-Son and the metaphysical, eternal background of this in the Logos concept, we have a final term of reason and imagination directed to Christology and its implication for theology.

St. John then turns to the doctrine of the Spirit. He personalizes the Spirit by naming him the Advocate or Comforter and by putting his role for the future on a par with that of the Son of God. He is to continue and complete the work of the Son, but in a new phase—in the life and ministry of the Church which is his Body.

John does not use the word "church" in his Gospel. But the reader who is a disciple will always fill in the picture. The Advocate who is to follow the crucified and risen Lord is the *alter ego Christi*, the soul of the Church and the Strengthener of individual believers. He is the Spirit of truth and love and source of both.

There is a certain problem about the apparent periodization of the Spirit in the Gospel of John. It seems that this evangelist sees a relation of successiveness in the eras of the Son and the Spirit. In Christian history this has been stretched at least twice into a concept of three successive eras and has ended in notable heresies.

The first heresy was that of Sabellius. We really know little about this greatly feared and excoriated heresiarch, but he may have been incited to his view of the trinitarian God and his works by the Johannine teaching about the coming of the Spirit of Truth. Sabellius is believed to have flourished about A.D. 200.

A similar thing happened in the high Middle Ages. A monk, Joachim of Floris (Fiore) was a prophetic visionary who was in some way a forerunner of St. Francis and the Franciscan movement. He divided history into three periods: the Age of the Father (the Law); the Age of the Son (the Gospel); and the Age of the Holy Spirit (in which monasticism will be universal and all will be peace and love; with discipline no longer necessary).

Both men misunderstood St. John and the doctrine of the Trinity. John must be read in the light of the New Testament and all Scripture taken as a whole.[4] Actually, in the Fourth Gospel the Spirit is invoked at the beginning of Jesus' ministry when John the Baptizer testifies to having seen the Spirit come down from heaven and rest on Jesus. The latter will baptize not with water but with the Holy Spirit.

In chapter 3, there is teaching about the Spirit. Presumably, our Lord's teaching here about the second birth and being born of water and the Spirit is proleptic. That is, it really refers to Christian truth and the life of the church in the future. Yet the Evangelist cannot have been unaware of the role of the Spirit in the Old Testament dispensation and the work of the prophets; he says clearly in Chapter 3 that the Spirit is like the wind that "blows where it wills; you hear the sound of it, but you do not know whence it comes, or whither it is going."

In chapter 4 in the conversation with the woman of Samaria at Jacob's well, Jesus tells the woman that "God is Spirit, and those who worship him must worship in spirit and in truth." In chapter 6 after the long discourse on the bread of life and eating his flesh and blood, Jesus takes his murmuring disciples to task. He tells them: "the Spirit alone gives life; the flesh is of no avail; the words which I have spoken to you are both spirit and life."

From everything it is clear that the sending of the Advocate after Jesus' death and return to heaven does not exhaust the role of the Spirit or limit his activity to a particular period or dispensation of sacred history. The Spirit proceeds from the Father (John 15:26) but he does so eternally, and his sending by the Son, in unity certainly with the Father, is a reprocession or special mission that should not be confused with the eternal going forth and activity of the Divine Spirit. He is "The Creator Spirit by whose aid/ The world's foundations first were laid" as well as the Spirit of Truth "whom I will send you from the Father."

A great deal more might be (and in further chapters will be) said about the resources that the second-century Church found in the New Testament as it grappled spiritually and theologically with Gnosticism and Marcionism. Unquestionably, also, the Old Testament was not simply a passive entity in this grapple for truth and God. It carried with it strong positive qualities of a theological character and impact that assisted the defenses of the mainline Church in this combat.

It is necessary to come to grips with theology in relation to Holy Scripture if we are to deal with the theological and doctrinal resources of the church or churches of the main line. Certainly there is a theology in both Testaments. Many books have been written on and entitled "The Theology of the New Testament" or "The Theology of the Old Testament." Yet it was possible for a Harnack and others to doubt the validity of such titles and to identify Christian dogma and theology with Hellenization. The great German historian not only declared that the Gnostics were the first theologians; he said also that Gnosticism, which is just Hellenism, has in Catholicism 'achieved half a victory.[5]

At Oxford (more than half a century ago now) I encountered the name and writings of an eminent New Testament scholar, William Sanday. Sanday was remembered as having said that in the New Testament we find "theology in solution." I do not know to what extent, if any, this scholar was influenced by Harnack and the Liberal School. His phrase is a suggestive one, but I think it does not go far enough.

Theology denotes in the very term reasoned talk about God and things related to God. This means creation, especially God's creatures able to think and reason—men and women. They are declared in Genesis to be created in the image and likeness of God.

In a very profound, imaginative account of Adam, the first man, we are told of his need of a helpmate. It was his privilege to name all the animals and he sought companionship with them. Doubtless he found some sense of relationship, some solace and comfort in them, as modern man assuredly does. On this, Scripture is silent. But Adam found in the animals, we are told, no adequate satisfaction. He found no helpmate. So Eve—woman—had to be created. She, too, though complementary to man, had to be, like him, created in the divine image.

Theology also means redemption—the rescue of erring, sinning, lost mankind—and restoration and recreation. This means sanctification—growth in wholeness or holiness, recovery of the divine image and likeness in vision, character, and ability to find and keep social harmony; in one word, love.

The traditional word for all this is salvation. Theology, from the point of view of the Bible, is as concerned with man as with God. This means intensive preoccupation, in Reinhold Niebuhr's comprehensive, summary phrases, with *human nature* and with *human destiny*.[6] Though Niebuhr, when one thinks about it, does not have much to say about the Church, talk of man necessitates the Church. And the Bible, in a real sense, begins and ends with the Church.

Dr. H. L. Goudge, Elizabeth the novelist's father, used to say that there were only two doctrines in the Bible: God and the Church. This has the limitation of most epigrams. It doesn't cover everything, but it is on target, it does hit a bull's eye. And it is highly relevant to the problem of identifying theology and getting hold of its relation to Scripture.

This invites a short excursis. A while ago, I became interested in a young Roman Catholic intellectual who is known in the secular, political area as a neoconservative. On dipping into his writings I found out that he is a considerable lay-theologian. And he gave me one of the most exciting experiences I have had in many a day.

Many of my readers—though by no means all—will recall that the book that really put Reinhold Niebuhr on the map was one called *Moral Man and Immoral Society*. It was published in 1932, and when I left Oxford and began work in Berkeley, California, in January 1933, as a chaplain at the University of California, I found that this book was a central topic of conversation.

It has been many years since I read this book, but I believe that it was essentially an attack on Liberalism as embodied in Pacifism and evolutionary social progress. It represented disillusionment with characteristic Social Gospel theology of the 1920s. Emil Brunner wrote of Niebuhr (much later) that "he aimed his guns at the optimistic American progress-philosophy at a time when on the whole it was still largely unchallenged."[7]

At any rate, in this book the rising theologian seemed to put the onus of blame and of abiding frustration on society, on human organization and institutions, rather than on the individual. I think he had not yet reached the emphasis on "the exceeding sinfulness of sin" and its place in the Christian scheme of things that were to characterize the mature thinker. One is tempted to say that he had not yet reached with his criticjsm into the central citadel of Liberalism. If we look into this inner sanctum we find, I believe, as my teacher, Harvard Dean Willard L. Sperry, used to say, that the first and paramount tenet of the Liberal creed is, "I believe in Man."

But to go on with this somewhat longer excursis than I had intended, I was astounded to find in Novak's big book *A Time To Build* (1967) an essay entitled "Immoral Man and Moral Society." Deliberately inverting Niebuhr's paradox, this young lay moralist and theologian points out the social nature and need of the human being, the role of the family, and the necessity of culture in general and the Church in particular.

This squares with Goudge's epigram and with

the order of things in Holy Scripture—an order that reverses most modernism. Thus the People and the Covenant are primary in the Old Testament; they are the object of the love, concern, and action of Yahweh. And they are the target of the prophets. Israel the people is a Church as well as a nation, and it is in the Church that salvation is found.

When we come to the New Testament, we confront a curious paradox. Our modern ideas are turned upside down. The earliest Christian writings are the letters of Paul. They appear to cover a period of thirteen to fifteen years, from 48 or 49 to 62 or 63. They are addressed to churches, but imply and speak constantly of the Church, regarded as a living organism which is the extension of the life and being of Christ the Saviour. It is through her Sacraments and in her nurture and fellowship that individuals are in Christ and have the Spirit. It would seem that in this context and as a matter of spiritual reality, not an authoritarian dogma, *extra ecclesiam nulla salus*, outside the Church there is no salvation.

The Gospels were produced in the Church and as a result of church needs and pressures. Tradition was clearly a strong element, for the Gospels could not have been written—in the second generation of the Christian churchly movement, from 65 to 95—unless somewhere sustained attention had been given to preserving two things: a rough outline of the ministry of Jesus, Messiah and Lord, with a detailed account of his passion and death, and a great body of his parables and sayings.

What we have said earlier about ear-memory versus eye-memory[8] need not be repeated, but it is germane here. It is, of course, likely that some sort of written notes or collection of sayings came into being earlier and underlie the first three or Synoptic Gospels, especially Matthew and Luke. The extraordinary thing is that these unique narratives do hang together and in a way are independent of the Church. With the exception of two passsges in Matthew,[9] they ignore the Church and really concentrate on Jesus, his life, teaching, ministry, and death and resurrection. The crux and proof of this is the dominating role of the Kingdom of God (heaven in Matthew) in the thought and teaching of Jesus. This is perhaps the strongest of all proofs of the essential authenticity of the Gospels and their account of the man Christ Jesus, thought of in the Church and at the time of their writing as the unique Son of God and Lord of the Church.

If we look at the rest of the New Testament, we see a history (Acts) and an Apocalypse (Revelation). Both are extremely church-centered. The Acts is a history of the Christian movement and Christian churches from the Ascension to Paul's appeal to Caesar and arrival in Rome. Revelation is the great Christian apocalypse based to a degree on Ezekiel and Jewish apocalypses like Daniel, but creative and profoundly original. It pivots on the seven churches of Asia, providing letters to each one, and exalts throughout the spiritual Christ, at once the Lamb slain from the foundation of the world and the Lord of history who will shortly return to bring this age of suffering and wickedness to an end and to inaugurate the era of the heavenly Jerusalem, coming down out of heaven, adorned as a Bride for her Husband.

If we take account of the Seven Letters of Revelation, we can say that all of the New Testament, except the Gospels and Acts, consists of letters in one form or another. So influential was the example and genius of Paul.

The letters are products of churches and church leaders and are addressed to churches, some specifically as in the case of Paul's authentic epistles; some by implication as in the case of the Pastorals (1 and 2 Timothy and Titus) and 2 and 3 John; and some generally, as with Hebrews, James, 1 and 2 Peter, Jude, and 1 John. The New Testament is thus to a considerable degree a book of the Church. It is a powerful witness to the inseparability of Christianity and the Church. It was through the establishment and functioning of churches that the Gospel spread and that Christianity overcame the might of the Roman Empire and, in fact, became the established imperial religion.

In the West the Church advanced even further. It succeeded the Empire as the source of what order there was and was the guardian through dark ages of the lamp of learning and civilization. In time, under the aegis of the Church, there was a rebirth of civilization which, in the high Middle Ages, rose to great heights. Moreover, just as Greece and Rome persisted through Medieval Christian civilization so tian civilization persisted and gave birth to the modern era with all its fantastic advances, discoveries, and alterations of life and outlook.

In the modern era the individual came into his own. The age of the autonomous person came into being. But this does not and cannot alter the social origin and conditioning of personality. In our immediate era the limitations of autonomy and individualism are all too clear. There can be no substitute for the family and the Church. Each needs and is made for the other. The State likewise is a divine ordinance, man being a political animal. It needs the Family and the Church, and without them will not do its work well and within proper limits. This is the reason why our Founding Fathers were constantly harping on the importance of religion and morality. They saw their necessity for ''good government'' and ''the happiness of mankind.''

In the present period of breakdown and crisis, which is likely to prove chronic and grow worse before it becomes better, the Church has an indispensable role. In this role lies a great opportunity. It is not impossible that instead of an indefinite post-Christian period we could see the rise of a new Christian and religious civilization. If we truly believe in God and if we are genuinely realistic about the sorry predicament of contemporary man and society and the reasons for it, this is certainly not such a strange belief or fanciful hope.

What I am saying is that with the Church and, by implication, the Christian family, we can speak meaningfully of "immoral man and moral society." Nor does the truth of this insight stop with religious community. Society, especially with our mass media, is immensely influential on all its members. The possiblities of good in a really good society are inestimable.

This, I must admit, seems like dreaming at the present moment, but it adds up to good sense. Nor dare we forget the power of vision. "Where there is no vision the people perish."[10]

In the second century the Church faced a grave crisis in its own life. It was basically a theological crisis. What was the faith of the Church? What was the character of the Good News of the Gospel of Christ? What was the nature and extent of Christian salvation?

These were the real issues in the massive controversy over Gnosticism and Marcionism. What were the theological resources available to the Church at this time, which in fact enabled her to meet this critical life-and-death emergency? The issue, remember, was the Old Testament, Jewish monotheism, the concept of a living Creator God, active also in history, and the meaning for human life of the life, death, and resurrection of Jesus Christ.

The succinct answer can be put under two heads. The Church had the Christology of the New Testament. She had the theology of the Old Testament. Each of these was a priceless treasure possessed of great offensive virility in the clash of theological ideas.

It must be added that the actual Scripture of the Church at the inception of the controversy was solely the Old Testament. This was part of the problem. The canon of the New Testament had still to be hammered out in final, authoritative form. But the process of attaining such an addition to Scripture was well under way, and most of our present New Testament was known and in use. Justin Martyr is our authority for noting that in the embryonic liturgy of the Eucharist at this time (150), the memoirs of the apostles were read or the writings of the prophets, as long as time permitted.[11]

In the Gospels one can trace the working of the mind of the early Church. Mark plunges right into the ministry of Jesus. He begins with a quotation from Isaiah that introduces John the Baptizer, then devotes a paragraph to John. John baptizes Jesus, and the Holy Spirit descends on him like a dove and drives him into the wilderness to be tempted. He begins straightway (a favorite word with Mark) to preach the Kingdom of God, calls the first four disciples, and at Capernaum on the Sabbath asserts his divine authority by casting out of a demented soul an unclean spirit.

This demon or devil recognizes Jesus, though the people do not, and hails "Jesus of Nazareth" as "the Holy One of God . . . come to destroy us." By verse 28 of chapter 1, his fame has spread throughout all Galilee.

Mark then proceeds, breathlessly as it were, to press forward with his exciting narration. It is easy to imagine how this excitement was communicated to the first readers of this fast-paced biographical chronicle, principally devoted to acts and events. Parables are given, and sayings associated with them, but the teaching is secondary. The figure of Jesus and the drama and wonder of his Passion are primary in this Gospel, as they are in the letters of Paul. Thus we are given a double but coincident insight into the soul of the primitive Church, well before its first, white-hot period is over.

With Matthew and Luke we can see a certain cooling off. Both Evangelists reflect curiosity as to the origin and background of Jesus. Matthew begins with "the genealogy of Jesus Christ, the son of David, the son of Abraham." His research starts with Abraham and carries the generations to Joseph, "the husband of Mary, of whom Jesus was born, who is called Christ." Then he gets into the birth and infancy of Jesus, apparently handling the subject of his miraculous birth from the point of view of Joseph. Then he tells the story of the wise men, featuring the title "King of the Jews" as applied to the child and thus introducing King Herod, the Flight into

Egypt, and the Slaughter of the Innocents. In all this, the Evangelist is in no hurry, and it is chapter 3 before he has reached John the Baptizer and Jesus' Baptism.

Matthew will now follow Mark's outline, with significant interpolations. The first is to present the classic account of the temptation of Jesus. We are so used to this that we are likely to miss its extraordinary, utterly unique character. It takes a genius like the Russian Shakespeare, Fyodor Dostoevsky, to drive this home, as he does in ''The Legend of the Grand Inquisitor,'' orginally written as a chapter in the novel, *The Brothers Karamazov*. In this truly dazzling, incredibly stirring rendition of the three temptations against the background of the Lord's return in the darkest days of the Inquisition in Spain, Dostoevsky writes, speaking through the Grand Inquisitor:

> The statement of those three questions was itself the miracle. If it were possible to imagine simply for the sake of argument that those three questions of the dread spirit had perished utterly from the books, and that we had to restore them and to invent them anew, and to do so had gathered together all the wise men of the earth— rulers, chief priests, learned men, philosophers, poets—and had set them the task to invent three questions, such as would not only fit the occasion, but express in

three words, in three human phrases, the whole future history of the world and of humanity—dost Thou believe that all the wisdom of the earth united could have invented anything in depth and force equal to three questions which were actually put to Thee by the wise and mighty spirit in the wilderness? From these questions alone, from the miracle of their statement, we can see that we have here to do not with the fleeting human intelligence, but with the absolute and eternal.

The second interpolation follows an expanded version of Mark's account of Jesus' preaching and healing, and of his fame in all Galilee and in Syria and in all Judea and from beyond the Jordan. At this point—in chapters 5, 6, and 7—the Evangelist gives us the immortal Sermon on the Mount, which stands as a Mt. Everest in the whole world of ethical preachments and pronouncements.

This process is repeated in several installments. Matthew uses Mark, appropriating 90 percent of his Gospel, but does not hesitate to modify his source and to insert blocks of teaching wherever it suits his purpose. This applies also to Matthew's passion narrative, which is essentially Marcan with additions.

Luke, obviously, is very much the historian. He writes from sources, beginning with Mark, on whom he is less dependent than Matthew. These sources at times seem to coincide with one of Matthew's: hence the hypothesis, less popular today than fifty years back, of a second written document called Q for *Quelle*, the German word for source, which was a collection of sayings.

Luke is in even less of a hurry than Matthew and exhibits a viewpoint as Greek in a cosmopolitan way as the latter's outlook and appeal are Jewish. He goes Matthew one better in the matter of genealogy, tracing Jesus' descent back to Adam, but does not get to this till the end of chapter 3.

Luke's chapter 1 (not of course so divided by him) has eighty verses and is one of the longest in the Bible. It begins, following a short author's preface, with Zechariah and Elizabeth, the parents of John the Baptizer, and an angel's miraculous appearance and promise to them. Then Luke turns to the maiden Mary, the angel Gabriel's anouncement to her, her response in the Magnificat, the birth of John, and Zechariah's exultant prophecy in the Spirit. All this in chapter 1. In chapter 2 we have the Journey to Bethlehem, the birth in a stable, the vision of the shepherds and their pilgrimage to the Christ-child, his circumcision and Simeon's blessing of him in the temple, and, finally, the account of his childhood and disappearance in the temple at the age of twelve. Chapter 3 is devoted to John the Baptizer, in some detail, then introduces Jesus, his Baptism and the descent of the Holy Spirit, with the beginning of his ministry at age 30, followed by the genealogy already referred to.

Luke is now leaning upon the Marcan outline, but he is more free than Matthew and introduces new events, such as the first visit of Jesus to his home synagogue in Nazareth, which apparently began well but ended in an angry scene.[12] Other events unique to Luke that are worked in early are the miraculous catch of fish (leading Simon Peter to fall at Jesus' knees, saying, "Depart from me, for I am a sinful man, O Lord")[13] and the tender, exquisite account of the woman of the city with the ointment.[14]

By the end of chapter 9, Luke has Jesus setting his face to go up to Jerusalem. This begins what is often called Luke's special section. In it he inserts blocks of teaching and includes such unique materials as the stories of the Good Samaritan and the Prodigal Son. This section does not end until 18:30.

There is powerful symbolism in Luke at this point, which supports the idea that he is the bridge-writer among the four Evangelists, coming well in between Mark and Matthew, on the one hand, and John, on the other. I have already introduced a partial qualification of this view in pointing out the advanced Christology of Matthew. To a certain extent Luke the humanitarian humanizes Jesus.

Yet there is little doubt that Luke, with a keen sense of artistry expressing theological conviction, sees this journey up to Jerusalem as having a deep symbolic meaning. This is brought out in the New English Bible in a way that no other version I know of brings out. These translators render 9:51 thus:

> As the time approached when he was to
> be taken up to heaven, he set his face reso-
> lutely toward Jerusalem, and sent mes-
> sengers ahead.

His ascension is at hand, and the journey to the Holy City which is before him is a part of his ascension. Luke's Gospel will, of course, end with the Ascension as the Acts of the Apostles will begin with it. And Luke is the only Evangelist to give us an account of the Ascension as a specific happening.

Enough has been said to show the complementary and at the same time unitive character of the Synoptic Gospels in relation to Paul, who could say:

> Wherefore we henceforth know no man
> after the flesh: even though we have known
> Christ after the flesh, yet now we know him
> so no more.[15]

It is not remarkable that this statement attracted the Gnostics and especially Marcion. It seemed right up their alley and of course caused them to wrench and maim Paul hopelessly. But it is not surprising that such a passage, taken with the general thrust and emphasis of Paul christologically, tempted these Spirituals.

The Synoptic Gospels are another matter. Small wonder that the Gnostics, confronted by them, set themselves to composing new and different Gospels.

As Paul was a providential man, so were our first three Gospels of the same directing Providence. They provided the necessary balance between the human and the divine in Christ, and in effect negated forever dualism and Docetism.

The author of the Epistle to the Hebrews, whom I am calling Apollos, made at this point a signal contribution to New Testament Christology and, therefore, theology and the theological resources of the early Church. What his inspiration was, we cannot know for sure. It is a temptation to ascribe it to the appearance of Mark or possibly Luke. At any rate, though he can refer to the pre-existent Christ as Philo Judaeus did of the Logos, reaching even higher than his predecessor, Paul, he is at the same time constrained to set before his reader a Jesus who is fully human, as clearly so as in the Synoptic Gospels.

Apollos does this in a moving and compelling way, as is especially appropriate in a work entitled "To the Hebrews." It is unnecessary here to quote all the relevant passages, but we can note that his Jesus was truly tempted, truly suffered, truly prayed with strong crying and tears, and truly died. Thus did our great High Priest prepare himself for his heavenly office of merciful intercession, having himself learned obedience and reached perfection by the things that he suffered.

I am unaware of notice being taken of Hebrews by the Gnostics, but Clement of Alexandria (c. 180) supplies our earliest reference to the present title of this highly original and brilliant epistle. It is first quoted by Clement, bishop (or presbyter) of Rome, in his Letter to the Church at Corinth (known as 1 Clement), which is usually dated A.D. 96. So Hebrews was well known from an early time.

With regard, finally, to John, already presented as a key theologian and still to be treated in detail, it is sufficient to note that he supplied the capstone to New Testament thinking about the meaning and being of the Christ. For this evangelist-prophet-theologian, Jesus is more than the Messiah, though he is that emphatically. He is more than the Lamb of God, though he is called that by no less a witness than John the Baptizer at the beginning of the Gospel proper. He is the God-man come down from heaven, sent by the Father, the God no one has ever seen, to reveal his will and his very nature. He came because of the love of the Father. "God loved the world so much that he gave his only Son, that every one who has faith in him may not die but have eternal life."[16]

John, like the other New Testament writers, does not develop very much the nature and being of God apart from Christology and its sweeping implications. He does, in addition to what he tells us of the love of God, refer to God as an active, working God, even on the Sabbath; and he implies the omnipresence of God and the rightness of a universal worship of a God who is Spirit. By the introduction of the Logos, he invites and renders inevitable the introduction of Greek ways of conceiving of the Divine in relation to the world of change. In his full doctrine of the Incarnation and of the person and mission of the Spirit of Truth, he all but enunciates a doctrine of the Trinity. Yet the God of John remains essentially Hebraic, modified only by the dazzling light of Christ. And he assumes with the whole apostolic and subapostolic church the truth and canonical validity of the Old Testament. Its expectations and prophecies are seen as fulfilled in the One who has come, Jesus Christ, the King of the Jews and the Saviour of the world.

It remains to examine the scriptures of the Old Testament to see what they have to say theologically for themselves and whether they are as bankrupt as the Gnostics and Marcion claimed them to be. This Book, we must remember, is what the Church carried into the Graeco-Roman world as the second century wore on. It is the authority to which the Christian must appeal, along with the nascent but as yet fluid and unauthorized New Testament.

This is shown in a striking way in the middle of the century by Justin Martyr, in his *Apologies* and still more in his lengthy and detailed *Dialogue with Trypo*, a rhetorical argument with a Jew which Greeks as much as Jews were expected to overhear. Justin, of course, like all Christians of that time, is not confined to the letter of Scripture but has at hand all the conveniences of allegorical interpretation and exposition. The letter nevertheless is bound to make an impression, even if unconsciously. It is there and can hardly avoid registering in an intelligent mind, irrespective of the rationalizations permitted by the allegorical route.

In the case of Marcion, though not of the Gnostics generally, this sense of reality and dubiety operated with decisive consequences. He rejected allegory and stayed with the letter of both Hebrew and Christian scriptures. The result was his wholesale rejection of the first and his drastic recasting and rewriting of the second.

Looking at all this in retrospect, it is not hard to understand the difficulties which the Graeco-Gentile mind had with large sections of the Old Testament. The Hebrew mind does seem to have been surprisingly untroubled by contradictions, though the Book of Job and the Prophecy of Jonah should not be overlooked. The doctrine of development was not available for the ancient mind, and the educated Greek was trained in logic. This is the key to much of the objection to the Old Testament and the God of the Hebrews raised by the Gnostics and by Marcion and his followers.

On the other hand, the remarkable theological developments to be found in the Old Testament stand out in their purity and impressiveness, even if they could not have been seen in a clarifying developmental context. We are able to see rather readily the results of the Deuteronomic reform and the still more emphatic and outstanding impact of the priest-theologians behind the P stratum in the Pentateuch and manifest no doubt in Second Isaiah and other later prophets. Then there is the role of individual genius in the prophets generally, the Psalms, and the Wisdom literature.

To take specifically the idea of God in the Old Testament and the Apocrypha, it moves in a long sweep tied together by the conservative instinct of religion in contrast to philosophy. Essentially, what we have in Hebraic theology is the rationalization of a tribal deity, Yahweh. It is this singular movement and structure of thought that made possible the unique Hebraic and biblical idea of God.

This God is quite different from the deity of Hinduism or Mahayana Buddhism. It is different from the God of Greek philosophy or classical, recurring mysticism. It diverges sharply from the climax of modern philosophical speculation in Europe, namely, the absolute idealism of a Hegel, a Bradley or Bosanquet in England, and a Royce or Hocking in America. The identification of this metaphysic of God and the whole world yields, or certainly tends to yield, what William James called a block-universe.

What is the difference between the biblical deity and the Absolute of metaphysical and mystical philosophy? It is that the God of the Bible remains the living creator God, the God active in history, and the loving God so concerned about his human children that he acts in various ways for their salvation— their redemption and sanctification.

To put the matter another way, the Old Testament reveals a movement from polytheism to henotheism, or monolatry—the worship of a superior deity among the gods—followed by a jump to absolute monotheism. This development is so prominent, as a matter of fact, and so emphatic, that it can hardly be missed. It does not require an evolutionary theory or a general doctrine of development in order to detect and isolate the situation in Holy Scripture.

This absolute being—the one and only God—is the Creator of the world, visible and invisible, but he is distinct from the world. The world of creatures stands over against him.

This outlook is at the opposite end of pantheism. It was well described by Samuel Taylor Coleridge, who, according to my English mentor at Washington and Lee University, Dr. Edgar F. Shannon, was the greatest metaphysical mind England has produced. He contrasted Christian theistic doctrine with that of the philosopher Spinoza, a Jew anathematized by the Synagogue. For Spinoza, Coleridge said, God minus the world equals zero. For Christianity and the Bible, God minus the world equals God. The difference in the two theologies is immense.

The absolute special monotheism of the Bible basically created by Jewish theologians made a stir in the world long before the Christian era. It impressed the Romans who gave the Jews a special status prior to the great revolts. The classic Christian Apologists in the second century later took the line that the remarkable revelation given Moses and the prophets antedated Greek philosophy and was responsible for the knowledge of God found in the Greek tradition.

One wonders why this line of thought and the power of Old Testament monotheism at its best and highest made no more impression on the Gnostics. The reasons, one guesses, are philosophical and psychological.

Philosophy was always a reality in the Roman period, before and after Christ. Schools of philosophy flourished, and itinerating philosophers were no novelty. Justin, it will be remembered, continued to wear his philosopher's cloak even as a Christian. At Alexandria, for example, philosophy was a persisting enterprise; Philo Judaeus was an older contemporary of Jesus. Ammonius Saccas, the teacher of both Origen and Plotinus, is thought to have been a Christian. Plotinus knew about Christianity as well as Gnosticism, which he criticized, but elected to be a Platonist and brought to birth a rarified and rather beautiful mystical Neoplatonism.

It seems certain that the Gnostics were heavily influenced by philosophy and especially by Plato, with his thoroughgoing transcendentalism and sharp distinction between knowledge and opinion. But there was also a strong dualistic trend, sharpened by Oriental influences. There was the salvation interest characteristic of the period, which turned people to religion. And there was preoccupation with evil, not only sin and wickedness but stupidity and meaning-lessness.

With all this, there was undoubtedly some animus, some feeling, about the Jews. There is a potentiality of this in the Gospels and Paul. As we have seen, there had been two terrible Jewish revolts, fierce and very bloody. The second, and the second destruction of Jerusalem occurred in A.D. 132-135, and the period immediately following this is the time of Marcion and of the eruption of Gnosticism. It would seem that anti-Semitism was a definite factor in the rise and proposals of the Gnostic heresy.

From this point of view the steadfastness of main-line Christianity and refusal of the great Sees and of important and influential theologians like the Old Catholic Fathers to modify the central Creed of the Church or to let go the calling and training of Israel, embedded so fundamentally in the Old Testament or Covenant, are immensely impressive phenomena. It is impossible not to see the hand of God and the guidance of the Spirit of Truth in what happened.

Theologians were at hand or were raised up who hewed to the main line of tradition and who stayed with an active and revealing God, witnessed to alike in the Old Testament and in the Christian Scriptures rapidly coalescing into an authoritative canon. The chief champions of orthodoxy and of the nascent Great Church were Irenaeus, Tertullian, and Hippolytus.

Of these Irenaeus was the most central and the most profound, though he was less flashy as a rhetorician than Tertullian. The latter had been a lawyer and he was great at making a case. He is also important as the first great phrase-maker and formula-fixer in the history of the doctrine of the Trinity.

There is nothing in Irenaeus to equal the purple rhetoric of Tertullian, the prosecuting attorney, arraigning Marcion before the bar of tradition and reason. In the Preface of his *Five Books Against Marcion* he starts out with a stinging description of Euxine[17] Sea, ''self-contradictory in its nature, and deceptive in its name,'' and of the barbarous inhabitants who live around it in Pontus. Then he proceeds:

> Nothing, however, in Pontus is so barbarous and sad as the fact that Marcion was born there, fouler than any Scythian, more roving than the waggon-life of the Sarmatian, more inhuman than the Massagete, more audacious than an Amazon, darker than the cloud, (of Pontus) colder than its winter, more brittle than its ice, more deceitful than the Ister, more craggy than the Caucasus. Nay more, the true Prometheus, Almighty God, is mangled by Marcion's blasphemies.
>
> Marcion is more savage than the beasts of that barbarous region. For what beaver was ever a greater emasculator than he who has abolished the nuptial bond?

What Pontic mouse ever had such gnawing
powers as he who has gnawed the Gospel
to pieces?

Nevertheless, Irenaeus was the central and
essential theologian. His name means "Peace Man,"
and he has been called the most Christian of the
Fathers. McGiffert describes him as "one of the few
really original and creative thinkers in the history
of the Church."[18] Harnack says of him: "The
Christianity of this man proved a decisive factor in
the history of dogma in respect of its content."[19] Paul
Tillich, in the context of an exposition of Irenaeus,
writes: "When I go into these matters, I am always
surprised how much better the theology of the ancient
church was than the popular theology which developed in the nineteenth century, how much profound-
er and more adequate to the paradox of Christianity,
without becoming irrationalistic, nonsensical, or ab-
surd."[20]

Irenaeus was born in Asia Minor and was a
product of the rich Christianity of that area. In his
early youth he had seen and heard Polycarp, martyr
bishop of Smyrna, and he may have studied at
Rome. His mature life was spent in Gaul as presbyter and bishop. Though unrelenting to the Gnostics, he was disposed to tolerance for the Montanists
and the Quartodecimans (those who stood for always
observing Easter on the 14th of Nisan).

As a theologian, Irenaeus is basically biblical,

with an orientation derived from the Greek grasp of salvation as transformation of the whole nature of man. Of New Testament writings he is especially indebted to Ephesians. He is a great churchman as well as a probing and original theological thinker.

Irenaeus is centrally preoccupied with salvation, what it is and how man obtains it through Christ, God, and man. Possibly because of the basic error of the Gnostics but also in accordance with the fundamental thrust of the biblical outlook, he emphasizes the ultimate unity in the divine economy of creation and redemption. They are distinct, since man in the person of the first Adam fell away from the estate in which he was created and the purpose God had for him. The development of human nature that was broken by the disobedience and fall of Adam was resumed in Christ and carried to a victorious conclusion. In other words, Adam—humanity—was fulfilled in Christ. God's vision and purpose in creating man in his image and likeness was accomplished in the manhood of Christ. If we want to know what the fullness of humanity is, we must look at him.

Irenaeus appears to have been grasped by Paul's powerful idea, near the beginning of Ephesians, of recapitulation or gathering up into one in Christ all things, both in heaven and on earth. He built on these words his conception of the history of salvation.

Ireneus distinguished between the image of God, which connotes reason and freedom, and the divine likeness, which is the capacity for immortality.

Man was made in the image and was destined to attain the likeness. But in falling away from God, Adam and mankind after him became subject to death. Man could no longer attain the goal of immortality, God's attribute by nature.

The purpose of the Incarnation was to restore to manhood and man what had been lost in the Fall. In Christ was realized the final predestined development which was God's purpose in the creation of man. And those who are in Christ share in his perfected human nature, united with divinity.

In one of his loftiest and most memorable declarations, Irenaeus writes: "The Word of God, our Lord Jesus Christ, on account of his infinite love, became what we are, in order that he might make us what he is."[21] He continues, going to the heart of a doctrine that lies at the very heart of biblical religion, namely, revelation:

> For in no other way could we have learned
> the things of God, unless our Master,
> existing as the Word, had become man.
> For no other being had the power of
> revealing to us the things of the Father,
> except his own proper Word."[22]

Here we see Irenaeus drawing on the thought of John, as in his concept of all things being summed up in Christ, both things heavenly or spiritual and things earthly or humanity in all its aspects and stages, he draws on the Paul of Ephesians. These two New Testament theologians, it should be remembered, are the ones the Gnostics saw promise in and tried to appropriate. Irenaeus saw in them the sheet anchor of the truth as it is in Christ, the Lord of the Church and the Saviour of the world.

In another very vivid and quotable sentence Irenaeus sums up and reenforces the very heart of the Johannine evangel. "And through the Word himself who had been made visible and palpable, was the Father shown forth, though all did not equally believe in him; but all saw the Father in the Son: for the Father is the invisible of the Son, but the Son is the visible of the Father. And for this reason all spake with Christ when he was present [upon earth] and they named him God."[23]

Irenaeus is critical for the Gnostic-Marcionite crisis and Christianity owes a great deal to the balance and persistent, steady fidelity of the Peace-Man. At times tedious as a writer and seemingly imprisoned in the careful consideration of minutiae, he nevertheless had a feel for pivotal points and true fundamentals. The Christian Church owes him an immeasurable debt.

Irenaeus, of course, did not live or write in a vacuum. He had predecessors and relied heavily on sources. The latter were basically New Testament writers, Paul and the Evangelists. Also, he fully accepted the Old Testament scriptures as inspired by the Holy Spirit and the gift of God to the Church. He labored mightily, as his predecessors from the apostles on had done, to interpret the Old Covenant, and the prophets who operated under it as a covering umbrella yet were inspired to show remarkable creativity and even novelty in development, as a Christian sourcebook. Allegorical exegesis was, of course, an essential ally in this, but the lofty endpoints of development in the idea of God, the expectation of a Messiah, and the mission of Israel to the nations and the Gentiles were the aces, so to speak, of Christian apologetics.

Before we go on to consider the "First Theologians" on whose shoulders Irenaeus, his Old Catholic colleagues and all future mainline theologians must inevitably stand, we shall do well to summarize Irenaeus' contribution as a central theologian and creative Catholic churchman by laying out *in extenso* his original version of the *regula fidei* or creed going back to the apostles and his stunning paean in praise of the holy Catholic or Universal church.

Bear in mind that all this was written well within the enigmatic, disturbed, and free-wheeling second century. Here are the pillar passages:

> The Church, though dispersed throughout the whole world, even to the ends of the earth, has received from the apostles and their disciples this faith:
>
> [She believes] in one God, the Father Almighty, Maker of heaven and earth, and the sea, and all things that are in them; and

in one Christ Jesus, the Son of God, who became incarnate for our salvation; and in the Holy Spirit, who proclaimed through the prophets the dispensations, and the advents, and the birth from a virgin, and the passion, and the resurrection from the dead, and the ascension into heaven in the flesh of the beloved Christ Jesus, our Lord, and his [future] manifestation from heaven in the glory of the Father "to gather up all things in one," and to raise up anew all flesh of the human race, in order that to Christ Jesus, our Lord, and God, and Saviour, and King, according to the will of the invisible Father, "every knee should bow, of things in heaven, and things in earth, and things under the earth, and that every tongue should confess" to him, and that he should execute just judgment towards all . . . .

As I already observed, the Church, having received this preaching and this faith, although scattered throughout the whole world, yet, as if occupying but one house, carefully preserves it. She also believes these points (of doctrine) just as if she had one soul, and one and the same heart, and she proclaims them, and teaches them, and hands them down, with perfect harmony, as if she possessed only one mouth.

For, although the languages of the world are

dissimilar, yet the import of the tradition is one and the same. For the churches which have been implanted in Germany do not believe or hand down anything different, nor do those in Spain, nor those in Gaul, nor those in the East, nor those in Egypt, nor those in Libya, nor those which have been established in the central regions of the world.[24]

But as the sun, that creature of God, is one and the same throughout the whole world, so also the preaching of the truth shineth everywhere, and enlightens all men that are willing to come to a knowledge of the truth. Nor will any one of the rulers in the Churches, however gifted he may be in point of eloquence, teach doctrines different from these (for no one is greater than the Master); nor, on the other hand, will he who is deficient in power of expression inflict injury on the tradition . . . .

Nor does it follow because men are endowed with greater and lesser degrees of intelligence, that they should therefore change the subject-matter (of the faith) itself, and should conceive of some other God besides him who is the Framer, Maker, and Preserver of this universe, [as if he were not sufficient for them], or another Christ, or another Only-begotten.[25]

1. *adv. Prax.* 2 and 3 Theophilus of Antioch had used the word *trias* (Greek), but made it refer to God and his Word and Wisdom, not Father, Son, and Holy Spirit (*ad Auto*. II. 15).

2. viii. 16; x. 48; xix. 5

3. Assuming with the NEB that the shorter reading of xxiv. 52 is the correct one.

4. cf. *Articles of Religion*, **XX**: ''The Church hath power to decree Rites or Ceremonies of Faith: and yet it is not lawful for the Church to ordain anything that is contrary to God's word written, neither may it so expound one place of Scripture that it be repugnant to another.''

5. *Op. cit.* I, p. 227

6. The reference is to his Gifford Lectures in two volumes, *Human Nature* and *Human Destiny*.

7. In *Reinhold Neibuhr*, Ed. Kegley and Bretall, p. 29

8. *supra*, Ch. I, pp. 12-13

9. xvi. 18 and xviii. 17

10. Proverbs xxix. 18

11. *Apol.* I. 67. By these memoirs Justin apparently meant the Gospels: see 66. cf 6

12. Luke iv. 16-30

13. v. 1-11

14. vii. 36-50

15. II Cor.v. 16. RV. It is no doubt difficult to be certain of Paul's meaning in his use in this verse of *sarx* (flesh), but the AV and RV at least give the reader what Paul said. The RSV and still more the NEB present an interpretation as a translation.

16. iii. 16. NEB

17. Means ''hospitable.''

18. *Op. cit.*, p. 132

19. *Op. cit.*, II, p. 236

20. *Op. cit.*, p. 45
21. *Op. cit.*, V. Preface
22. *Ibid.* V. 1. 1
23. *Ibid.* IV. 6. 6
24. Referring probably to the churches of Palestine.
25. *Ibid.* I. 10. 1, 2, and 3

Chapter Five

Paul
The Rabbi

Christianity, greatest and most influential of the world religions, began as an offshoot of Judaism. The Christian Church had its origin as a kind of sect, an enclave, within the Israel of Jerusalem. The first Christians were all practicing Jews who added to the religion of the Law the absolute and inextinguishable conviction that the Messiah (or Christ) had come, and that his name was Jesus.

Names have a life and a power all their own. It should not be overlooked that the word "Christians" originally meant "Messianists." The name "Jesus" is Greek for a familiar and patriotic Hebrew name, "Joshua." Joshua means "the Lord, the Saviour."

Jesus was a Galilean, but of a proud and fully Jewish family, descended from David, the greatest king of Israel. His disciples were all Jews, and the chosen, select twelve, symbolizing the Twelve Tribes, became the original Apostles. Judas, who had betrayed the Master and subsequently met an ignominious death, had to be replaced by Matthias. The latter was chosen by lot over Joseph the Just.

The Apostolic college was not, however, a closed corporation. At some point, clearly after Pentecost but probably quite early, James the Lord's brother came into the picture and was given the primacy in the Jerusalemite church. It is tempting to believe that his conversion and commitment came after the Crucifixion and Resurrection.

Paul in 1 Corinthians 15, in listing the appearances of the risen Christ, says: "Then he appeared to James, then to all the apostles. Last of all, as to one untimely born, he appeared also to me."

The first appearance, according to Paul, was to Cephas (Peter), "then to the twelve." This would indicate that James and others had been added to the Apostolic College, as in due course was Paul himself. It is possible, though purely a speculation, that the inclusion and elevation of James broke the ice and was responsible for the expansion of the office of Apostle.

James was a strict Jew who added belief in Jesus as the Christ or Messiah to the religion of the Law. His position as president of the Apostles and in some sense head of the primitive Christian community must have made for conservatism in the relation of converts to the Law. We can be fairly sure about this in view of the history that follows and which, because of Paul and Luke, we know a good deal about.

We must not, however, get the impression that the Christian enclave and assembly (*ecclesia*) within

Judaism was a quiescent, self-satisfied body. All the information we have, written up in the first chapters of the Acts, forbids any such supposition.

There was a Pentecost; the Spirit came down upon the assembled believers with tremendous power; and the little body overflowed with dynamic energy and enthusiasm. We say that Pentecost was the birthday of the Church, and certainly from the beginning this body was a missionary organization. It drew people in: consider all the tongues and nationalities listed in the Pentecost narrative and the evidence both of Stephen and of Paul's persecutional activity. Clearly many non-Jews had from the first been added to the church, and apostles had gone out to Antioch and Damascus and other cities preaching Christ and establishing churches.

This being the situation, it was inevitable that problems connected with Judaism and the Law would arise. They would have arisen even if there had never been a Paul. There is an inkling of such tension in Acts 6, where we are told that "when the disciples were increasing in number, the Hellenists murmured against the Hebrews because their widows were neglected in the daily distribution." The result was the establishment of the diaconate. The first of the seven deacons appointed was Stephen, destined to be the first Christian martyr and a powerful influence on a prominent Pharisee named Saul, of the city of Tarsus but then dwelling in Jerusalem.

The story in Acts 10 of Peter and a centurion

of the Italian Cohort named Cornelius at Caesarea is striking in this connection and appears to show that the issue of the Law in regard to food had arisen prior to Paul. According to this account, Peter had a vision from the Lord that bore on the question of ceremonial laws concerning clean and unclean foods. Peter was led by this vision to conclude that there was no such thing as unclean foods in God's eyes and that God "shows no partiality, but in every nation anyone who fears him and does what is right is acceptable to him."[1] He then proceeded to have Cornelius and three of his Gentile friends baptized "in the name of Jesus Christ."

When "the circumcision party" in Jerusalem criticized him for going to uncircumcised men and eating with them, Peter stoutly defended himself, recounting his vision and decision to baptize Gentiles. "In the face of this," we are told that "the critics were silent."[2]

From the testimony of Paul in Galatians there appears to be some doubt about Peter's steadfastness on the issue of the Law and even about his representation to the circumcision party in Jerusalem concerning the Caesarean episode. Paul calls Peter, in contrast to himself, the apostle entrusted with the Gospel to the circumcised, and accuses him of having been two-faced on the issue of eating with the Gentiles at Antioch.[3] The truth of course could be, and probably was, that Peter vacillated from time to time on this complicated, burning question.

In any event, the first formidable challenge that faced the new religion was its relation to the Jewish Law. Implicit was the issue of universality of appeal and the possiblity of outreach to all races, nations, and peoples. The infant Church met this problem and surmounted a very high hurdle, thanks to the conversion and genius of a learned rabbi, a pupil of Gamaliel but a man of fiery temperament, who would later refer to himself as having been a Pharisee of the Pharisees. This man was Saul of Tarsus, of the tribe of Benjamin, leading persecutor of the new sect of the Nazarenes or Messianists. His conversion is the most important event in Christian history, next to the advent and career of Jesus himself. If the name of Jesus is indeed not so much written as ploughed into human history in the vivid apothegm of Emerson, the role of Saul looms as a factor of decisive moment in the total consequence.

In the fact of Saul's conversion, in the quality of his zeal, spirit, and personhood, and in the preservation of his letters, it seems as though for a second time we see with crystal clarity the intervening hand of God. His conversion was drastic, radical, and total. On his way to seize and do away with the misguided but guilty followers of the Nazarene, nearing the ancient city of Damascus, he suddenly saw something like a bolt of lightning flash from heaven. It knocked him to the ground, and as he lay there blinded, he heard a voice that said, "Saul, Saul, why do you persecute me?" And he said, "Who are you,

Lord?'' And the voice said, "I am Jesus, whom you are persecuting."[4]

Saul arose from the ground but could see nothing. It was necessary for his traveling companion to lead him by the hand into Damascus. "And for three days he was without sight, and neither ate nor drank."[5]

There have been many conversions, many men and women turned squarely around, before and since this experience of Saul on the Damascus Road. None on record has been more decisive or unconditional; and none has been more productive of far-reaching consequences. The details of what followed need not be repeated here. It is sufficient to say what Paul (his new Greek name) said, as many years later he gave his testimony with superb eloquence before King Agrippa and Bernice his Queen in the great audience hall at Caesarea, surrounded by Festus the Roman governor, the military tribunes, and many prominent men of the city. After recounting his experience on the Damascus Road, describing the "light from heaven, brighter than the sun," the voice speaking in the Hebrew tongue, and his conversation with the resurrected and living Jesus, he said, summing up all:

> Wherefore, O King Agrippa, I was not
> disobedient to the heavenly vision.[6]

Obedience, trust, and love—these are the cardinal attributes of Paul—missionary, apostle, thinker, but, above all, the free slave of Christ. This was a man of strong emotions and affections. When he had found himself and knew who he was, his love knew no bounds. He must be regarded as one of the great lovers of history, though not in the usual sense of such a phrase.

It was to Christ, who had died for him on the cross, that Paul's love went out most strongly. There was no tension for him in thinking of God and Christ. Here the Gnostic could find nothing favorable or encouraging about him. The love of God was shown in Christ; Christ was a Son, the Beloved; it was by the divine will that he who was Lord and Christ had left the heavenly realm, emptying himself of a form of being like to that of God himself, and assuming the form of a man, indeed of a servant, and going obediently out of sheer love to a hideous death, death on the Roman gibbet, the cross.[7]

Since Paul, as a Jew, thought of God as essentially transcendent and was hardly able to think of a crucified God or a God who found his glory in sacrifice, his heart and soul went out to the servant-Son who had held nothing back and given his all to save the sinful and the ungrateful. So phrases like "the love of Christ" and "the grace of our Lord Jesus Christ" were are constantly on his lips.

Paul was a highly trained rabbi. He was naturally talented in mind and ability to think; and he turned the full light of his intellect on this reality that had become for him the center of existence, the Christ: who he was, what his meaning for sinful man was, what his death had accomplished, why the Father had sent him, and what still lay in the future, by way of completion and fulfillment of the whole purpose of God.

Paul, in short, was a theologian; if not exactly a systematic theologian in the modern sense, he did approach various problems and issues connected with God and man and tried to give answers to them— the answers he felt were indicated by the light of Christ and what it shed on the being and will and purpose of God, who is over all, blessed forevermore. But the most important thing for Paul, the pearl of great price and the object that called forth his deepest love, was Christ crucified and risen, Christ the vicegerent of the Father reigning now and extending his saving grace to all who believed, Christ who will reign until he overcomes all enemies, including Death, the last dread adversary, and turns the kingdom over to the Father, who will then be all in all.[8]

> Christ! I am Christ's! and let the name suf-
> fice you,
> Ay, for me too He greatly hath sufficed;
> Lo with no winning words I would entice
> you,
> Paul has no honour and no friend but
> Christ.[9]

Christ, I suggest, became "all in all' to Paul after his conversion. It is very possible that this did not come to full flower at once. We have only Paul's occasional letters to go on, along with Acts. Some of the letters are more impassioned and expressive of his personal love for Christ than others. On reading them through with this point and issue in mind, it seemed, oddly, that 1 and 2 Thessalonians were the least warm of them all in the expression of deep emotion and devotion centering on the person of Christ.

These letters are of course taken up with the expectation of the Messiah's imminent return and with problems arising from this state of mind among the believers. Perhaps as time passed and the Apostle realized the greatness and power of the present life in the Church and in Christ, he was led to dwell more and more on the crucified Lord and to be lost in the wonder of the deliverance that his love had brought.

The letters that seem to throb most with the deep feeling of Paul for Christ are 1 and 2 Corinthians, Galatians, and Philippians. Ephesians, too, has some strong devotional celebrations. Romans, which is the closest to being a comprehensive theological treatise and is the most rabbinical of all the letters, has perhaps the supreme description of "the love of Christ" and identifies it with "the love of God in Christ Jesus our Lord."[10] In general, Romans brings God steadily into the picture and discusses his ways, providence, dispensations, and purpose in sending his son into the world. From chapter 12 on, Paul gives us in Romans a summation of Christian ethics, which recalls and invites comparison with Jesus' Sermon on the Mount in St. Matthew.

It would be a mistake to suggest that Paul is ever unaware of God as Father, as loving, and as the ultimate agent in the advent, life, death, and resurrection of Jesus the Christ. But, as has been emphasized in an earlier chapter,[11] Paul is a kind of mystic and his mysticism is a Christ-mysticism. Unlike John, this does not in Paul's mind and experience spill over into and become one with a God-mysticism.

Further, it is Christ who is in a special way Lord of the church. In the sacrament of baptism, the believing initiate is mystically one with Christ in his Death and Burial and in his Rising again. This is viewed as a rebirth from death into life. Henceforth, the Christian is *in Christ* and has become a new creation. The classic expression of this is in 2 Corinthians 5:17—

> Therefore, if any one is in Christ, he is a
> new creation; the old has passed away,
> behold, the new has come.

Paul's thought is saturated with being "in Christ." It is the meaning of meanings for him; he is constantly referring to it; it is the reason for the Church and the heart of the new and ultimate religion. This leads him to dwell on his own relationship to Christ and to express with fervent eloquence its wonder and its transforming power.

To the Corinthians in his first letter after upbraiding this Church for its serious division into parties, he says that when he had come to them, his testimony to God was not in lofty words or high-sounding wisdom. Rather, he said, "I decided to know nothing among you except Jesus Christ and him crucified."[12] A little further on, he adds that, following the commission of God given him, he, like a master-builder, laid a foundation. And that foundation stands for every Corinthian Christian and every man. "For no other foundation can anyone lay than that which is laid, which is Jesus Christ."[13]

In 2 Corinthians, which is a very moving, a very tender, and a very loving letter, there is a word of great power almost at the beginning, as Paul sets out to compose what was certainly not an easy appeal to write or dictate. In the context of saying that he had wanted to visit Corinth again but had not, and denying that he is a vacillating person, a worldly Yes and No man, he says:

> As surely as God is faithful, our word to
> you has not been Yes and No. For the Son
> of God, Jesus Christ, whom we preached
> among you, Sylvanus and Timothy and I,
> was not Yes and No; but in him it is always
> Yes. For all the promises of God find their
> Yes in him.[14]

This epistle closes with what Episcopalians as Prayer Book Anglicans call the Minor Benediction. To many Protestant communions it is the Major and most frequently used Benediction. And it is Paul's most succinct trinitarian pronouncement. These are the familiar words:

> The grace of our Lord Jesus Christ, and
> the love of God, and the fellowship of the
> Holy Spirit be with you all.

Galatians, I believe, is one of the supreme writings in all Christian literature. It is also a very personal and at times a very emotional letter. In this composition we see into the mind as well as the heart of the Apostle in a special way. At the center is the meaning of Christ, and he has very much in mind his deep and so precious relation to the Lord Christ.

Paul is concerned about a false gospel that has been preached in the churches of Galatia. He speaks sternly about this. "Even if we, or an angel from heaven, should preach a gospel contrary to that which we preached (before) to you, let him be accursed."[15]

This gospel, Paul goes on, is not man's gospel. "For I did not receive it from man, nor was I taught it, but it came through a revelation of Jesus Christ." Here we see exposed for a single instant the raw nerve of the central conviction of the great apostle to the Gentiles. Then, going on to review what all have heard, how he persecuted the Church of God, seeking to destroy it, he says: "And I advanced in Judaism beyond many of my age, so extremely zealous was I for the traditions of my fathers."

What did Paul then do? Not what we should have thought, had we only the Acts as an authority for his biography. "But when he who had set me apart before I was born and had called me through his grace, was pleased to reveal his Son to me, in order that I might preach him among the Gentiles, I did not confer with flesh and blood, nor did I go up to Jerusalem to those who were apostles before me, but I went away into Arabia; and again I returned to Damascus.'' It was not until after three years, he says, that he went up to Jerusalem to visit Peter and to see James, the Lord's brother.[16]

Paul pursues his argument about the Law against the Judaizers at Galatia, but in the midst of it, emotion takes over logic: ''I have been crucified with Christ; it is no longer I who live, but Christ in me; and the life I now live in the flesh I live by faith in the Son of God, who loved me and gave himself for me. I do not nullify the grace of God, for if justification were through the law, then Christ died to no purpose.''[17]

Coming back to his main argument, he justifies and explains the Law as a tutor until Christ came, bringing justification by faith and freedom from the status of slaves, since the heir, as long as he is a child, is no better than a slave. He also implies that human enslavement was more than the bondage of the Law, since ''when we were children, we were slaves to the elemental spirits of the universe.''[18]

At this point Paul brings forward an idea that is exciting indeed and that he obviously sets great store by, the freedom of the Christian man, in Luther's phrase, or, in Paul's tremendously preferred expression, "the freedom wherewith Christ has made us free."[19] Paul exulted in being out from the Law's bondage, in the consciousness of sonship under a Father-God, and in being a spiritual heir, a joint-heir with the special Son, Jesus the Christ.

Here our concern is not the theological *how* of this, but the fact and the grateful love Paul has for Jesus, whose sacrifice accomplished it all. There is, however, a passage in another of Paul's choice shorter epistles, Philippians, which seems to combine a kind of theological overview with his surpassing love of Christ. Paul again refers to his extreme Jewishness and his zeal for the Law, which led him to blame-lessness in its observance but also to persecution of the Christian Church. He then declares:

> But whatever gain I had, I counted as loss for the sake of Christ. Indeed I count everything as loss because of the surpassing worth of knowing Christ Jesus my Lord. For his sake I have suffered the loss of all things and count them as refuse, in order that I may gain Christ and be found in him, not having a righteousness of my own, based on law, but that which is through faith in Christ, the righteousness from God that depends on faith; that I may know him and the power of his resurrec-tion and the fellowship of his sufferings, becoming like him in his death, that if pos-sible I may attain to the resurrection from

the dead.

Not that I have already attained this
or am already perfect; but I press on to
make it my own, because Christ Jesus has
made me his own.[20]

Finally, there is the great tribute to the love of
Christ in Ephesians, a unique epistle masterful in its
maturity and finality as reflecting the mind of Paul.
This tribute is within a prayer and is followed by one
of those supreme doxologies to which the Apostle was
given. This is the amazing prayer:

For this reason I bow my knees before the
Father, from whom every family in heaven
and on earth is named, that according to
the riches of his glory he may grant you to
be strengthened with might through his
Spirit in the inner man, and that Christ
may dwell in your hearts through faith;
that you, being rooted and grounded in
love, may have power to comprehend with
all the saints what is the breadth and length
and height and depth, and to know the love
of Christ which surpasses knowledge, that
you may be filled with all the fullness of
God.[21]

Incidentally, this passage is one that tells especially against Gnosticism and the attempt of both
Marcion and the Gnostics to appropriate Paul and
utilize him for their purposes. On all fours with Ephe-

sians in this respect is the immortal lyric hymn of the Apostle to love in 1 Corinthians.[13] Here Paul says specifically that whereas "love never ends...knowledge will pass away."

In this inspired tribute, so universally admired, revered, and loved, the love of which the Apostle speaks is that which he calls on Christians to exemplify. "Make love your aim," he says to the Corinthians at the end of the chapter. (And of course for him there was no division or formal indication of transition at this point). The fact that Jesus or Christ is not named or in any way referred to in the great love chapter is arresting, but I believe makes the impact of Paul's thought even stronger. The Lord Christ is, of course, the inspiration of all that the Apostle says about agape, a word that as a noun occurs only in the New Testament. He is the source of this highest, ultimate spiritual quality. It is because the Son of God came out of love and lived and died in love that the Spirit of love invades and gives to naturally selfish human beings the power to follow Christ in agape—a love like to his and the heart and soul of Christianity.

It was said of the Jewish philosopher, Spinoza, by Novalis that he was a God-intoxicated man.[22] I believe that it can and should be said of Paul the Apostle, a Jew who in his own way was as broad and as independent as Baruch Spinoza, that he was a Christ-intoxicated soul. For him Christ Jesus was the be-all and end-all of his being. For all of Paul's rever-

ence for the God of Israel and all the nations and his
ascription to this God of all might, majesty, dominion, power, and praise, Frederic Myers does not put
the case too strongly when he concludes his poem on
the great apostle:

> Yea thro' life, death, thro' sorrow and
> thro' sinning
> He shall suffice me, for He hath sufficed:
> Christ is the end, for Christ was the be-
> ginning,
> Christ the beginning, for the end is Christ.

What of Paul the theologian? He had been
trained as a rabbi, and in some ways, as the Epistle
to the Romans shows, he remained a rabbi after his
conversion and even in the midst of his stirring career
as the great missionary to the Gentiles. By this I mean
that he reasoned like a rabbi and used the Scriptures
(the Old Testament) like a rabbi.

The example that immediately comes to mind
is Abraham and his two sons, one by Hagar, the
bondwoman, the other by Sarah, his wife and, of
course, a freewoman. Paul sees in Abraham, who believed in the promise of God, the prototype of justification by faith, not by the works of the Law. "So you
see that it is men of faith who are the sons of Abraham."[23]

God made a covenant with Abraham, Paul goes
on to say, 430 years before the giving of the Law, and
the latter could not annul the former. This leads to

Paul's explanation of the Law, as having been added because of transgressions and remaining in force until the coming of the offspring to whom the promise had been made. Until then, until faith should be revealed, the Law was our tutor or custodian. But when Christ came, the whole situation was altered. "For in Christ Jesus you are all sons of God, through faith. For as many as were baptized into Christ have put on Christ."[24]

Further along, Paul picks up the significance of Abraham's two sons by different and contrasting mothers. This, he says, is an allegory. "These women are two covenants. One is from Mount Sinai, bearing children for slavery; she is Hagar. Now Hagar is Mount Sinai in Arabia; she corresponds to the present Jerusalem. But the Jerusalem above is free, and she is our mother."[25]

There is no certainty about the date of Galatians. I remember that when I was in seminary, there was a view that it was the earliest of Paul's letters: it was placed before 1 Thessalonians and dated before 49. This seems to me quite impossible. But I do not see putting it after Romans, either. Rather, it has the earmarks of being a kind of overture to the more elaborate and systematic tackling of the problem of the Law and its relation to the Gospel in Romans.

Galatians, of course, was an occasional letter directed to a burning concrete problem whereas Romans was intended by Paul as an introduction addressed to the most important church in the Empire.

It was his purpose to visit Rome, possibly en route to Spain. Paul knows that he is known in Rome and desires that this knowledge shall be accurate. Possibly he wishes to correct two misapprehensions of his position: that he is antinomian—that is, against law and free to do as one pleases, and that he is anti-Jewish. In this epistle we find his most elaborate and definitive treatment of Israel's failure to accept Christ, and the reconciliation of this with God's purpose in history.

Precisely because he has this broad general aim and is not obliged to deal with specific, critical, local issues or problems, Paul in Romans gives us the most synoptic and comprehensive presentation of his outlook as a Christian teacher and thinker. Let us see if we can summarize succinctly this pivotal epistle.

Romans is a brilliant production. It is one of the world's great writings. It is unique in the field of theological literature. It marks Paul as a theologian of consummate ability. It also shows us the way in which the mind of a great rabbi works when applied to the supreme issues of religion against a controversial background.

As I have thumbed through Romans over and over and brooded on the mind and heart of the Apostle, torn, sorrowful, and yet absolutely clear in his conviction respecting God and his gracious providence, it has come to me that we have before us in this work something like a majestic tapestry or a gigantic wall painting. Paul is operating on a tremendous canvas and is employing, to stick to the second image, a vast brush.

Like John Milton centuries later, he is bent on explaining and justifying the ways of God to man. He even goes further and at one point reaches out to all nature—to a world groaning and travailing in pain, from the beginning until now. At the same time, as always, he insistently advances the Gospel and glorifies Christ as Lord and Saviour of the whole race of men—men locked in sin and under judgment without exception.

After a particularly felicitous opening, a kind of summary doctrinal preface, which precedes the Apostle's customary cordial greeting, he pays tribute to the renowned church of Rome and declares his intent to visit the Christians there and to preach the Gospel to them. After this, much as in 1 Corinthians though more simply and summarily, he sets the stage by affirming and defining the gospel of salvation as God's righteousness through faith, "to the Jew first and also to the Greek."[26]

This propels Paul into his celebrated arraignment of the whole human race as mired in sin and wickedness and unable of themselves to extricate themselves. With thunderous eloquence he delineates the corruption and moral decadence of the Roman Empire and Greek culture. In many respects Paul might have been describing present-day America and Europe.

The Jews, he goes on, may not presume to sit

in judgment of the Gentiles. They are under the Law
of Moses and are judged, too, by their actions. The
Gentiles have a law inscribed on their hearts: Paul
here shows his knowledge of the Stoic natural law.
The Jews are no better off. Quoting Scripture widely,
he arraigns them for their immorality and lawlessness
and the mockery they make of circumcision. The true
circumcision is of the heart.

All persons are equally guilty: this is the human
predicament and the verdict of Scripture. But God
has provided an answer.

> But now, quite independently of law,
> God's justice has been brought to light.
> The Law and the prophets both bear wit-
> ness to it: it is God's way of righting wrong,
> effective through faith in Christ for all who
> have such faith—all, without distinction.
> For all alike have sinned, and are deprived
> of the divine splendour, and all are justi-
> fied by God's free grace alone, through the
> act of liberation in the person of Christ Je-
> sus.[27]

Paul adds that all human pride is excluded and
that God is the God of Gentiles as well as of Jews.
This leads him to review systematically his special argument regarding Abraham and the promise made
on the ground of faith.[28] Abraham was a prophecy
of God's remedy, namely, justification through faith
and peace with God through our Lord Jesus Christ.

Paul exults in the wonderful salvation God has provided: how Christ died for us while we were yet sinners, which is God's own proof of his love toward us and desire for our reconciliation.

But this rabbi is not about to rest in simplicity. Instead, he plunges from exultation over peace and reconciliation because of love into perhaps the most closely knit argument in all his epistles: the entry of sin, and through sin death into the world through the disobedience of one man, Adam, and the contrasting redemption ''through the grace of the one man, Jesus Christ....For as through the disobedience of the one man the many were made sinners, so through the obedience of the one man many will be made righteous.''[29]

Sin was multiplied by law, but grace immeasurably exceeded it, issuing in eternal life through Christ. If anyone should take this to mean, persist in sin that grace may abound (antinomianism), he has completely forgotten that the Christian has died in sin. That was the meaning of his baptism into union with Christ and his death—death unto sin and resurrection unto life. Paul dwells at length on this— the end of the dominion of death and Christ's gift of life and freedom now and forever. ''For sin pays a wage, and the wage is death, but God gives freely and his gift is eternal life, in union with Christ Jesus our Lord.''[30]

To a certain extent in this epistle Paul is writing in enlarging circles; and now in the famed seventh chapter he draws on his own experience of sin and the desperate inner conflict he once knew of two warring principles or laws, the law of God in his inmost self, in which he delighted, and another law in his bodily members, opposing the law approved by reason and making him the prisoner of sin.

Paul gets very personal at this point, exclaiming almost vehemently,[31] which is somewhat surprising in view of the character of this letter, intended as a self-introduction to a church where he is not personally known. One feels that at this point, as in other letters, the Apostle was carried away on the wings of passionate feeling. Though a thinker, and a man of determined will, he was above all a man of feeling. He truly felt that love was the greatest thing in God and man, and 1 Corinthians 13 is as autobiographical as this chapter of Romans.

With this tremendous build-up in terms of realistic diagnosis and dissection of the natural man's predicament, the way is cleared for Paul to dwell on the mighty act of divine rescue. This is the theme of Romans 8—a chapter that would be bound to rank high in any attempt to select the paramount chapter or chapters of Holy Writ.

Romans 8 winds up a long and fundamental section of this most systematic of all Paul's letters. His theme has been Sin and Salvation, the Law and the Gospel, the equality in need of Jew and Gentile, the parallelism of Adam and Christ, and the existential predicament of rational but morally hobbled man. It remains to round out and clarify and properly glorify God's answer—his act of rescue in Christ and the meaning of this for the life of believing and responding man.

"The conclusion of the matter [then] is this."[32] For the Christian or person united with Christ there is no condemnation; the old law is replaced by the life-giving law of the Spirit which sets one free from the law of sin and death; the level of the lower nature whose outlook spells death is replaced by the spiritual level, created by the Spirit of God and of Christ dwelling in the Christian and bringing forth new life in the whole being.

Moreover, the Spirit that the Christian has received is the opposite of slavery and fear. It is the Spirit of adoption and sonship, making us cry Abba! Father! And as God's heirs and Christ's fellow-heirs, we share his sufferings now so that we may share his splendor and glory hereafter. Nor is this confined to human beings. All of nature suffers, too, and awaits liberation. The whole universe is destined to be freed from pain and the shackles of mortality and to be given a share in the liberty and splendor of the children of God.

We, that is the Christians, those being saved, have the first fruits of the Spirit based on hope, by which we are saved. But we still do not see and, like the creation or Nature, we continue groaning inwardly as we wait for adoption as sons, which will mean the redemption of our bodies. There is, it must be admitted, a residual duality in Paul, which seems at times more Greek than Jewish. Recognizing thus our weakness even as saved, Paul invokes the might and wisdom of the Spirit, who knows both our hearts and the will of God and can be counted on to intercede for us forcefully, with sighs too deep for words or groanings unutterable.

With this thought of deep comfort (or strengthening), Paul brings to an end his attempted summation of God's answer of rescue, which is the coming of Christ and the work of the Spirit. But before leaving the subject and shifting to a new theme, he shows the intensity generated in him by what he has just said and by the whole ambitious effort of summing up in depth for the Roman Christians the Gospel that he preaches. The conclusion of this chapter reveals the depth of Paul's faith and the power of his emotional nature. It is perhaps the paramount peroration of the New Testament. In wide areas of the modern Church it has replaced 1 Corinthians 15 as the favorite passage for use in burial services.

But characteristically, Paul first tries a final thrust of reason, drawing on the idea of the divine foreknowledge, predestination, election, justification, and glorification, in that order.[33] And since God does all these things, what is there to question? Is there any room left for concern? Who or what can separate us from the great thing that has changed all things—the love of Christ? With inspired and moving eloquence, Paul answers his own rhetorical questions. Nothing in all the world, or above it, or in future time, can conceivably separate us from the love of God, which is in Christ Jesus our Lord.

But now there is a troublous question. It preys on Paul's mind, and it is certain to be a constantly raised issue in Rome. The Gentile ministry is going well. The more daring prophecies of Holy Writ are being wondrously fulfilled. But what about God's ancient people, the Jews? Many individual Israelites have of course heard the Gospel and responded. But Jewry as a whole has not accepted Jesus as the Christ, the Messiah.

In the next three chapters of Romans, 9, 10, and 11, Paul wrestles with the tough question, Why? There can be no issue of the power of God or of his love. The answer must be found in his providence, his inscrutable wisdom, the hidden mystery of his will.

Paul shows in this very rabbinical section, studded with quotations from Scripture, how deeply and quintessentially Hebraic he is in his conception of God. The elect, a remnant, obtained by grace the salvation offered, ''but the rest were hardened, as it is written,

God gave them a spirit of stupor.''[34]

He does not, however, give up hope: when the full number of the Gentiles comes in, all Israel will be saved.[35]

The conclusion Paul reaches and sets down at the end of this very honest and significant discussion is much the same as the final conclusion of Job.

> O the depth of the riches and wisdom and knowledge of God! How unsearchable are his judgments and how inscrutable his ways! . . .
>
> For from him and through him and to him are all things. To him be glory forever. Amen.[36]

Paul now makes another major transition—it has been noted that Romans is the best thought out and skillfully planned of all Paul's known writings. He turns from theology to ethics, from how we should think and believe to how we should behave. Romans 12-15 is an impressive essay on Christian ethics: principles and behavior. Only the Sermon on the Mount excels it in this field, and only with this compendium of the Lord's teaching and sayings is it comparable.

For our purposes it is unnecessary to go into this aspect of Romans or of Paul's teaching, except to point out its acuteness, comprehensiveness, and practicality. Also, it confirms from a new angle the greatness of Paul as a Christian and an apostle.

It is appropriate and necessary for us to evaluate Paul the theologian from the point of view of the controversy that, during the second century and even later, threatened either to swamp the faith of the

Church and tear up its roots or to divert many Christians into an heretical counter-church.

First of all, Paul was well known. Whether the Chicago New Testament scholar, Edgar J. Goodspeed, is right or not in his theory about the early publication of a collection of Paul's letters, it is certain that they were collected and published and were well known from early in the second century. Of our New Testament, his letters were the best known part, with the possible exception of the Synoptic Gospels.

The Gnostics, we know, read both the Gospels and the letters. The same goes for Marcion. In view of the Nag Hammadi discoveries, it may no longer be correct to say that Paul was more influential than the Evangelists, including John, on the total Gnostic movement. But he was certainly pivotal in it, as Professor Elaine Pagels in her book *The Gnostic Paul* has demonstrated. From her researches it would appear that he might have been the starting point for the Gnostics in the Church, as definitely as he was for Marcion. Indeed, it is tempting to speculate that Marcion, a normal Gentile Christian, the son of a bishop, may have derived his fixation on Paul and his overmastering, tangential Pauline impulse from the Gnostic fantasy of a secret, different Paul who was really not of them (the Orthodox, mainliners), but of us!

Prior to the Nag Hammadi discoveries and to studies based on them, like that of Professor Pagels, it had been possible to make light of a Gnostic Paul, even though a Reitzenstein could hold that Paul was the first and greatest of the Gnostics. Examples are Bultmann, writing in 1947, who sees Paul as opposing a pneumatic-Gnostic movement in Corinth, and W. Schmithals who, in works published in 1971 and 1972, argues Paul's opposition to Gnostic opponents, instancing his preaching the kerygma of Christ crucified, his warning of coming judgment, his proclamation of the resurrection of the body, and his insistence on the priority of love over gnosis.

These are impressive points and conclusively point to the absurdity of claiming Paul as a Gnostic. And there is much more. Yet, as Ms. Pagels brings out, after noting the above points at the beginning of her book *The Gnostic Paul*, the Gnostic writer not only failed to grasp the whole point of Paul's writings, but dared to lay claim to his letters as a primary source of Gnostic theology. He was widely revered as the one apostle who was himself a Gnostic initiate. The great Valentinus, according to Clement of Alexandria, was a hearer of one Theudas, who had been a disciple of Paul.

There are a number of reasons for the Gnostic choice of Paul as their Apostle-founder, so to speak.

First of all, he was not a simple thinker. He no doubt struck the ordinary Christian as paradoxical and hard to follow. The author of 2 Peter is a witness to this. After commending Paul's helpful practical wisdom, he adds:

There are some things in his letters hard
to understand, which the ignorant and unstable twist to their own destruction, as
they do the other scriptures. You therefore,
beloved, knowing this beforehand, beware
lest you be carried away with the error of
lawless men and lose your own stability.[37]

There may be a reference here to the Gnostic
use of Paul as well as to his obscurity.[38]

A second reason for the appeal of Paul to the
Gnostics was the irregularity of his Apostolate. He
was not of the Twelve. He came as one born out of
the time. He knew Christ after the Spirit, not after
the flesh. Moreover, in Galatians he appealed to a
direct revelation that he had had from Jesus Christ.

Thirdly, there were obscure statements in Paul's
letters as well as doctrinal emphases that were lures
to Gnostics seeking for a source of their special secret
tradition. Thus in 1 Corinthians 2, after emphasizing
"Jesus Christ and him crucified" and nothing more,
he abruptly speaks of a wisdom for the mature and
"a secret and hidden wisdom of God." It is easy to
see how the Gnostics jumped at these words, but a
careful examination of the whole passage (vv. 7-9)
indicates that Paul may have had in mind God's wisdom hidden in his mind and in the counsels of his
will until the time was ripe for revealing it and putting
it into execution for man's salvation.

Then there is the account in 2 Corinthians 12,
under the heading of "visions and revelations of the

Lord,'' of having been caught up fourteen years back to the third heaven—truly into Paradise—and of having "heard things that cannot be told, which man may not utter." Paul, however, refrains from boasting of this, even though it would be the truth, and instead goes on to tell of the thorn given him in the flesh, a messenger of Satan, to harass him and to hold down his pride. Though he prayed fervently three times about this affliction, it was of no avail. Rather, the Lord said to him, "My grace is sufficient for you, for my power is made perfect in weakness."[39]

From this it is clear that Paul had once had an unusual mystical experience. But it was no more remarkable than the vision on the Damascus Road that led to his conversion and 180-degree turn-around in life and in his whole being. And it was apparently never repeated. The great mystics have said that their experience of union with God was ineffable; and that is essentially what Paul says of this vision.

He was beyond doubt of a mystical turn, but except for this experience, of which all that we know is that something seemingly overpowering and very remarkable happened—probably in the desert—Paul's mystic sense is directed toward the living and reigning Christ—God's son, the Lord Jesus. His mysticism, as we have seen earlier, is a Christ-mysticism. In all that he writes, *being in Christ* is explicit or implicit and utterly fundamental.

But Christ has no rival. All talk of aeons is

proscribed. In him the whole pleroma of Godhead dwelt in a bodily form; he is the head of all rule and authority. Anyone who denies this is the prey of philosophy and empty deceit, according to a human tradition, inspired by the elemental spirits of the universe (*stoicheia*).[40]

A fourth reason for the Gnostic infatuation with Paul was his semidualistic view of human nature, according to which the spirit or mind and the flesh were opposed, and indeed were strongly at war with one another. It is by no means certain that Paul's dualism was what Plato had in mind in his dichotomy of soul and body. In general, Oriental influence sharpened even this philosophical outlook, seeing the flesh as evil and radically and absolutely opposed to Spirit.

It was this dualism that most Gnostics and Marcions held in a stringent form. Paul's language about the flesh and his rooting the law of sin at war with the law of his mind in his fleshly members inevitably excited these Christian dualists and made them feel that here was *their* apostle.

In addition, Paul's original and creative idea of the resurrection as involving not flesh and blood but something continuous with the present body, which he called a spiritual body, stood out as something different from the Hebrew point of view and the teaching of the second-century Church. Paul's argument in 1 Corinthians is of course *pro*-Resurrection and is directed against the Corinthians who deny the Resurrection—in other words, Spirituals. But it would have been easy for the new Spirituals to have passed over or missed this fact.

Not to draw out too tediously this discussion, the Gnostics were attracted also to the apparent predestinarianism they found in Paul. Romans 8:28-30 and various verses in Ephesians 1-3 come to mind. But again they missed his emphasis on responsibility and on the democracy of faith. There is nothing in Paul to warrant the spiritual arrogance of the Gnostics and the relegation of the simple Christians to psychic or hylic classes, out of which they could never rise, with the consequences of this carrying over fatalistically into the life of the world to come.

Basically, Paul's revolt against the Law of Moses and his ingenious and at times far-fetched arguments attempting to prove the provisional and temporary role of the Law were what drew him to the attention of Church Liberals and Spirituals in the second century. His emphasis on Christian freedom could easily be pressed into service by those who wanted complete freedom, the Antinomians who are always at hand in the Church and elsewhere.

These are some of the reasons for Paul's peculiar role in church history. More than any other single figure, he was responsible for the emancipation of the Church from the leading strings of full Judaism. He made possible the idea of a new Covenant and the vision of an independent, universal Church for all people. But he was never able to become by his doctrine the founder or even the main inspirer of Christian theology. In Harnack's words, "Paulinism has proved to be a ferment in the history of dogma, a basis it has never been."[41] Earlier in his great work, he had remarked, "Paul's most peculiar (i.e. distinctive) thought acted on the development of ecclesiastical doctrine only by way of occasional stimulus."[42]

Neverthelss, the influence of Paul has been profound and it has been persistent. From time to time at critical periods, Paul has been rediscovered and associated with powerful and even revolutionary renewal. The two most notable instances are St. Augustine and Martin Luther. It is not accidental that both men are examples of twice-born souls in an extreme degree, as Paul of course was. The element of release from bondage and the oppression of sin and guilt and the joyous experience of freedom in Christ are common and conspicuous aspects of experience in all three men.

Paul's influence, however, was not confined to such classic types of radical conversion. Charles Bigg, who preached the Bampton Lectures before the University of Oxford in St. Mary's Church nearly one hundred years ago (in 1886), observed that down to the age of Irenaeus and the Alexandrines there was no trace of Paulinism to be found, except among the Gnostics.[43]

Clement of Alexandria, it seems, felt called on to apologize for treating "the noble Apostle," as he calls Paul, with the same deference as the Twelve. Nevertheless he does so, and "the working of the new leaven is seen at once in (Clement's) view of Knowledge, of the Resurrection, of Retribution. Indeed we may characterize this period as the first of those Pauline reactions, which mark the critical epochs of theology."

Bigg notes the contrast between Irenaeus and the Alexandrines, but sees Paul in different ways as a strong influence on both. "Hence Paulinism assumed very different shapes in the Western and the Eastern doctors. In the former, the antithesis of the First and Second Adam is already pointing the way to the Augustinian doctrine of grace, in the latter the vision of the great day, when Christ shall deliver up the kingdom to his Father, leads on to Universalism."[44]

The reference in the last phrase of this quotation is to Origen, the first systematic theologian in the full sense and one of the giants among Christian doctors in all ages. For him creation was a mighty drama in three acts. Creation in the biblical and commonly understood sense was an intermediate phase in human history.

There had been a catastrophic ante-mundane fall aeons before this world came into being. The role of the latter was redemption and restoration. It was a vale of soul-recovery and soul-making. In this, Christ the God-man, truly divine and truly and perfectly human, was a figure of central importance, but not in a manner that infringed on the freedom of the human will.

However, Origen was obliged to believe that all things would return to God, as in the beginning they had come out from him. Here he was mightily reenforced by Paul in 1 Corinthians 15. Here was a clear revelation of the only possible end, in Origen's view, of the mighty drama. "God shall be all in all." There will come a time when all things are put in subjection to him who must reign until he has put all enemies under his feet. "Then comes the end, when [Christ] delivers the kingdom to God the Father after destroying every rule and every authority and power."[45]

Origen found Paul's very original notion of resurrection helpful; Romans 8 influenced him in the outlook on the whole creation visualized there as well as in the ringing, concluding declaration about the unconquerable "love of God which is in Christ Jesus our Lord." Indeed, Paul, in these two seminal sections of his writings, Romans 8 and 1 Corinthians 15, along with Plato, inspired and to a degree directed the great Alexandrian's weighty and powerful theological construction.

As it was in the ancient Church and at the Reformation, so it has been in modern history. It was as he heard Luther's preface to his *Commentary on Romans* being read that John Wesley felt his heart strangely warmed and was able to leave behind the bondage of the law and to feel with certainty the freedom of the Christian man.

In our own century it was Paul who grasped the pastor-preacher, Karl Barth, even as the heavy guns were thundering across the border in France in the fierceness and futility of the First World War. The manifesto that converted Barth in the brooding and the writing and that turned the modern theological world upside down was his *Commentary on Romans*.

The brilliant rabbi who remains unsurpassed as a man of feeling, who was taken willing captive by the marvelous love of Christ Jesus, did not cease to be a rabbi and to think like one. He became the first and possibly the greatest Christian theologian. But because he came when he did in point of time, and because he was so steeped in the traditions of his fathers and the religion of his people, he was as much a witness to the Old Testament matrix of Christianity as he was to the dawn of a new order and the reality of a new being in Jesus, Lord and Christ.

This was especially true in relation to (a) the being and purpose of God, (b) the exceeding sinfulness of sin and its universality, and (c) a world-view in which history is the theater of the divine activity and is moving to a climactic fulfillment in a glorious eschatological drama. These key points could not be missed by any real student of Paul. Along with his incomparable concentration on the Lord Jesus, the Son of God "who loved me and gave himself for me," these theses made it certain that any attempt to gnosticize or platonize or even de-Judaize this apostle would fail.

A Marcion might be attracted to Paul and think that he alone understood him, but it would soon be clear that he totally misunderstood him. Similarly, a Valentinus might try to swallow Paul's Jewishness and make it digestible by means of allegorization, but its bones and sinews were bound to stick in his throat, as theologians as different as Irenaeus and the Alexandrians, Clement and Origen, clearly perceived.

It was Paul, the Christian rabbi, the teacher not the philosopher, who, thinking of his people "with great sorrow and unceasing anguish in my heart," could write:

> They are Israelites, and to them belong the sonship, the glory, the covenants, the giving of the law, the worship, and the promises; to them belong the patriarchs, and of their race, according to the flesh, is the Christ. God who is over all be blessed forever! Amen.[46]

Turning to the Gentiles, whose special apostle he was, Paul could say:

> But if some of the branches were broken off, and you, a wild olive shoot, were grafted in their place to share the richness of the olive tree, do not boast over the

branches. If you do boast, remember it is not you that support the root, but the root that supports you. You will say, "Branches were broken off so that I might be grafted in." That is true. They were broken off because of their unbelief, but you stand fast only through faith. So do not become proud, but stand in awe. For if God did not spare the natural branches, neither will he spare you.

Behold therefore the goodness and the severity of God: severity toward those who have fallen, but goodness to you, provided you continue in his goodness; otherwise you too will be cut off.[47]

I appeal to you therefore, brethren, by the mercies of God, to present your bodies as a living sacrifice, holy and acceptable to God, which is your spiritual worship.[48]

1. Acts 10:34-35
2. 11:18
3. *Gal.* 2:11-16
4. *Acts* 9:1-5
5. *Ibid.* vs. 9
6. *Ibid.* 26, especially vv. 12-19
7. *Phil.* 2:6-9
8. *1 Cor. 15:26-28 cf. RSV rendering: "that God may be everything to everyone."*
9. *Frederic W. H. Myers, Saint Paul*

10. 8:31-39
11. *supra.* Chapter II, pp. 65-66
12. 2:2
13. 3:10-11
14. I:16-20
15. I:8-9
16. Gal. I:11-20
17. 2:20-21
18. 4:3
19. 5:1
20. 3:4-12. RSV
21. 3:14-19
22. Novalis was a German Romantic poet who lived in the last part of the eighteenth century.
23. *Gal.* 3:7
24. *Ibid.* 3:26-27. The whole chapter develops this argument.
25. 4:21-28
26. I:16-17
27. 3:21-24. NEB
28. Chapter 4
29. 5:15, 19. NEB
30. 6:23. NEB
31. As in this climactic sentence, ''Miserable creature that I am, who is there to rescue me out of this body doomed to death? God alone, through Jesus Christ our Lord! Thanks be to God!'' (7:24-25)
32. 8:I
33. 8:28-30
34. 11:5-8
35. vv. 25-26
36. vv. 33, 36
37. 3:15-17
38. 2 Peter is the latest New Testament writing and could be as late as A.D. 140.
39. 2 Cor. 12:9
40. Col. 2:3-10 cf. v.20; also Gal. 4:3,9. These spirits or powers

inhabiting the planets and the stars were thought of as ruling over human life in resistance to the living and true God.

41. *Op. cit.* I, p. 136
42. *Ibid.* p. 92
43. *The Christian Platonists of Alexandria*, p. 53-54
44. *Ibid.* pp. 53-54
45. 1 Cor. 15:24-28
46. Rom. 9:4-5
47. *Ibid.* 11:17-22 RSV and AV
48. *Ibid.* 12:1 RSV

Chapter Six

Apollos The Platonist

The New Testament, as we have discovered, is
through and through a Christological work. It is dominated by the figure of Jesus and the conviction that
he is Lord. This is what makes his teaching important
and gives the reason for the preservation of his teaching and its incorporation in large blocks and to a
remarkable degree (when you consider the dates of
their composition) in the Gospels of Matthew and
Luke.

Other ideas about Jesus and his significance
appear along with the central conviction that he is
Lord. Basically, these are Messiah or, in Greek,
Christ; Son of God; and Divinity: or in some true
sense, God.

The middle term here is Son of God. It can be
an implication of Messiah, especially if Messiah is
understood, in the Danielic and Enochian sense, as
a heavenly being, the chosen of the Father anointed
by him and delegated to appear on earth, announcing
the imminent breaking in of the Kingdom of God.
Then, after his return to the Father, he reigns from

heaven until all adversaries are overcome and the kingdom completed and ready to be delivered up to the Father.

Such an outline recalls St. Paul and explains how an Albert Schweitzer can deny all Hellenistic influence on Paul and derive even his Christ-mysticism from Jewish messianism and apocalyptic eschatology. But Son of God can be given a Greek connotation and suggests a Divine as opposed to a super-angelic status. Whether Paul faced this at all, as in Philippians 2 and Colossians 1 and 2, is not clear. Schweitzer excludes Colossians from consideration along with Ephesians, but not Philippians.

But whatever the case with Paul, the Epistle to the Hebrews plunges at once into phrases implying divinity in introducing Jesus. In this respect, Apollos, if he was, as I choose, to believe the author of this Alexandrian-oriented treatise or rhetorical letter, stands in between Paul and John. This is the swelling trumpet call and celebration with which he begins:

> God who in former times spoke in fragmentary and diverse ways to our fathers by the prophets, has in this final age spoken to us by the Son whom he has made heir to the whole universe, and through whom also he created the worlds. This Son is the effulgence of the Divine splendor and the very image of the Divine being: and it is he who upholds the universe by the word

of his power.

When the Son had brought about the
purgation of sins, he took his seat on the
right hand of the Majesty on high, raised
as far above the angels as the Name he has
by inheritance is loftier than theirs.

For to which of the angels did God
ever say,

> "Thou art my Son,
>   today I have begotten thee?"

Or again,

> "I will be a father to him,
>   and he shall be a son to me."

And again when he brings the first-
born into the world, he says,

> "Let all the angels of God worship
>   him."[1]

We can see at once that Apollos was a man who
had studied rhetoric. In Roman and Greek times this
was standard practice. Three centuries later, Augustine was a professor of rhetoric. But this author,
evidently a preacher of oratorical power, was also a
philosophical theologian. Philo would have understood at once what he was getting at, theistically and
philosophically.

The Jewish Christians and others who read this
epistle might or might not have got the Philonic
echoes. But they would have appreciated the references to Hebrew angelology, which was popular in

the Judaism of that period. Apollos wishes to set straight any who might have thought of Jesus Messiah as the highest of the angels. Soon there will be Gnostics who will relegate the bungling job done by the Demiurge or Fashioner of the world to one or more angels.

The receivers of this oratorical or sermonic tract would understand, too, the preoccupation with the death and sufferings of the Son of God. Paul had said of the Cross of Jesus that it was a stumbling-block to the Jews and folly to the Greeks.[2] The Gospel of Mark seems to have been written, in part, as an explanation of the tragic passion and hideous death of God's anointed Son—the Christ. Apollos treats this issue abstractly rather than biographically, but he handles it with marked realism and sensitivity. He has, in fact, the clearest grasp of the two sides of Jesus, divine and human, human and divine, to be found in the New Testament. And this is the first subject he addresses, Jesus the Son of God, divine and human.

The sweep of Christology in the New Testament and in subsequent theology is toward the full divinity of Christ. The danger indeed was, as Paul's thinking in the earliest books of the New Testament shows, neglect of the humanity of Jesus. The Synoptic Gospels, especially the introductory sections in Matthew and Luke, reflect a growing maturity in the Church and go far to correcting the balance in preserving the full truth about the Christ.

One could say the same thing about Apollos in
Hebrews: he knew Paul well and shared his zeal for
the saving Gospel of the One who in heaven had
emptied himself, forsaking the form of God for the
form of a slave, in order to live and die for sinful and
ungrateful men. But of Jesus in the flesh Paul had
said little. It is this omission that the Gospels conspic-
uously correct.

It may well be that Hebrews reflects this same
impulse of realism respecting Jesus, the real human
being, who for the joy that was set before him endured the cross, despising the shame.[3] In any event,
the author of this masterpiece of eloquence puts
together the Lord from heaven of Paul, known according to the Spirit, and the Son of man who shared
our flesh, was tempted in all points as we are, yet
without sin, and shed real blood for our sins. It is
tempting to think that Apollos, who knew Paul well,
consciously sought a reconciliation of the Pauline emphasis with the countervailing trend of the Gospel biographies.

Actually, the central orientation of Hebrews
differs from Paul. There is little mysticism in it and
apparently little concern with the Sacraments, in
comparison with either Paul or John. There is in
Hebrews only one incidental mention of baptism and
none of the Supper of the Lord. There is, however,
a sacramental outlook from the standpoint of the
relation of things earthly to things heavenly.

Worship and the all-important matter of the

connection between earth and heaven, and heaven and earth, seem to be the central concern of the author of Hebrews. It is here that we descry the influence of Plato, though the Platonism is in the end subordinate to and modified by a motif that is neither Grecian nor Hebraic, but authentically Christian. Instead of time as the moving image of eternity, we see in Hebrews events of time entering into and shaping eternity.

Now we know that Apollos had taught at Corinth, arriving there after Paul, and that a faction had arisen claiming to be of Apollos. This indicates that he was a man of force with very definite views. Before going further with the analysis of the theology of Hebrews, let us look at two things: what scholars think generally about this epistle, and what we know about Apollos.

Scholars have been at sea about the Epistle to the Hebrews since the second and third centuries when Clement and Origen, "the Christian Platonists of Alexandria," refer to it. Origen, the greatest scholar of Christian antiquity, thought that Paul could not have written it, because the "verbal style of the epistle entitled 'To Hebrews' is not rude like the language of the apostle . . and its diction is purer Greek . . . But who wrote the epistle, in truth God knows."[4]

In the West, where Hebrews was known from the time of Clement, the third "bishop" of Rome, who quotes it in the letter from the church of Rome to the church of Corinth known as 1 Clement and

usually dated A.D. 96, there was doubt about its
authorship for centuries. Tertullian thought that Barnabas might have written it. Such scholars as Jerome
and Augustine had their doubts about Pauline authorship. Eventually, however, the habit of ascribing
it to Paul in the Eastern Church prevailed. Pope
Innocent I in 405 adopted Athanasius' view[5] that it
was by Paul and canonical.

At the Reformation Luther reopened the issue,
suggesting that Hebrews might well have been written by Apollos. Erasmus also doubted that it was by
Paul. The Council of Trent stayed with tradition, as
did the King James translators.

Luther's guess or judgment has been widely
reported by modern scholars and is regarded as the
most likely possibility. As J. H. Davies says, in his
Commentary on Hebrews in the Cambridge Bible
Commentary on the New English Bible, "If we wish
to choose a name, Apollos is the best."[6]

In choosing to follow this suggestion, as I have
done, I have been influenced by the information we
have on Apollos in the New Testament and by the
fact that there is no other real contender among the
figures mentioned and described in these Scriptures.

Admittedly, there is no direct evidence available, except the magnificent, original theological treatise which will always be known as Hebrews, though
the earliest reference to the title "To Hebrews" is
by Clement of Alexandria in about 180. The title may
therefore be later than the letter and may have origi-

nated as an interpretation of the purpose of the writing.

As a literary and theological production Hebrews has been much admired. Only Romans is comparable to it in length, structure, weightiness of content and argument, and intellectual level. Hebrews, it has been said, shares with Romans the right to be styled the first treatise of Christian theology.

It is a tempting speculation that Apollos came upon Romans either at some time when he was visiting the church in Rome or at some other church that possessed a copy. He admired it, was impressed by it, and was moved to embody his parallel but considerably different view of Christianity in relation to Judaism in a work of comparable stature and magnitude.

The difference in situation indicated by a comparison of the two concluding practical sections in the two Epistles must be taken into account by any theory that is to be credible and convincing. In Romans there is no critical situation to which Paul feels the need to address himself and so the ethical portion of the Letter is general, stating what he regards as fundamental guidelines of Christian conduct.

In Hebrews a critical situation is addressed by the author. Whether it is a condition of severe persecution, such as that under Nero in the 60s or under Domitian in the 80s or early 90s, or whether it is a more chronic condition of dissatisfaction on the part of Jewish Christians infecting possibly Gentiles as well, we cannot tell. The latter diagnosis would seem to be favored by the formal, argumentative character of the first nine chapters, and by the rather didactic and oratorical tone and form of the appeal to the heroes of faith in chapters 11 and 12. Also, the counsels and exhortations of chapter 13 are somewhat general, not entirely unlike Romans 12.

If the author was Apollos, and if reading Romans was responsible for the writing of Hebrews, the question arises as to why no one knew about it and left some record of the fact. We are, of course, guessing—any explanation is bound to be speculative in the extreme—but it is possible that Apollos was somewhat under the shadow of Paul, by this time a martyr, possibly for a considerable time, and hesitated to go public with his ambitious rival production. The manuscript went out without signature, very possibly from Rome or a quiet spot near Rome.

This is suggested by the brief personal conclusion of Hebrews, with its news of Timothy's release (presumedly from prison) and communication of greetings from "our Italian friends." It has been thought by some scholars that these last verses were tacked on by a later hand, but it is hard to see what the motivation for the addition would be. The magnificent Benediction (used in all Prayer Book Burial Services), which comes in the middle of the final personal message section, is bound to be by the author of the epistle.

As the reader might well expect, there is no agreement among competent students on the probable date of Hebrews; 1 Clement gives us an outside time—in the early 90s. Some have thought that the fall of Jerusalem with the destruction of the Temple would have been mentioned, if the work had been produced after that event. After all, its theme is the superseding of the Jewish sacrifices by the death and sacrifice of Christ. On the other hand, it would have been natural to mention the Temple sacrifices, if they were still being offered.

The fact seems irrefutably to be that the author, Apollos I believe, was inclined to ignore the Temple sacrifices. His argument turns wholly upon the cult of the Tabernacle in the Pentateuch and the Levitical sacrifices. He is steeped in the Greek Septuagint version of the Old Testament, and it is this that he assumes his readers to know and to have before them. The Judaism that he has in mind is not that of Jerusalem and the Temple, but the synagogue Judaism of the Dispersion.

As to the problem of the date of Hebrews, since we are not looking for a specific fierce persecution, we are not forced to choose between the middle 60s and the early 90s (Nero or Domitian). A period after the fall of Jerusalem, with its psychological impact on all Jews and many Jewish Christians, seems logical. Also, we must allow for the impact of the concern for the human, historical Jesus which found expression in the Synoptic Gospels (65 to 85). Somewhere in this period, possibly between 70 and 75, Hebrews most likely was produced.

Now for the credentials of Apollos. It seems to me that they are impressive if we are looking for someone who could have written such a book as Hebrews. The sources are the Acts, Paul in 1 Corinthians, and Titus. St. Luke in the Acts gives us a relatively lengthy and certainly an intriguing portrait of Apollos. It is contained in chapters 18 and 19. Paul had left Corinth after a long stay there during which he founded the Corinthian church. He went to Syria, taking with him his hosts and fellow tentmakers, Priscilla and Aquila. From there they went to Ephesus where he left his friends, as he took a ship en route to Jerusalem, to observe a feast there.

Paul landed at Caesarea, went up to Jerusalem to ''salute the Church,'' then went to Antioch and after that made a lengthy tour ''over all the country of Galatia and Phrygia in order, strengthening all the disciples.''

Then, Luke says, a certain Jew came to Ephesus. He was named Apollos and was born at Alexandria. He was an eloquent man, powerful in the use of the scriptures. He had, Luke says, ''been instructed in the way of the Lord and was full of spiritual fervor; and in his discourses he taught the facts about Jesus accurately, though he knew only John's baptism. He now began to speak boldly in the synagogue, where Priscilla and Aquila heard him; they took him in hand and expounded the new way to him in greater detail."[7]

After a time Apollos expressed a desire to go across to Achaia (a district in Southern Greece on the Gulf of Corinth) and was supported in this by the brotherhood at Ephesus, who wrote the congregation at Corinth to make him welcome. Arriving in the southern city, from the beginning he was very helpful to those who by God's grace had become believers, "for he strenuously confuted the Jews, demonstrating publicly from the scriptures that the Messiah is Jesus."[8]

The Apollos narrative ends with the dry statement that "while Apollos was at Corinth Paul travelled through the inland regions till he came to Ephesus,"[9] where he was to stay for a period of two years. There is, however, a possible clue of importance in what immediately follows respecting baptism and the Spirit.

Luke had stated that Apollos had received (known) only John's baptism. Now we are told that at Ephesus Paul found a number of converts who, when asked, "Did you receive the Holy Spirit when you became believers?" replied, "No, we have not even heard that there is a Holy Spirit."

The upshot is that Paul finds that these converts, too, had received only John's baptism. Telling them that this baptism was a token of repentance, but that people were to put their trust in the one who was to come after John, even Jesus, he arranges for their baptism into the name of the Lord Jesus. Paul then laid hands on them, and the Holy Spirit came upon them and they spoke in tongues of ecstasy and prophesied. These men numbered about a dozen.

Bearing in mind the minimal emphasis on baptism and the Eucharist in Hebrews, and that we are nowhere told that Apollos was rebaptized in the name of Jesus, it is possible to see evidence of a significant character for a major difference with Paul. And, of course, as a result of his stay and ministry in Corinth, there was a faction that claimed to be not of Paul but of Apollos.

We shall, momentarily, be taking a closer look at the doctrinal teaching of Hebrews but two things may be noted and stated starkly while we are on the subject of baptism and the Spirit. The Spirit is mentioned in Hebrews only seven times.[10] Four are significant references, while three are merely formal, indicating what the Nicene Creed in its Constantinopolitan recension will confess, namely, "who spoke through the prophets." Certainly this work is not a pneumatic document in the manner of Paul's Letters or Luke's two-volume work or even Mark and Matthew.

The other notation concerns the omission of any reference to the Lord's Supper or the Eucharist. This raises profound questions, especially in view of the emphasis of Hebrews on sacrifice for sin and the high priesthood of Jesus the Christ, the Son of God. The blood of Christ for this theologian is all-important, but it is shed once for all for sin and there is no repetition of sacrifice as in the rites of the Tabernacle. It is as if the idea of partaking of the Body and Blood of the crucified Lord Jesus were not in the ken of this teacher, preacher, and theologian.

We must return to consider this aspect of Hebrews, but we can note here that it represents a line of development in some contrast to Paul, John, Ignatius of Antioch, and the sacramentalism which survived as central in the mainline, Orthodox and Catholic church. Apparently, we have to do with a point of view that is at once Hebraic and Platonic, but owes nothing to the mystery religions or the mystical sacramentalism which became powerful and attractive in the Hellenistic and Roman world. No wonder Apollos left his mark in Corinth!

We have still to examine the material on Apollos in 1 Corinthians and Titus, but it is doubtful that it will add anything of a substantive character to the data already before us. There are three places where Paul mentions Apollos. The first is in 1 Corinthians 1, where right off the bat, to speak colloquially, Paul raises the question of divisions and quarrels. Here he notes four factions: a situation in the Church where each member is saying, "I am Paul's man;" or "I am for Apollos;" or "I follow Cephas;" or "I am Christ's."[11]

Paul is dismayed by this and uses strong language in criticizing it. He reviews the word or doctrine of the Cross and its seeming folly: yet it is the power of God and the wisdom of God. He recalls his first appearances and preaching in Corinth. He had refrained from delving profoundly into the hidden wisdom and secret purpose of God, not realized by the powers that rule the world when they crucified the Lord of glory.[12] This leads him into the nature of the Spirit of God and the perfect knowledge of the Spirit, who is alive and active and has been given freely to us by God himself. Yet Paul had dealt initially with his converts as infants in Christ, giving them milk to drink, not solid food.

This brings him back to the subject of divisions in the Church. This time he notes only the factions of Paul and of Apollos. And who are they? Only God's agents. He, Paul, planted the seed, and Apollos watered it; the garden is God's. Or, to change the metaphor, you are God's building. The foundation is Jesus Christ himself, and there can be no other.[13]

In chapter 3 there is a further mention of Paul, Apollos, and Cephas; and in chapter 4 he begs his "friends to view himself and Apollos as examples and learn not to go beyond the things which are written; that no one of you be puffed up for the one against the other."[14]

In the final "greeting" section (chapter 16) Paul says that he has strongly urged our brother Apollos to go to Corinth "with the others," but it was not at all his will to go now;[15] he will come later when he has opportunity. It would appear from this statement that Apollos had a mind of his own and was not easily swayed from a decision made. In Titus 3, near the end of the epistle, Apollos is mentioned along with Zenas the lawyer and the writer urges Titus to help them on their travels and see that they lack nothing.

It is surely noteworthy and speaks well for Paul that in all his references to Apollos there is nothing in any slightest way small or critical. He takes him and his ministry at Corinth at face value and is only concerned to have the Corinthian disciples look deeper and be more mature as Christians. There is nothing whatever that bears on the information contributed by Luke in Acts respecting John's baptism and the coming down of the Holy Spirit on baptized converts when Paul lays hands on them.

Paul does say early in 1 Corinthians that he thanks God he had not baptized any of his converts except Crispus and Gaius (and on second thought the household of Stephanas). It also appears in Acts 19 that Paul did not himself baptize the twelve Ephesian converts, but did lay hands upon them.

Paul does say in 1 Corinthians that God sent him not to baptize but to preach the Gospel.[16] As to Apollos' views and as to the significance of the minimizing in Hebrews of the two Sacraments of the Gospel, we must remain in ignorance.

It is time now to analyze the thought of Apollos in a work given an epistolary form but which in reality is a homily or exhortation. It is a rhetorical masterpiece; no other New Testament writing compares with it in oratorical power.

We can see the preacher in Hebrews. It may well be that much of the material in the work has been used not once but many times in expounding the Scriptures (the Old Testament in Greek) and proclaiming the Gospel. When the Alexandrian Jew, Apollos, reached Ephesus and made himself known in the Church, it was perceived that he was very eloquent, powerful in his use of the Scriptures, and fervent in temperament. After he got to Corinth, a church he must have heard of, for he wanted to go there, he was judged to be especially helpful to believers, for he concentrated on confuting the Jews by demonstrating in public address that "the Messiah is Jesus."

There is a great deal of exhortation in Hebrews, and it is not concentrated in particular sections, as toward the end. Rather there is in the Epistle a continuous rhythm of doctrine and exhortation. This makes it difficult to find a clear outline of the argument. I have looked through a large number of efforts at grasping the whole in summary form. None is entirely convincing or satisfactory.

The summation that appeals most to me is the broad topical outline employed by the NEB translators. They sum up the sweep of the argument as follows:

>   Christ Divine and Human
>   The Shadow and the Real
>   A Call to Faith

This analysis has the value among other things of calling attention to the three great sources of the author's thought and to his skill in constructing a credible and brilliant synthesis of these three vital traditions. Hebrews is an amalgam of Christianity, Judaism, and Platonism. The Christian strain is dominant, but there is a strong witness to the Jewish background. Plato and his ideas are invoked as a way of explaining the transitory character of the Jewish institutions of worship and of underwriting the perfection and permanence of heaven and the heavenly realities to which Christians look, now that Jesus has made a full expiation for sins and has ascended to the Father's side, a High Priest forever after the order of Melchizedek.

Platonism, to be sure, is modified. The Christian fact, Christ divine and human, is dominant. In accomplishing the great work of man's redemption and establishing forever his royal priesthood, Jesus had to leave the heavenly household and realm where he was the effulgence of the divine splendor and the vicegerent of God in creation, and become one of us. He had to realize our weakness and experience our sufferings, even to be tempted in all points as we are, yet without sin. Above all, he was not exempt from our final trial but tested death for every man and poured out on the cross his precious blood. And without blood there is no forgiveness of sins!

This identification with human beings, this realistic expiatory sacrifice for sins by the Son of God and the Son of man, and this equipment for eternal priesthood are everlastingly significant. The eternal order takes up into it the action in time of the Son of God. He is now forever at the right hand of God as our Intercessor and High Priest.

> So now, my friends, the blood of Jesus makes us free to enter boldly into the sanctuary by the new and living way which he his opened for us through the curtain, the way of his flesh. We have moreover a great priest set over the household of God.[17]

Much is made by Apollos of the new Covenant in Christ's blood which is considered to be the fulfillment of Jeremiah's famous prophecy.

> Here we have also the testimony of the Holy Spirit: he first says, 'This is the covenant which I will make with them after those days, says the Lord: I will set my laws in their hearts and write them on their understanding;' then he adds, 'and their sins and wicked deeds I will remember no more at all.' And where these have been forgiven, there are offerings for sin no longer.[18]

This reasoning is the premise for a rather terrifying doctrine which we know obtained for long in the ancient Church: the doctrine that there is no forgiveness for postbaptismal sin, or in the thought of Apollos, of sin after the acceptance of the forgiveness provided by the blood of Christ and repentance. This is the succinct statement of this stern teaching:

> For if we wilfully persist in sin after receiving the knowledge of the truth, no sacrifice for sins remains.[19]

This relentless argument ends with the severe observation:

> "It is a terrible thing to fall into the hands of the living God ."[20]

Such a perfectionistic demand was bound to prove unrealistic and counterproductive, but it had the good effect of making people think seriously about themselves and sin and salvation prior to and at the time of conversion and Baptism. The view enunciated classically by Apollos in Hebrews persisted at least until well into the fourth century.

Constantine, the first Christian emperor and the sovereign who made Christianity the established Church of the empire, put off Baptism until his deathbed. Ironically he who had convoked the First General Council, which had condemned Arius and affirmed the full divinity of Jesus Christ, the only Son of God, was baptized in 339 by an Arian bishop, Eusebius of Nicomedia.

Slightly different and yet basically similar was the case of the great Aurelius Augustinus (354-430) —St. Augustine of Hippo. His devout Christian mother, Monica, was a great influence on his life, but she was prudent and was only too well aware of the perils that awaited a young man in the sexually permissive climate of North Africa. Also, Augustine's father was a pagan. Accordingly, Aurelius had never been baptized despite his mother's piety, and it was not until his conversion in Milan in 387 that this remarkable young man, destined to be one of the giants of theology in all ages, received the Sacrament of Holy Baptism.

If Apollos' position in Hebrews is classically Christian in its creative Christocentric outlook and reasoning, and draws heavily on Judaism in its intensive concentration on sin and its centrality in religion, he leans on Platonism in explaining the inadequacy and transitoriness of the forms and types in the Judaism of the First Covenant. The Jewish forms were shadows of the real, copies of the everlasting realities set in heaven.

Apollos, like Paul, appeals to Abraham and his two irrevocable acts of promise and oath. Particularly impressive was the presence of the priest Melchizedek, who is without father or mother; who has no lineage at all, and hence is a type of the eternal order and eternal priesthood. It is in this succession that Jesus comes, entering in through the veil, and "having become a priest forever in the succession of Melchizedek."[21]

The perfection of Jesus as High Priest and of the new order now obtaining in heaven but reaching down to earth is emphasized. The imperfection of the Levitical priesthood was revealed in the shift to another priest who was in the succession of Melchizedek, not of Aaron. The earth-bound rules were cancelled, "since the Law brought nothing to perfection; and a better hope is introduced, through which we draw near to God."[22]

In the fullness of time, the shadow has passed that the real may be revealed. Things on the earth have their patterns eternally in the heavens, and this is exemplified in the Mosaic and Levitical order of things.

This the inner shrine behind the curtain or veil, where the High Priest alone may go at the time of high sacrifice, is the temporary representation of an everlasting order into which "Jesus has gone as a forerunner on our behalf, having become a high priest forever after the order of Melchizedek."[23]

Jesus is separated from the old Covenant and inferior order where a succession of priests was required, since "he holds his priesthood permanently, because he continues forever . . . He has no need, like those high priests; to offer sacrifices daily, first for his own sins and then for those of the people; he did this once for all when he offered up himself. Indeed the law appoints men in their weakness as high priests, but the word of the oath which came later than the law, appoints a Son who has been made perfect forever."[24]

Now, says Apollos, at the beginning of chapter

8, we come to the point of what we have been saying.[25] We have a high priest seated at the right hand
of the throne of the Majesty in heaven, a minister
in the sanctuary and true tent set up not by man but
by the Lord. He is in contrast to the priests offering
gifts under the Law. "They serve as copy and shadow
of the heavenly sanctuary, for when Moses was about
to erect the tent, he was instructed by God, saying,
'See that you make everything according to the pattern which was shown you on the mountain.'"[26]

One of the arresting things about Hebrews is
the degree to which it is worship-centered. For its
author, the important thing about the old Law and
Covenant was the Cult, the rites of worship. For him
these were classically those laid down by Moses under the instruction of the Lord God. They were the
rites of the Tent or Tabernacle. He must have
known, of course, the Temple worship, which was
the same, only grander and more spectacular. But
for reasons that are obscure he chooses to ignore the
Temple. He blanks it out as if it had never existed.
I believe that this is because the Temple has in fact
been wiped out—it is indeed as if it had never been.
This is bound to have been and to remain a poignant
and painful fact. But for the Christian it is irrelevant. For him the newer rites are here. His worship
is directed to heaven, where the suffering Son of God,
now our High Priest forever, is at the right hand of
the Majesty and Glory of the Universe. Moreover,
the type of heavenly worship for the Alexandrian

especially and the Jew of the Dispersion generally is that described and laid out in glowing detail in the Book of Moses, the so-called Law.

It is, I repeat, quite remarkable, and in notable contrast to the meaning of the Law for Paul the Rabbi, that for Apollos the Law means primarily worship. In chapter 9 he describes vividly and dramatically the worship of the earthly sanctuary: the full physical layout and the ritual actions of the priests and the high priest. Particular stress is laid on the second curtain and the Holy of Holies into which only the high priest can go, and he only once a year, and then with blood. This is seen as a symbol for the present age, the Holy Spirit indicating that as long as the outer tent is still standing, the way into the sanctuary is not yet opened.

All is changed, however, when Christ appeared as a high priest of the good things that have come, and through the greater and more perfect tent not of this creation entered once and for all into the Holy Place, taking not blood of bulls and goats, but his own blood, and "thus securing an eternal redemption."[27]

Then comes a declaration of transcendent significance. "Therefore he is the mediator of a new covenant, so that those who are called may receive the promised eternal inheritance, since a death has occurred which redeems them from the transgressions under the first covenant."[28] We are then given an impressive description of the role of blood under the old Covenant. The Law was not simply given and that was that. No, even the first Covenant was not ratified without blood. When Moses had declared every commandment to the people, he took the blood of calves and goats, with water and scarlet wool and hyssop, and sprinkled both the book and all the people, saying, "This is the blood of the covenant which God commanded you." Similarly, he sprinkled the tent with the blood and all the vessels used in the worship. "Indeed," says Apollos, "under the law almost everything is purified with blood, and without the shedding of blood there is no forgiveness of sins."[29]

To us who tend to shrink from blood, all this seems not only involved but on the repulsive side. Yet we can see its deep significance. The blood is indeed the life. Look at the case of Dr. Barney Clark, first example of a human being living on with a completely unfleshly, mechanical heart, but still living because the blood is being pumped and is reaching his organs through the system of arteries and veins.

The point our author is making, to repeat, is that if "the copies of the heavenly things" had to be purified with the rites of the Law, the heavenly things required even better sacrifices, which Christ has provided by entering not into a sanctuary made by hands, "a copy of the true one," but into heaven itself, to appear now and forevermore in the presence of God on our behalf.[30] Thus Christ, who has put away sin once for all by the sacrifice of himself, is at the center of our worship, our life, our hope, and our faith. "For by a single offering he has perfected for all time those who are consecrated."[31]

Once again, the prophecy of Jeremiah 31 comes to mind. This new Covenant has been executed. It is in force. It is final. It is God's perfect gift to mankind in Christ. All the Christian needs to do is to see this with full assurance of faith and live with others of the brotherhood, not forsaking the assembling of themselves together, in the confidence of a great reward.

The trouble, however, is that not all are finding it easy to persist in this vigorous, enkindling faith. Many are finding it difficult, whether from persecution and disapproval, or from the comfort of the accustomed reliance on old thought-ways or the difficulty of the perfectionistic demands of the new and living way in Christ, which hardly takes account of human frailty and liability to repeat sins.

So Apollos, who must have been something of a spiritual firebrand, an evangelist and preacher aglow with the glory of the new righteousness of a perfect covenant as well as the joy of a worship joining earth with heaven itself, turned in his book to concentrated exhortation. There had been exhortation before, interspersed with and lightening his chain of argument and reasoning. This is an Alexandrian. He is trained in the Scriptures. He is also an accomplished rhetorician. He is a master of words. Moreover, he seems, despite his intellectualism and logical bent, to be aware of human feelings and the universality of passion and sufferings, for he was aware of and placed strong emphasis on Christ's sufferings and temptation. His view of the Son of God had shown a discerning, remarkably balanced understanding of the blending and union in him of divinity and humanity.

Now, the chips are down. The picture is complete. What God has done and what he offers is clear. The call is to stand firm, to be steadfast in faith and hope, to abide in the army of the faithful, giving no ground to faintness of heart or loss of courage.

So the preacher—for that he surely was—turns with versatility and impressive power to call to faith. First, he defines faith—in a celebrated sentence.[32] Then, he calls the roll of the heroes of faith in Israel's long, checkered history and by implication in recent fierce persecutions.

This section of Hebrews is at once very Hebraic and is touched with the element of transcendence and otherworldliness with which Alexandria is synonymous and which represents the touch of Plato and Platonism. Thus Abraham occupied him some time in his roll call of heroes and leads him to various reflections. Of the father of the faithful, he declared, "For he was looking for the city which has foundations, whose architect and builder is God."[33] A little further along, still dwelling on Abraham and those closely related to him, he reflects: "These all died in faith . . . having confessed that they were strangers

and pilgrims on the earth.'' They could have turned
back but did not, for their desire was ''for a better
country, that is as heavenly.'' Which desire God
honors, ''for he had prepared for them a city.''[34]

This language was to influence St. Augustine
when, as mighty Rome was falling, he brooded on
the city behind all human habitations and communities; and in particular was stirred and inspired by
the climax of assurance Apollos was led to sketch out,
still absorbed with the dream of the city for which
the heroes of faith were looking but as yet had not
found.

> Aim at peace with all men, and a holy life
> for without that no one will see the Lord
> . . . Remember where you stand: not be-
> ore the palpable, blazing fire of Sinai, with
> the darkness, gloom, and whirlwind, the
> trumpet-blast and the oracular voice,
> which they heard, and begged to hear no
> more; for they could not bear the com-
> mand, 'If even an animal touches the
> mountain, it must be stoned.' So appall-
> ing was the sight, that Moses said, 'I shud-
> der with fear.'
>
> No, you stand before Mount Zion
> and the city of the living God, heavenly
> Jerusalem, before myriads of angels, the
> full concourse and assembly of the first-
> born citizens of heaven, and God the judge
> of all, and the spirits of good men made

perfect, and Jesus the mediator of a new
covenant, whose sprinkled blood has better things to tell than the blood of Abel.
See that you do not refuse to hear the voice
that speaks . . . The kingdom we are given
is unshakable; let us therefore give thanks
to God, and so worship as he would be
worshipped, with reverence and awe; for
our God is a consuming fire.[35]

Such is the tapestry of thought boldly sketched
out by the most original theologian produced by the
Christian Church in the first century of her existence.
There is and can be no absolute proof of his identity, but Apollos is the only figure of whom we have
any knowledge who could possibly fill the bill. There
are several things about the Christianity of Hebrews
that are notable and unusual.

The aim of the work is to distance Christianity
from Judaism. The old Covenant has had its day.
It has done its work, played its role in the economy
of God. Something new and different, infinitely
superior in quality and meaning has rendered it
obsolete. The temporary and changing has been
replaced by the Eternal and Unchanging.

Yet Hebrews is essentially a Jewish work. The
extent to which it was ignored by the Gnostics, in
contrast to Paul and John, is an indication of this.
Its ideas and categories, for all the transposition in
sphere from the temporal to the eternal, are Hebra-

ic through and through.

The Jew thought in concrete images and symbols. Abstraction was never his forte. In Hebrews we find the ultimate imagery still drawn from the Bible: God is the living God, who makes and keeps Covenant, and who is both Judge and Saviour. Jesus is the Son whose obedience is perfect. It has led him to the understanding needed by the High Priest who is man's perpetual Advocate and Intercessor. Nor is real sacrifice and the shedding of blood left behind. True, both have taken place once for all but their reality and efficacy have simply been translated and transferred to the heavenly sphere, where they abide as the everlasting basis of the forgiveness of sins and the reconciliation of God and men. And finally, sin is the human problem and only by atonement through sacrifice can a guilty man become acceptable to a holy God.

Hebrews, in short, represents a transmutation and transplantation of the Hebrew sacrificial system to the eternal heavenly sphere, conceived in quasi-platonic categories. Furthermore, worship remains the dominant interest of Apollos.

The imperfect, repetitious sacrifices of the Mosaic and Levitical system have given place to the perfect, unchanging, eternal worship of Heaven, with which the Church on earth is linked.

The Pharisaic aspect of Judaism, the aspect of the Law that loomed so large in the experience and spiritual difficulties of a Paul, seems to have no existence for Apollos.

At the same time, Hebrews strikingly shows the influence of time and history as the arena of the divine purpose and activity. It is here that a harvest is garnered for eternity. Thus, though the forms laid up in heaven after the manner of Plato supply the patterns of the earthly tent, the Jewish sacrificial system including the Levitical priesthood, and the old Covenant or Law—the perfect realities in all these areas came about through the action of the living God in and through his Son, obedient unto death. In the fulness of the Time (*Kairos*), all was fulfilled and lifted up into the existing but not completed Heavenly City, the city whose architect and builder is God.

This same problem, posed by the juxtaposition in Christian thought of Hebraism and Platonism, will ultimately come before the Christian Fathers and Doctors in a more philosophical form. In the end there is a synthesis of sorts with the ball going back and forth between philosophers and theologians. Nevertheless, biblical dynamism and historicism manage in the main to maintain themselves. Static categories have to give way to creative personal vitalities. The Incarnation, Christianity's cardinal contribution to religion and philosophy, dominates life and thought for all Christians.

How could it be otherwise?

1. i. 1-7. A translation from the Greek, consulting a number of versions.
2. I Cor. i. 23
3. Hebrews xii. 2. cf. Philippians ii. 5-9
4. Quoted from Origen by Eusebius, *Eccl. Hist.*, vi. 25
5. 39th Easter Letter in 367. The position of Hebrews in eastern MSS is between 2 Thessalonians and I Timothy. In western MSS it occupies the position to which we are accustomed: after Philemon and before James.
6. p. ii
7. 18:25-26, NEB
8. *Ibid.* vv. 27-28
9. 19:1
10. cf. NEB In this version only six references are visible. In one of the most important references to "the eternal Spirit" (ix. 14) the phrase is eliminated by a paraphrase. If the instinct of these translators is sound, which I doubt, my observation of a formal rather than a vital sense of the Spirit in Hebrews would be strengthened.
11. i. 12. NEB
12. ii. 1-10
13. iii. 1-11
14. vs. 6. RV. There is a textual problem here resulting in many different translations, but the moral is clear.
15. vs. 12. There is another textual problem here. RSV adopts the reading "God's will." NEB follows AV and RV but with a free translation.
16. i. 14-17
17. x. 19-21
18. x. 15-18
19. x. 26
20. x. 31
21. vi. 20
22. vii. 18-19
23. vi. 20
24. vii. 24, 27-28

25. cf. viii. 1. NEB
26. viii. 1-5
27. ix. 12. cf. vv. 1-12
28. ix. 15.
29. ix. 22.
30. vv. 23-24
31. x. 14.
32. xi. 1. One of the best translations reads: "Faith gives substance to our hopes, and makes us certain of realities we do not see." NEB
33. xi. 10
34. vv. 13-16
35. xii. 14-29 (with some elisions). NEB

Notes on Chapter Six

The Problem of the Eternal and the Temporal

This is a problem that has been with Christian thinkers as well as philosophers across the centuries. It is still with us, though there is probably less concern and more doubt about solving it among contemporary theologians than was the case two generations ago, or even one.

Hebrews is the one New Testament book that raises this paradox and problem in an acute and specific form. For this reason and in the interest of clarity, it seems well to sum up the aspects of the epistle that at once illuminate and intensify the metaphysical problem of time and eternity. At the risk of being slightly repetitive, I am attempting to lay out such a summary and comment on the problem, but am doing so in a detached appendix to Chapter VI.

Hebrews taken as a whole involves knowledge and impact derived from three systems: Judaism, Christianity, and Platonism. Judaism is present both as background and progenitor; it represents the Old Covenant between the living God and his special, chosen people. This Covenant was much more than an idea; it was a sacramental reality, expressed and realized through rites of worship.

Christianity is the New Covenant relationship established by the gracious God through his only and eternal Son, Jesus the Christ, divine and human. It is notable that in the thought of Hebrews the New Covenant could only be established through the mediation of one who was human in the truest, most realistic sense. This Son is also divine, but in the sweep of the extended argument involving priesthood, atonement, and intercession the human side receives the dominant emphasis.

The thesis of Hebrews is that a new and greater rite is here, a Christocentric system that supersedes the Mosaic system and that is manifestly superior to the older worship and its rites. It is in affirming this superiority that the author, Apollos of Alexandria we are calling him, draws on the Platonic idea and world-view. Alexandria was to be the extension of Athens in the Christian era, the birthplace of Neoplatonism and the nursery of Christian Platonism. Already by the time of Jesus it was making its influence felt in Jewish circles, and in the person and thought of Philo was in process of melding with Judaism and issuing in a syncretistic mix.

In his Letter to the Hebrews Apollos does not go to anything like this length, but he does find it convenient to invoke the Platonic model of the archetypal, heavenly idea or form and its earthly copy.

Melchizedek, King of Salem, who met Abraham
returning from the slaughter of the kings and set before him bread and wine,[1] is the type of an eternal
priesthood, preceding the Aaronic priesthood. This
eternal priesthood is fulfilled in Jesus, "holy, blame-
less, unstained, separated from sinners, exalted about
the heavens." Jesus, the High Priest "seated at the
right hand of the Majesty in heaven is a minister in
the sanctuary and true tent set up not by man but
by the Lord."[2]

This line of imagery and thinking is elaborated
in chapters 8 and 9. The priests under the law "serve
a copy and shadow of the heavenly sanctuary; for
when Moses was about to erect the tent, he was instructed by God, saying, 'See that you make everything according to the pattern which was shown you
on the mountains.'"[3]

The same logic is then applied to the eternal
High Priest and a Holy of Holies transcending everything created and earthly. "But when Christ appeared as a high priest of the good things that have
come, then through the greater and more perfect tent
(not made with hands, that is, not of this creation)
he entered once for all into the Holy Place, taking
not the blood of goats and calves but his own blood,
thus securing an eternal redemption."[4]

There is clearly a touch of the Platonism of Plato
in this epistle and the passages just cited are perhaps
the only instance of such specific Platonic influence
in the New Testament. It is equally clear that the Pla-

tonic model is subordinate to the biblical and Christian concept of time and process. These are related to the eternal order, but in the Christian manner of conceiving time and eternity, not the Platonic.

For Plato time is the moving image of eternity. For the New Testament and Christianity the Eternal may break into time: God is the living Lord and the form of his creative and revealing, redemptive action is the temporal order. The Incarnation occurs in time; the sacrifice of Jesus, though expressive of his inward and doubtless eternal obedience, is effected through his death on the cross; and his presence and work in heaven as Paraclete or Advocate are possible because of his earthly life, death, and resurrection.

Thus it is clear that Christianity endows time with a very special value, standing in this respect against all ahistorical systems whether of religion or philosophy. William Temple, the great scholar-archbishop who once dreamed of a modern *Summa* that might map the universe of reality, admitted this and is celebrated for his emphasis on the decisive breach of Christianity with all idealisms. Christianity, he declared, "is the most avowedly materialist of all the great religions."[5]

At the same time the great archbishop, who had been trained in philosophical idealism in the Oxford schools and had had as his Master at Balliol Edward Caird was unable to give up intellectually the necessity for a perfect cosmic and universal whole—an ultimate eternal perfection. So in *Nature, Man and God* he goes to great lengths to square the circle.

His general idea is that the harvest of time is the content of eternity, the *totum simul* that constitutes the everlasting vision and consciousness of God. But he recognizes that there are serious objections to all previous efforts to posit and comprehend this view of the whole.

Accordingly, the archbishop attempts to posit and construct a picture based on drama in relation to the dramatist, enriched by the analogy of the father in a human family. These examples help but do not suffice to solve the intellectual problem. We are too limited in our knowledge of the Infinite, Divine Nature.

What we must say, on the one hand, is that history cannot make any difference to God. For God is eternal and the Eternal is not successive. "But in another sense History makes a great difference to the Eternal; for if there were no History or if History were other than in fact it is, the Eternal would not be what the Eternal is."[6]

Temple thus left unsolved the ultimate problem, but the horn of the dilemma as just quoted left him open to attack by proponents of strict orthodoxy. Such a one was Professor Leonard Hodgson of Oxford, and Temple was deeply disturbed by the professor's onslaught. He wrote me of it in successive letters early in 1944, complaining either that Hodgson had not understood him or that he had failed to say what he had meant to say.

Actually, the reality is that the problem of time and eternity is insoluble by the human mind in the terms of either philosophical or theological orthodoxy. There has to be a give at some point, in one direction or another. Temple, I believe, was profoundly right in insisting that history reflects what the Eternal is, and therefore makes a great difference to the Eternal. Or, in concrete terms, "it is not incidental to God's eternity that Christ lived and suffered and triumphed in the process of time." If that had not happened, "it would prove His eternal being to be other than Christianity believes."[7]

The point of what might seem a somewhat abstract excursus is that while Apollos in Hebrews invokes against Judaism the Platonic doctrine of ideas, he is ultimately guided by Christianity, the child of Judaism, in meeting ultimate reality in time and process and positing its eternal significance.

What of the significance of Hebrews in relation to the special problem of our investigation, namely, Gnosticism and its desire to jettison the Old Testament and Hebraic influence?

First of all, Hebrews is very Jewish even in opposing Judaism. This opposition, like St. Paul's, was not absolute. But because of the latter's polemic respecting the law and circumcision, he could be construed as anti-Jewish. This would be impossible in the case of Hebrews.

Apollos' essential argument is that in his life, death, and priesthood Jesus is the fulfillment of the

Old Covenant and the Jewish sacrificial system. He brought in a new and enlarged Covenant, lifting the way to God to a higher level. The temporal is fulfilled in the Eternal but is not repudiated. The Old Testament in all that it directed and provisionally established remains a perpetual witness to the new and lasting Covenant *sealed in the blood of Christ.*

Hebrews is both a powerful affirmation of what is and a forceful, repetitious exhortation to live up to reality. In both streams of tendency the material utilized is very Hebraic and scriptural; there is comparatively more citation of Old Testament writings than in any other New Testament book. One gets an insight in reading this book into the enormous emphasis in Alexandrian and other Christian circles on the Septuagint Old Testament, and the part ''prophecy'' and example played in the life and thought of the early Church.

There are numerous indications throughout the New Testament of the worship life of the Church. It would, however, be hard to assemble from the various hints and apparent ritual implications available any clear picture of Christian worship. In 1 Corinthians 11:17-32 (cf. 10:16-19) we find a picture of the eucharistic supper of the Lord at a very early period, including important sociological information. But except for the breaking of bread and sharing the cup as part of a common meal of the church fellowship, we are told little of the ritual patterns of church worship.

There is, for example, nothing in the New Testament comparable to the description around A.D. 150 of characteristic church worship that we have in Justin Martyr's First Apology (LXVII):

> And on the day called Sunday, all who live in cities or in the country gather together to one place, and the memoirs of the apostles or the writings of the prophets are read, as long as time permits; then, when the reader had ceased, the president verbally instructs, and exhorts to the imitation of these good things. Then we all rise together and pray, and, as we before said, when our prayer is ended, bread and wine and water are brought, and the president in like manner offers prayers and thanksgivings, according to his ability, and the people assent, saying Amen; and there is a distribution to each, and a participation of that over which thanks have been given, and to those who are absent a portion is sent by the deacons.

Hebrews does not exactly fill in this picture for the apostolic or sub-apostolic church. But it does present a vivid picture of a Church that lives by worship, with some indication of the parallels seen in the worship of Israel as set forth in the Books of Moses. The Temple at Jerusalem and its worship, though grander and more elaborate, were modeled on the ancient use.

I have often said that the Church is first of all a worshiping community. This has always been true, and Hebrews indicates the influence from the earliest time of Jewish worship on Christian worship. It indicates that the primary paradigm in this respect was not the Synagogue but the sacrificial rites of the primitive Tent of Meeting as continued in the Temple in Jerusalem. It portrays with stunning vividness the centrality of Christ Jesus in the life and worship of the Church—the Christ Jesus who was crucified, who poured out his blood, who was made sin for us, who was raised from the dead, who ascended into heaven, and who, now at the right hand of the Eternal Power and Glory, is our faithful and understanding High Priest.

At some point, we know from Justin, the worship of the Synagogue was reproduced in a Christian adaptation as the preparation for the Eucharist—the Ante-Communion, so to speak. But the earliest worship was sacrificial, still in or around the Temple or as Hebrews indicates a form of words and/or acts paralleling but transforming the ancient rites through the new and eternal Covenant inaugurated by the death (body broken and blood poured out) of Christ. But the dead Messiah is also the eternal High Priest, forever personifying and recalling the one sacrifice once offered.

From the point of view of our concern with Gnosticism and Marcionism, this realistic sacrificial emphasis of Hebrews was a strong counterweight.

Its Jewishness and dependence on the Old Testament
were too marked to be ignored or allegorized away.

Another prominent feature of Hebrews follows
in the same direction. It is a book of faith, not of
knowledge. In this it continues the main thrust of the
Jewish tradition. Obedience and faithfulness are the
watchwords of exhortation in this epistle. And when
the author searches for examples with a view to
inspiring believers, Jews or others, who may be
wavering, he is led to the Old Testament.

Out of its pages he calls the roll of heroes of the
faith: Abel, Enoch, Noah, Abraham, Sarah, Isaac,
Jacob, Moses, Rahab the harlot, Gideon, Barak,
Samson, Jephthah, David, Samuel and the prophets.
It is a stirring list, to which he adds the unknown and
unremembered heroes, martyrs and others who
suffered and died for their faith. Last of all is Jesus
himself—"Jesus who, for the sake of the joy that lay
ahead of him, endured the cross, making light of its
disgrace, and has taken his seat at the right hand of
the throne of God."[8]

The concluding Benediction of this book is the
majestic blessing used in all English Prayer Books for
the Burial of the Dead. We cite it in conclusion, in
the NEB translation:

> May the God of peace, who brought up
> from the dead our Lord Jesus, the great
> Shepherd of the sheep, by the blood of the
> eternal Covenant, make you perfect in all

goodness so that you may do his will; and
may he make of us what he would have us
be through Jesus Christ, to whom be glory
for ever and ever! Amen.

1. Genesis xiv. 17-20
2. Hebrews vii. 26; viii. 2
3. viii. 5
4. ix. 11-12. cf vv. 1-10. Also x.1
5. *Nature, Man and God*, p. 478
6. *Ibid.*, p. 447
7. p. 448
8. xii. 2. NEB The roll call is in chapter xi.

Chapter Seven

John
The Incarnationist

We come now to dwell on the high point of the New Testament and of Christian literature perhaps for all time. We have had occasion several times already in this book to emphasize the transcendent importance of the Fourth Gospel and its author. Beyond any doubt it is a work of genius that carries to a climax a development of thought and experience unique in the history of religion and that constitutes a phenomenon which, if not strictly incomparable, is without parallel in its beauty and originality.

For the Christian the Gospel of John represents the apex and consummation of the self-revelation of the living God which is the inner core and continuous central thread and theme of the library of scriptures or writings that we know as the Bible. From this point of view it is richly significant that John (who, whoever he actually was, will always be for us the Fourth Evangelist) was inspired to repeat, as he began his Gospel, the very words with which the unknown priest-theologian who wrote Genesis 1 began his majestic Creation narrative.

Thus this priest-theologian wrote:

In the beginning God created the heavens
and the earth.

And John—possibly a priest of the high priestly
family, possibly a Christian prophet, and certainly
a profound theologian—wrote:

In the beginning was the Divine Reason,
the Word.
And the Word was with God,
and the Word was fully Divine.[1]

John's prologue is in its own way a succinct and
very compressed account of Creation. But this
dominating interest is not the long past but the recent present. For at long last the Logos-Light has broken in in full splendor: the living God has not only
spoken; he has appeared, acted, manifested himself
so that all might see his true glory.

Prior to this, John will say, no man has ever seen
God. He is very serious about this, though it seems
to contradict some important Old Testament Scripture which incidentally Paul had accepted, though
he, too, sees a new and marvelous glory of the Divine revealed in the face of Jesus Christ.[2]

John's interest from first to last is Christological. In a sense there is nothing new in this. The New
Testament, as we have seen, is through and through
a Christological document. Jesus the Christ, Son of
God and Lord, is at the center nearly everywhere.

Nowhere is there the human interest and curiosity that we associate with biography.

Moreover, there is going on throughout the New Testament a continuous, insistent Christological development. The symbol and at the same time the proof of the dominating faith-concern of the Church from the beginning is the priority of Paul in the chronology of Christian literature.

Other elements came into consideration, as the writing of the Gospels shows, but the balance is in no way upset or reversed. The Gospels are all theological treatises as well as in a limited manner biographical chronicles. They were written "from faith to faith," as the German Johannes Weiss said.

There is theological, or more precisely, Christological development in the Gospels and it is here that we find the key to John. His Gospel has always been seen to be different, to have something about it that is special and highly distinctive. This aroused some adverse criticism in the second century, as the controversy between the Jews en bloc and Jesus and his disciples in the Gospel in effect predicts as well as reflects.

There was in the late second century a faction of conservative and otherwise orthodox Christians who disliked the teaching of the Gospel by then coming to be associated with John the Son of Zebedee and denied that it had been written by an apostle. These people, who became known as "Alogi," opponents of the Logos doctrine, asserted that this Gospel had been written by the Gnostic, Cerinthus.[3]

Nevertheless, it had a wide circulation from an early time, as has now been proved by manuscript evidence, and in the ancient Church exerted unrivaled influence both as "the spiritual gospel" (Clement of Alexandria c.180) and in the fashioning over both the Ante-Nicene and the Conciliar periods of Christian doctrine and dogma.

In modern times, beginning around 1800, with the advent of the "Higher," or literary and historical, criticism of the Bible, controversy swirled with particular breadth and intensity around the Fourth Gospel. It is easy to see why this should be so. The Gospels are portraits of Christ Jesus, and the fourth and last of them is so different and unique in distinctiveness, and at the same time compellingly powerful, that it was bound to raise many questions.

There has been no letup in this scholarly ferment, and today there is actually more complexity and contradiction of ideas in the Johannine criticism than perhaps in any previous generation. It would be possible at this point to get into this morass and to go on and on for many pages, reviewing theories, hypotheses, speculations, bold and clever guesses, and endless, repetitive arguments about the Fourth Gospel—its genesis, antecedents, formation, redactions, and authorship.

There is here a great, still unplumbed mystery. And the world loves a mystery. Look at the fantasia of writing books and developing theories about the plays of Shakespeare. As a Harvard M.A. in English literature, with clear ideas about all this settled long ago, I discovered to my amazement in 1956 that one of the most prominent Harvard professors in the department of political science was dogmatically sure that Shakespeare never wrote any of the plays attributed to him. I also learned that he was not simply an oddity in this matter, but that there was considerable ferment in at least some Harvard circles respecting this strange and stubborn obsession.

Or, one might consider the assassination of President John F. Kennedy. Books about this, involving high intelligence, diligent research, and the imaginative elaboration of complicated theories, continue to pour off the press. It appears that neither the pundits nor the public will ever allow this traumatic national tragedy to be put to rest.

It is probably that the mystery of John's Gospel will never be conclusively settled and that scholars and others will never cease to probe and speculate both on what is known and what is not known. There are fashions in scholarship, and they come and go. In this case the facts are severely limited; so there is room for almost indefinite guessing and putting forth of more or less plausible hypotheses. The rearrangement of prejudices is a deep bent of man, and in few areas is it more manifest than in biblical scholarship.

I propose to eschew here any involved critical introduction and, instead, to get at once to the main aim of this chapter which is the presentation of John as a theologian. In the course of this and in the necessary analysis of his Gospel, I shall have occasion to give my position on fundamental critical isues and positions. But I hope to keep first things first.

John's Gospel is best understood as essentially a theological composition, transposed into the forms and terms of a unique literary genre, the Gospel. St. Mark apparently initiated this literary-theological or literary-Christological form; and he speedily found successors. There were, of course, a great many more of these, and of gospels produced by them, than have come down to us. Today, thanks to the Nag Hammadi find, we know more of these and more about the total phenomenon that resulted in a voluminous literature which included gospels, than was previously possible.

The New Testament, as we have seen, is theological through and through, but in the total canonical writing gathered together in this work, we find three principal theologians. They are Paul, Apollos (taken in this book as the author of Hebrews), and John, the author or final redactor of the gospel bearing his name. He very probably wrote at a later date the First Epistle of John, but even if he did not, the influence of the Gospel on the Epistle is so great that for practical purposes the two can be grouped together.

In the past the tendency was strong to see a very close relation among these three Christian thinkers.

Clement of Alexandria began this with the first two, supposing that Paul had written Hebrews originally in Hebrew and that Luke had translated it into Greek. Origen queried this, but eventually thought that a disciple of Paul might have written it. In any case, the ascription of Hebrews to Paul won the day, and this highly original and distinctively unPauline treatise was placed by the Scripture canonists among his letters.

No similar problem arose in antiquity as between Paul and John, except that the Gnostics who tried to appropriate both must have felt there were similarities. Marcion, on the other hand, found Luke as his man and as *sympatico* with the thinker he imagined Paul to be. John he repudiated despite his gospel of love.

In modern scholarship it is a different story. Historians like Harnack and his disciple McGiffert found a close affinity betwen Paul and John, a view spiked by the eschatology-centered Albert Schweitzer. The latter saw Paul as still within the Jewish mental orbit, whereas the key to John was, in his view, acceptance of Hellenistic ideology and purposive outreach to Hellenists.

I see broad parallels, of course, and analogies here and there in the first three Christian theologians, but the individual differences are more striking than the similarities. We have seen this clearly in the case of Paul and Apollos. With each thinker concerned with the relation of the Gospel of Christ to Judaism, it is remarkable how they diverge in the paths they travel and the ultimate concepts they reach. It is not that they reach contradictory positions—indeed, they complement one another handily enough—but their basic orientations are diverse and almost nonintersecting.

There is development, too, in the complete distancing by Apollos of the new Christian Covenant from the old and inadequate system of sacrifices. He uses Platonism to enhance the inadequacies and transiency of Judaism and to exemplify the eternal perfection of the victorious and risen Christ as High Priest at the Father's side.

With John we come to a resolute and far-seeing theologian and Christologist. What he does in a nutshell is to hold up the Christ of the Church's faith and worship in A.D. 90 or 95 as identical with the Christ who came into the world as a flesh-and-blood human being, walked and talked among men, laid down universal truths about God and man and eternal life and judgment, endorsed the basic institutions of Baptism and the Holy Eucharist, called and indoctrinated and commissioned disciples, and accepted as the way of true glory the sacrifice of suffering and death, this being attested to by his rising from the dead, leaving the tomb empty, and appearing to Mary Magdalene and on several occasions to his disciples.

According to the Synoptic Gospels—all three of them—at a critical point in his ministry, Jesus asked his disciples who they thought he was. The answer was the Messiah or Christ, with some elaboration in Matthew's version.

In the Gospel of John the approach is wholly different. The reader is told from the start who the man Christ Jesus is and why he has come. There is no development in the Johannine portrait. Different titles and terms are used and expanded. But the Gospel begins with a mighty affirmation, that the Logos—the Divine Reason who is the Word—has come personally into the world that he has created. He has done this, not spectrally or as an evanescent apparition, not as a Homeric god or a Hindu avatar, but with absolute realism. He has become flesh and has dwelt among men as a man. And at the other end of the story, Thomas the Doubter falls on his knees and exclaims, "My Lord and my God!"

The purpose of Christ's coming is revelation and salvation, both terms being interpreted in the broadest and most sweeping way. There is nothing narrow or merely conventional or negative in what he opens up for men and women to view. It is as if with his gracious words he asks us to look down far vistas, breathtaking in their sweep and beauty as they reach beyond the farthest horizons out into the Infinite and the Eternal.

The reader of John's Gospel is told right off that as many as accept the Logos-Light which has broken in full brilliance into a darkened world, will receive divine authority to become children of God, born not only of blood or of the will of the flesh or of the will of a man, but born anew, from above, of God himself. Then, after the stupendous fact of the Incarnation has been announced, we are told that man beheld a divine glory, the very fulness of Grace and Truth. And finally, reminding us that no one has ever seen God, John says: "But God's only son, he who is nearest the Father's heart, he has made him known."

So far, the Prologue—John's inspired, uncannily compressed, verbally simple, philisophically unlimited introduction to a Gospel. There is no production in the world remotely comparable to it.

Now he plunges into the narrative, which it is the business of a gospel to carry. Like Mark, he begins with John the Baptizer, only dealing more elaborately with John's deprecatory words about himself and turning the encounter of Jesus and the Baptist into a three-day drama. The second day, when he sees Jesus coming toward him, he utters a remark that annihilates any element of progressive development or human tentativeness on his part. He says, "Behold, the Lamb of God, who takes away the sin of the world!" And in bearing witness to the descent of the Spirit on Jesus, he neglects even to mention that the Lord was baptized, and that he, John the Baptist, had performed the baptism.

The third day leads into a drama of no little excitement. The curtain rises on John standing with two of his disciples. Again beholding Jesus as he walks along, John says, "Behold, the Lamb of God!" This causes the two to follow Jesus, who first queries them a little sharply, then encourages them. "Come and see", he says, and they stayed the day with him.

One of these was Andrew, who finds his brother Simon and says to him: "We have found the Messiah" (which means "Christ"). On the spot Jesus tells him he "shall be called Cephas" (which means "rock"). These parentheses are put in for the benefit of the Greek reader who may not understand the Aramaic words "Rabbi," or "Messiah," or "Cephas." (The Greek translation of Cephas is, of course, "Petros").

An intriguing aspect of this drama is that nothing more is said about the second disciple of the Baptist. It has been speculated that he might have been "the beloved disciple," a Jerusalemite and a member of the high priestly family, who had become a disciple of John. These encounters had been near Jerusalem.

The first chapter of the Gospel concludes with Jesus deciding to go up to Galilee. Here he finds Philip and calls him to discipleship. Philip then finds Nathaniel of Bethsaida, and the dramatic encounter ensues in which Jesus praises him as an Israelite in whom is no guile and tells him that he had seen him under the fig tree before Philip had called him. Nathaniel amazed, exclaims, "Rabbi, you are the Son of God! You are the King of Israel!" Then Jesus answers him—there is a crescendo in this extremely dramatic scene—"Because I said to you, I saw you

under the fig tree, do you believe? You shall see
greater things than these." Then Jesus adds, concluding the scene and the chapter, "Truly, truly, I
say to you, you will see the heaven opened, the angels of God ascending and descending upon the Son
of man."

There are some intriguing and arresting omissions also in this narrative. This is all we are given
about the calling of the Twelve. Nor are James and
John, the sons of Zebedee, so much as mentioned.
Only in the appended chapter 21, where seven disciples are accounted for, do the sons of Zebedee come
in for specific mention.

Chapter 2 begins with the first of the Seven
Signs, the spectacular but symbolic miracle of the
turning of water into wine at Cana of Galilee. From
then on through chapter 11, we have a narrative al-
ternating between miraculous signs and striking,
sometimes startling discourses.

The motif of rising and increasingly bitter controversy with "the Jews" is woven into this alternat-
ing pattern. This is the Evangelist's way of bringing
out the all-important background of his pronouncements respecting Christ and who he is and what he
means. The Synagogue and the Church have reached
"A Parting of the Ways," and the major reason is
the Church's faith in Christ as divine and worhsip
of him as one with the Father, his only-begotten
Word and Son.

Perhaps the sharpest and most sensational example of this comes in the latter part of chapter 8. This chapter begins with a characteristic saying of Jesus:

> Again Jesus spoke to them, saying, "I am the light of the world; he who follows me will not walk in darkness, but will have the light of life."

This leads into controversy with the Pharisees over his bearing witness to himself. Then it moves into the sin of unbelief and dying in one's sins, and now is with "the Jews;" and a spreading argument ensues that centers around Abraham and the children of Abraham. Soon it reached heights or depths of great bitterness. Jesus suggests that they who would murder the Messiah are children not of Abraham, but of the Devil, a liar and a murderer from the beginning. The Jews call him a Samaritan, and say he is deranged, he has a demon.

It is not one of the lovelier portions of "the spiritual Gospel," but the upshot of the argument is immensely vital from the standpoint of the overwhelmingly divisive issue. Jesus says, "Your father Abraham rejoiced that he was to see my day…The Jews then said to him, You are not yet fifty years old,[4] and have you seen Abraham? Jesus said to them, Truly, truly, I say to you, before Abraham was, I am. So they took up stones to throw at him; but Jesus hid himself, and went out of the temple."[5] What John is saying is that the Christ partakes of the timelessness of God and in his eternal being is on a level with Yahweh.[6]

Thus we see clearly that the Prologue is not, as some have claimed, an afterthought or an attention-getting preface not really integrated with the great body of the Gospel. Christology in John has reached its zenith: Christ is God made man; he faces men and women from the Godward, not the manward side. He is sent by the Father and speaks the very words of the Father. This is the central conviction of this evangelist who very probably was a Christian proph-et, with an ontological psychology continuous with that held by the prophets of Israel over the centuries and accepted by all Jews as well as Christians.

I first heard this view of John expounded by Canon B.H. Streeter, author of *The Four Gospels* and, in my day, provost of Queen's College, Oxford. If John thought of himself as a prophet, the writing of a gospel in which he set out to correct mere history in the blazing light of the divine Son whom the Church knows and worships along with the Eternal Father and the Spirit of Truth proceeding from him would not raise any special problem. He would have felt himself speaking or writing the word of God under the inspiration of the divine Spirit—the Spirit of prophets.

In addition, we need to understand the differ-ence between our modern ''scientific'' view of his-tory and the basic outlook of ancient writers. For us literal truth is what truth means; our search is for facts on as extensive a scale as possible, taking great pains to insure their accuracy and non-contradiction either by other facts or prejudicial and one-sided interpretations. We do recognize that in the writing of biography or history, selection, shades of emphasis, and subjectively influenced interpretation are unavoidable.

Even in our scientific day, history cannot be totally scientific. It remains to a degree an art, and a very fine art at that. The history of history demonstrates this, and I believe that contemporary historians are more and more realizing and accepting this reality.

Anyway, in ancient times historical truth was viewed less rigorously than with us. It was closer to poetry or embroidered chronicles and there was manifestly less concern about contradiction and inconsistency. A case in point, massive in scale, is Old Testament history. We have to say that in the main the first great division of the Bible is a history book. But it is a very curious history book. It was against the Hebrew instinct to revise by excision or the elimination of either repetitions or contradictions.

A fascinating example is the two Creation accounts of Genesis. They are very different. The dovetailing and/or juxtaposition of the basic histories J, E, D, and P illustrate the same point. Then there are the overlapping and often dissonant histories of Kings and Chronicles. It is surely one of the supreme oddities of human nature and human history that generation upon generation of human beings, just as smart as we are, could have accepted and implicitly believed in the plenary verbal inspiration and the infallibility of Holy Scripture.

When we come to the New Testament, the situation is little changed in comparison with the Old. Sixty years ago, I used in a freshman Bible class at Washington and Lee University a Harmony of the Four Gospels, and at that time they were still in wide use in theological seminaries. This is no longer the case, as far as I know. But the trend in Johannine studies, as well as in other aspects of Gospel criticism has been one of rapid motion, with a vast diversity of results, but on the whole a strengthening of the older view of the superior historicity of John in a number of points and a breaking down of the departture it represents from the Synoptic tradition.

I must confess, I find in much of what I read a fatal violation of the elementary law of contradiction, laid down so long ago by Aristotle. The force with which the great Roman Catholic lay theologian F. von Hügel applied this in his monumental essay on the Gospel of John for the 11th edition of the Encyclopaedia Britannica has long filled me with admiration. There are important points at which I believe the Baron's stringent pronouncements can be moderated; and I am certainly not immune to considering and learning whatever continuing research and responsible, prudent scholarhsip can teach. At the same time, I believe that von Hügel was right in his conviction that, from the point of view of relative historicity in career and in teaching, one must make a choice between the Synoptists and John.

This is no way forecloses the judgment that John may be nearer the absolute truth and meaning of Jesus than any other Gospel or writing or body of writings in the New Testament. For it remains true that if the Bible has any meaning beyond presenting a varied and fascinating assortment of Hebrew literature, it is a book in which the one, living and true God is the chief actor and is working out his purpose for mankind. This action comes to a climax in the annex of scripture known as the New Testament. All parts of this annex are inspired and contribute to the most amazing story in the history of religion.

This is the story, first, of a deeper involvement of the Lord God in his world. He decided to enter into history in person. The account of this is the Christology of the New Testament accompanied by an unprecedented outpouring of the Spirit of the Lord.

But there is a second stage and aspect of the Divine program. The one, living and true God had it in his purpose to go worldwide. Not that anywhere he had ever left himself without witness in some measure. But he determined now to make his tri-personal move and revelation universal. The knowledge of it was to go out to all races and nations. The name given to this unheard of, though not entirely un-prophesied enterprise was the Evangelium or Good

News—in English based on Old English, the Gospel.

Paul's Letters are to various churches and to us are memoirs in which he expresses his affection, expounds the Gospel, and applies it both to church life and to individual conduct. The other large feature of the New Testament or Covenant is a quadrilateral of accounts of the career of Jesus Christ, the son of God, Lord of the Church and Saviour of mankind. They are called collectively The Gospel according to Matthew, Mark, Luke, and John.[7]

The subject of each Gospel is the Lord of the Church, Christ Jesus. We are told in each case how he came, what he did and said, what he decided God called him especially to do, and the tragedy of a judicial execution (by crucifixion since he was not a Roman citizen) followed by two mighty deeds of God—the resurrection of Jesus from the dead, and the resurrection in vibrancy and sustained power of the action of the Spirit of God—the same Spirit that had spoken of old through the prophets.

John wrote at a time of radical transition and decision. A moment of mighty destiny had come. The Church could no longer look with high expectation either upon the old Israel as a whole or upon the generality of individual Jews. In a sense, the fundamental decision was that of God's ancient people, to whom the Jesus of history had felt primarily sent. Paul in Romans, as early as A.D. 57, had seen the hardening of the hearts of his people as far as Jesus Messiah was concerned. What amounted to at least a halfway house in the relations of Jews and Christians had been reached in less than a generation after the Crucifixion and Resurrection.

It was the destiny of a Christian mystic and prophet at Ephesus, the most profound thinker of the first age of Christianity, to grasp the meaning and the opportunity of "the religious situation" in the decade of the 90s—the seventh since the Crucifixion. We are bound to call him John and that may well have been his actual name. According to an interesting bishop of Hierapolis in Phyrgia named Papias, there were two Johns at Ephesus as the century approached its close.

Somewhere around A.D. 130, Papias published a very unusual treatise in five books entitled *Expositions of Oracles of the Lord.* Unfortunately it has not come down to us save in several intriguing excerpts preserved by Eusebius in his *Ecclesiastical History.* Apparently, the object of the older churchman was to gather what information he could on the gospel history from oral traditions he had collected from persons who had been members of the apostolic circle.

The two statements of Papias most often cited are those concerning the Gospel of Mark in relation to Peter at Rome and the oracles (*logia*) which are said to have been composed by Matthew in Hebrew (meaning possibly Aramaic). Many scholars have posited an identification of the second document with the hypothetical collection of Jesus' sayings called Q.

A third statement of tremendous import, quoted

from Papias by Eusebius, is this.

> And if ever any one came who had been
> a follower of the elders, I would inquire as
> to the discourses of the elders, what was
> said by Andrew, or what by Peter, or what
> by Philip, or what by Thomas or James,
> or what by John or Matthew or any other
> disciples of the Lord; and the things which
> Aristion and the elder John, the disciples
> of the Lord, say. For I did not think that
> I could get so much profit from the con-
> tents of these books as from the utterances
> of a living and abiding voice.[8]

Eusebius clearly states that these two Johns
mentioned were different persons, though this has
been disputed. It should be noted that the tense in
the second part of the statement is the present tense;
and Eusebius takes this to mean that Papias was himself a hearer of Aristion and the presbyter, or elder
John. Eusebius also mentions the "two tombs in
Ephesus, each of which, even to the present day, is
called John's." Finally, Papias, according to Eusebius, used testimonies from the First Epistle of John
and from First Peter likewise.

Scholars are generally agreed that John the
Evangelist was a Jew who, if he was not directly influenced by Philo Judaeus of Alexandria, had experienced the same Hellenizing current and ferment
that had affected Philo so deeply and such apocry-

phal writers as the author of the Wisdom of Solomon
and Jesus ben Sirach, who wrote Ecclesiasticus. Ecclesiastes, attributed to King Solomon and for that
reason admitted to the Jewish canon, shows Greek
influence, but of a more worldly and even cynical
strain.

John is more Jewish than Greek, but he is above
all a Christian who exalts the Son of God and sees
the need for a gospel that would interpret for Graeco-
Gentiles everywhere the Saviour who was sent from
God and who was God in the person of the Philonic
Logos. As an example of the impulsion to universality, which is so powerful as a motive in the theology
and Christology of John, consider the episode written up in chapter 4 in dramatic detail of Jesus' encounter with the woman of Samaria at Jacob's well,
near Sychar in that country.

This episode with the doctrine embedded in it
is, I suggest, one of the most far-reaching and revolutionary declarations, not only in St. John or in the
whole New Testament, but in all Holy Scripture. It
is a manifesto of freedom, spirituality, and universality in worship. The Jews held that Jerusalem alone
was the place of true and proper worship. The
Samaritans, a mixed race despised by the Jews, considered that Mount Gerizim, hard by the one-time
dwelling of Jacob, was the abode of Yahweh and the
only seat of authentic worhsip.

Jesus unhesitatingly and with sovereign authority dismisses both the Jewish and the Samaritan

claims and with this dismissal rejects all localism in worship—spatial, racial, or particularistic in any measure. He speaks at this point very much in a prophetic vein but with words that are apodictic in conviction of certitude.

> Woman, believe me, the hour is coming when neither in this mountain nor in Jerusalem will you worship the Father. You worship you know not what; we worship what we know, for salvation is from the Jews. But the hour is coming, and now is, when the true worshipers will worship the Father in spirit and in truth, for such the Father seeks to worship him. God is Spirit, and those who worship him must worship him in spirit and in truth.[9]

It should be noted that in this declaration of universal worship, a theological pronouncement of the utmost moment is included. God, Jesus declares, is in substance or being spirit. All materiality, all physicality, is ruled out. This has wide implications. The Jews were not a philosophic race; their theology tended to be anthropomorphic. The presumption is that they thought of God, as they certainly thought of angels, in terms of visual and material and probably human images. On the Greek side, the Stoics were ultimate materialists. Fire they considered the absolute stuff of being, and God in their thinking was in substantial nature material not spiritual.

So it could be said that in the passage where John shows his Jewishness and pays this people the high compliment of saying that their knowledge in worship is of the true God and that "salvation is from the Jews," he awards the palm to the Platonists in distinguishing spirit from matter and identifying the divine with spiritual substance or form of being. Unquestionably, we have here one of the most influential as well as most fundamental pronouncements in the history of theology.

It happened many, many months ago that I was leading a Bible study group on John, and we reached the fourth chapter and the encounter with the woman of Samaria. I was so carried away with the originality, profundity, and sheer brilliance of this episode that I sat down afterward to develop a check list of its outstanding features. Here is the gist of what I came up with:

> 1. Outreach to a race related to the Jews, ethnically and religiously, but despised by them.
>
> 2. Outreach by Jesus to women in the person of a woman of spirit and sensitivity, despite her record of sexual looseness. (John employs a technique similar to that used in Jesus' encounter with Nathaniel, the Israelite without guile. The woman who is unnamed is surprised to find that this forceful Jewish stranger, who pays no

attention to ordinary tabus respecting the
other sex, knows that she has had five hus-
bands and is presently living with a man
not her husband).

3. Jesus' humanity is shown by his weari-
ness that causes him to rest by the well of
Jacob and ask the woman for a drink when
she comes to draw water. This leads to a
discussion of the living water which, Jesus
says, wells up into eternal life. This is the
gift that he has to offer, and the desire for
such water along with his supernatural
knowledge of her character leads to the
woman's conversion.

4. Through the woman many Samaritans
believed in Jesus and asked him to visit in
their city, which he and his disciples did,
with very fruitful results. Thus Jesus' appeal as ''prophet,'' Messiah, and Saviour
of the world and the universal power of the
Evangel are driven home.

5. The success with the Samaritans follows
a short homily to his disciples on food and
fields white unto the harvest, treated as a
parable of fruit unto eternal life in which
sower and reaper rejoice together. A strong
emphasis on evangelism!

6. John uses this attractive, good-humored,
warmly human dramatic medium as a
springboard for the universalism of Chris-

tianity and a statement on both the being
of God and the nature of worship that are
final for all time.

7. The episode follows the nocturnal visit
to Nicodemus, a ruler of the Jews, and the
theological dialogue on spiritual rebirth
including a firm reference to the sacrament
of baptism. The dialogue leads into a discourse on why Jesus the Son came into the
world and the salvation he brings—all because of God's love for the world.

8. Jesus, as the one who comes from
heaven and utters the words of God,
receives added emphasis by the introduction for the sixth time of John the Baptizer,
who hails Christ as the Bridegroom and the
Son whom the Father loves and into whose
hand he has given all things.

9. All this as immediate backgorund for the
bid to non-Jews through the Samaritan
woman and her compatriots and the issu-
ance of the Great Charter of Spiritual
Worhsip, cannot be accidental.

Such reflections as these drove home to me the
combination of artistry and audacity that the Gospel of John reflects from start to finish. There is no
book in the New Testament or probably in the entire Bible that displays in structure and execution a
keener finesse or surer workmanship. The author

knew exactly what he was doing and carried through his bold design with fantastic verve, economy, and brilliance. John's Gospel is a consummate work of art as well as a theological masterpiece.

I do not mean to imply that this Gospel, which affirms history and values grounded in temporal reality, yet betrays a sovereign freedom, whether calculated or spontaneous in the manner of the prophet, in the treatment of received facts, is no more than a sublime fictional creation. This is to misunderstand and to ignore the peculiar relation between history and faith that characterizes all biblical scripture.

John knew not only the Old Testament through and through, as did all learned Christians through his generation, but also the central cumulative tradition of the Gospel already crystallized in a plurality of written works. Ephesus was a cosmopolitan city, the meeting place of ideas, cultures, and religions; and it was a premier publishing center. There has been much discussion as to whether the Fourth Evangelist knew and had before him the other Gospels. Most scholars have felt he knew Mark and probably Luke, though since the advance of form-criticism a school has arisen that denies contact with any other Gospel. Few students have detected the influence of Matthew. Some knowledge of the Christology of Paul seems to have been assumed by historians of doctrine and dogma, as for example Harnack and McGiffert. Von Hügel implies the same as when he writes: ''The Fourth Gospel, inexplicable without St. Paul and the fall of Jerusalem, is fully understandable with them...In character it is profoundly 'pneumatic', Paul's super-earthly Spirit-Christ here breathes and speaks, and invites a corresponding spiritual comprehension.''[11]

These words recall and quite possibly were influenced by an unforgettable passage in Harnack following his characterization of the Johannine writings as the most marvelous enigma that early Christian history presents:

> Here we have portrayed a Christ who clothes the indescribable with words, and proclaims as his own self-testimony what his disciples have experienced in him, a speaking, acting Pauline Christ, walking on the earth, far more human than the Christ of Paul and yet far more Divine, and abundance of allusions to the historical Jesus, and at the same time the most sovereign treatment of history.[12]

Water has flowed under the bridge since these great men, one a Roman Catholic layman, the other the classic Liberal Protestant, wrote, and there are strong reasons to posit more connection with the facts of Jesus' ministry through a distinct eyewitness tradition than they could conceive. I am, for example, convinced that the Beloved Disciple was an historical figure, not a creation existing only in the imagination of John the Evangelist. But I have never believed that this disciple could have been John the son of Zebedee.

I find Father Raymond E. Brown convincing in his assessment of the evidence here, along with professor Oscar Cullman.[13] The possibility that the unnamed disciple of John 1:35-40, the companion of Andrew and co-disciple of the Baptist up to that point, was the disciple who was to become the one whom Jesus loved, is intriguing and attractive. No better instructed guess has been found. The important and, I believe, decisive issue is the Jerusalemite background and connection with the family of the high priest which some disciple possessed if there is an authentic tradition uniquely preserved in John's Gospel. I do not see how the Galilean fisherman, John, can be fitted in here.

The Beloved Disciple is very important in the story laid out by John the Evangelist and is probably idealized. Again, Brown is convincing in much that he says in this connection. But I do not think we are allowed by the evidence available to us in its full totality to minimize the powerful Christological drive of John and the impetus it gave to the logic and organization of material in his Gospel. He is a theologian and stands at a certain point in the development of faith and doctrine in the Church. The overshadowing reality that he is proclaiming under the form of a narrative gospel is the Divine Christ, the eternal Word in human form, the Saviour of the world, the true Messiah and King of the Jews, and the only Son, whose words are the Father's words and whose life and death are the perfect mirror in which we behold the Father himself.

> Philip saith unto him, Lord, show us the Father, and it sufficeth us. Jesus saith unto him, Have I been so long time with you, and dost thou not know me, Philip? He that hath seen me hath seen the Father.[14]

We have here indisputably a pillar declaration, a foundation assertion, on a par with the Incarnation passage of 1:14-18. In such affirmations and confessions of faith we reach the heart of the Evangelist's mind and his intentionality in writing. Clearly he is more interested in this than in preserving or following any given tradition, whether it be in the Gospel of Mark or Luke or some other tradition, even one associated with the Beloved Disciple. This is not incompatible with his use of material gathered from one or all of the traditions available. But in using them he would not have hesitated to mould them to his design and overmastering purpose.

If this general view is correct, we have a key to a number of things, though we shall not always be able to determine what is in his special tradition and what represents an alteration relative to his primary purpose. Several examples will clarify this point.

It is generally or at least widely held that John's chronology of a three-year ministry is to be preferred to the Synoptic scheme. I believe this to be a correct judgment.

A second issue concerns the date of the Last Supper and therefore of the Crucifixion. It has been generally held that John's correction of the Synoptists at this point is reliable and that Jesus' final meal with his disciples was not to keep the Passover sacrifice but a solemn fellowship meal of some sort that took place on the previous evening.

The late Frank Gavin (professor at the General Theological Seminary, New York) believed that the Last Supper was what he called a Kiddush. At least I heard him argue that late one evening in 1931 at the home of Professor Levy, professor of Oriental Studies at Cambridge University. (My wife and I had met the Levys, a charming, friendly couple, on the Geneva-Paris train in the early autumn of 1930 and they had invited us to spend a weekend at Cambridge.)

The eminent liturgiologist, Dom Gregory Dix, is sure (a) that St. John was right in saying that the Last Supper was an evening meal 24 hours before the actual Passover, and (b) that this farewell meal was the formal supper of a *chaburah* (a group of friends: from *chaber,* a friend).

Of late, German scholarship has been swinging back to the Synoptic view, that, as the first three Gospels unanimously say, the Last Supper was a Passover meal. This has influenced current English thinking. Professor E.J. Tinsley in his Cambridge Bible Commentary on Luke writes:

Recent research seems to favour the interpretation of the last supper as a Passover
meal. In that case Mark and Matthew give
us the real time-sequence, and John has
moved things back because of his 'Lamb
of God' theme; in John Jesus is crucified
just at the time when the Passover lambs
were being killed. Compare Paul's 'our
Passover has begun; the sacrifice is
offered—Christ himself,' 1 Cor.5:7[16].

This means that John held the Crucifixion to
have occurred on Nisan 14, whereas the Synoptists
date it as Nisan 15. Both sources agree on the day
of the week, Friday. This is regulated by the fact that
the next day was the Sabbath and that the Resurrection occurred on the first day of the week, Sunday.
The difference is not too great, for in either calcula-
tion the Passover is fundamental.

It is of some interest that the original Church
celebration of Easter began on the first day of Passover, 14 Nisan. The church in Asia stuck stubbornly
to this dating of Easter and its proponents were
known as Quartodecimans (Fourteenth men). It was
not until Nicea (325) that this controversy was settled. It will never be possible to settle the issue of the
day of the month on which Christ was crucified. But
John had a motive for his emphasis. From chapter
1, when on successive days John the Baptizer witnesses to Jesus as the Lamb of God that takes away

the sin of the world, we can see how strongly he was drawn to this metaphor and foretype. In the Revelation, which came out of Asia and was probably related to the Johannine circle, the lamb is a major symbol. It is even spoken of as "slain from the foundation of the world."[17]

A more difficult problem—on any view of John—is the ommision of the institution of the Eucharist. One frequently encounters the cliche that the reason for this is the desire not to profane the Christian mystery by divulging it to non-Christians. In view of the eucharistic language of chapter 6, which in literalistic verbal realism goes beyond all the insitution accounts, of which there are four, this explanaiton lacks cogency.

It is more likely (a) that John's Gospel is written to be read at two levels, by thoughtful God-seekers as well as church members; (b) that John wishes to hold up the Divine Son made man as communicating his life while he lives and not merely after his death; and (c) that he sees the living parable of a Christ, coming from God and going to God, who washes his disciples' feet, as the most eloquent way of pointing to the glory of Love, which is sacrifice, and which is about to be expressed in the death of God for man.

Is this living parable a transcript of literal happening, or is it John's way of driving home the meaning of history? In the Gospel of Mark, Jesus says, after James and John have asked to sit on his right hand and on his left, arousing the indignation of the other ten disciples,

> You know that those who are supposed to rule over the Gentiles lord it over them, and their great men exercise authority over them. But it shall not be so among you; but whoever would be great among you must be your servant, and whoever would be first among you must be the slave of all. For the Son of Man came not to be served, but to serve, and to give his life a ransom for many.[18]

Even more striking from the viewpoint of suggestiveness is Luke's placing the dispute over which disciples should be regarded as the greatest after the institution of the Eucharist; and giving this version of Jesus' injunction to them:

> But not so with you; rather let the greatest among you become as the youngest, and the leader as one that serves. For which is the greater, one who sits at table, or one who serves. Is it not the one who sits at table? *But I am among you as one who serves.*[19]

These passages could have inspired John's drama of the foot-washing. Or it could have come down from the Beloved Disciple in a special tradition. Logic, however, indicates that an action so special would have found its way into the basic oral tradition to which conservatives on John now appeal and would have been noted by Mark or Luke. The leap from the words recorded by them to the act described by John is not a great one.

One other divergence between John and the Synoptists must be noted, namely, the time of the cleansing of the Temple. The Synoptic tradition places it on Monday of Holy Week following the Triumphal Entry on Palm Sunday. John unhesitatingly places this at the beginning of Jesus' ministry, a short time after the first great miracle at Cana in Galilee, when he changed water into wine on a large scale. The time chosen for this assertion of Messianic authority was the Passover. From Cana Jesus had gone to Capernaum with his mother, brothers, and disciples. But with the Passover at hand, he proceeds to Jerusalem and makes a clean sweep of driving out the sellers, money-changers, and all animals.

This sign of the Advent of the Messiah in John may have reflected two Old Testament prophecies concerning the Day of the Lord. The first is Malachi 3:1 ff.: "the Lord, whom ye seek shall suddenly come to his temple...but who may bide the day of his coming...and he shall purify the sons of Levi." The second is Zechariah 14:21: "And there shall no longer be a trader in the house of the Lord of hosts on that day." These prophecies were fulfilled in Jesus' sudden action and in its thoroughness. Only in John is there mention of the sheep and oxen and the whip of cords.

There is another aspect of John's handling of this event which is characteristic of the symbolism that he constantly employs. The Jews challenge his action, demanding a sign as authority for his drastic action. Jesus replies, in words drawn possibly from Mark 14:58 (the Trial of Jesus), "Destroy this temple and in three days I will raise it again." There are two prophecies implicit in this, though John of course writes with the benefit of hindsight. "Destroy" means, "Go on in the manner you are doing and you will bring destruction on the Temple at the hands of the Romans." But Jesus continues, "in three days I will raise it up again," meaning his own body, the temple or shrine of God's presence in the Incarnate One, and thinking perhaps of the extension of the body of the risen Lord in the Church, the new Israel.

This symbolism could not have been intelligible to the Jews, and they reply with a comparative, literal calculator of 46 years, the time it had taken to build the Temple. But to John's readers Jesus' words describing the sign asked for are full of meaning. The Jews' mention of 46 years may represent an historical note of importance. Herod the Great had begun rebuilding the Temple in 20-19 B.C. This would give A.D. 27 or 28 as the date of the cleansing of the Temple.

The first two chapters of this highly original and artistically chiseled Gospel are arresting. First the Prologue, then the witness of John, with which the calling of disciples is dovetailed.

Underlying the second chapter is a profound unity which a casual reader may miss. The theme is the new order that has come in with the Christ, the word and Son of God and the Saviour of the world. The old order is passing, replaced by the new. A wedding feast in which the last and best wine comes from the miraculous transformation of water is the joyful sign of the Good News, embracing a new Bridegroom and marriage, that of Christ with his Church.

> From heaven he came and sought her
> To be his holy Bride.

Then as we have seen, Jesus moves swiftly to cleanse the Temple and to predict both its destruction and his own resurrection. Again John is saying, The old system is finished; the new has come. The Temple and its sacrifices are outmoded; a new and better worship is at hand.

Thus the basis is laid for the enunciation of two foundation teachings; the new birth associated with both water baptism and the work of the Spirit, and the universality of the Gospel and of spiritual worship corresponding to the omnipresence of the God who is Spirit.

Archbishop Temple thinks that chapter 6, presenting the sign of the feeding of the multitude followed by the realistic eucharistic discourse, originally followed chapter 4 and there is a certain logic in this. On the other hand, John was well aware of the Syn-

optic tradition and of the healing side of the Lord's
ministry. It would be natural for him to think about
this and work it in without further delay. In any event
Jesus, returning to Cana, heals the son of a prominent government official who has been at the point
of death.

Then, going back to Jerusalem because of a
feast, Jesus goes to the pool of Bethesda with its five
porticoes or colonnades filled wth sick and disabled
people. Here he heals a man who has been ill for
38 years. This act, in addition to emphasizing the
work and power of Jesus as a healer, introduces the
matter of Sabbath observance, a subject also dealt
with in the Synoptic narrative. Again we get a liberating utterance: the Son is lord of the Sabbath and
in working on that day is imitating the Father. This
great statement about the Father working eve until
now in the Sabbath context would appear to call in
question not only the Sabbath laws of Moses but their
basis in God's resting on the seventh day. The work
of God's providential care is never-ending.

The closeness of the Father and the Son is emphasized in the strongest fashion and the delegation
of judgment to the latter is proclaimed. It is notable
that around the events of the narrative there is a
drumfire of controversy with the News; and it always centers on the person and authority of the Son.
This is the sticking point for them, while for John
it is the crux of his Gospel.

The setting of the great sixth chapter is simi-

lar: a great sign in the miraculous multiplication of
the loaves and fishes and moving in controversy to
the food that does not perish and Jesus' discourse
on the bread of life. This leads into a discourse on
the Eucharist, though not overtly—on the necessity
of eating his flesh and drinking his blood if one is
to attain eternal life.

From this controversial but fundamental section, the element of controversy is stepped up and
culminates in the bitter argument over Abraham,
his witness to the Christ, and the latter's self-
identification with "I AM" or Yahweh, the God of
Israel.[20]

The narrative once again swings from discourse
to action and in chapter 9 we have the deeply moving story of the man born blind. This highly dramatic episode begins with another liberating
pronouncement by Jesus, this time on the problem
of evil. "Rabbi, who sinned, this man or his parents?" asked Jesus' disciples. "Why was he born
blind?" To which the Lord replies, "Neither did this
man sin, nor his parents: but that the works of God
should be made manifest in him."

Without stopping, Jesus continues in words of
grace and power, "We must work the works of him
that sent me, while it is day: the night cometh, when
no man can work. When I am in the world, I am
the light of the world." Then he makes clay with his
spittle, anoints with it the eyes of the man born blind,
and tells him to wash in the pool of Siloam. The man

receives his sight, and there is a great to-do among his parents, neighbors, and the Jews, with the issue of the Sabbath raised and of the veracity of the parents and the man himself. He stands up for the wondrous truth stoutly and is expelled from the synagogue. Then, when Jesus finds him, he confesses his faith in his benefactor as the Son of God "And he said, Lord, I believe. And he worshipped him."[21]

The drama concludes with a specimen, rich in dramatic irony, of the special teaching of John about judgment, not as external, but as internal, imminent in the choice forever going on between light and darkness. Here as occasionally happens, Jesus speaks not of "the Jews" but of the Pharisees.

> And Jesus said, For judgement came I into the world, that they which see not may see; and they which see may become blind. Those of the Pharisees which were with him heard these things, and said unto him, Are we also blind? Jesus said unto them, If ye were blind, ye would have no sin: but now ye say, We see: your sin remaineth."[22]

If we follow Profesor A.M. Hunter's excellent outline of the content of John's Gospel,[23] the revelation to the world continues through three more chapters—11 and 12. The only parable specifically introduced by John—and it is more of an allegory than a parable, for there is no story in it—is the similitude of the Good Shepherd. Actually the Greek says literally, "I am the beautiful Shepherd," and this is useful as a tacit reminder that beauty is a fundamental aspect of reality and in the Greek tradition is thought of as ultimately one with the Good or goodness.

The place of the shepherd in Hebrew life and tradition is an important one and need not be rehearsed here. It is a natural symbol for Christological application and it would be surprising if John had not availed himself of it. The 23rd Psalm comes immediately to mind, but Ezekiel 34 is probably the primary inspiration for John. Ezekiel here draws up a powerful indictment of the shepherds or rulers of Israel. Over against their selfish infidelity and heartless neglect of the sheep, the prophet paints an ideal picture of the Shepherd which the Lord God promises through the prophet that he will be, as he comes personally to the resuce and upbuilding of the flock.

This ancient ideal is seen by John as fulfilled in Christ. In contrast to the false teachers, rulers, and messiahs or would-be saviours, who do not really care for the sheep, he calls them by name and offers them life in abundance.

The test of the Good Shepherd is the willingness to die—to lay down his life for the sheep. Only Jesus has done this. Therefore he is the good and beautiful Shepherd: and he is also the Door—the one entrance into the sheepfold, which is the new and true Israel.

But this fold, which is the remnant of Israel, does not exhaust the sheep of Christ. Other sheep he has, not of this fold; these he must bring also so that there will be one flock and one shepherd. The good Shepherd of Israel is also the Saviour of the world.

In further controversial argument, which characteristically follows this discourse, Jesus declares that he and the Father are one.[24] He also parries the charge of blasphemy brought against him by Jews who threaten to stone him. They say, "We stone you for no good work but for blasphemy; because you, being a man, make yourself God."[25]

The raising of Lazarus, which occupies chapter 11, is perhaps the climax of the revelation of Christ to the world, in the careful plan of John's gospel. This sign is the most spectacular of the seven narrated in the Gospel. In contrast to parallel miracles of the kind in the Synoptics, John deliberately contrives details to make the feat of raising Lazarus truly wonderful and overpowering. The absoluteness of the Saviour's power over death and as "the Resurrection and the life" is played up the full.

Moreover, this sign is done openly before a crowd of "the Jews," many of whom believed because of it. The decided impetus it gave to Jesus' cause and mission determined the chief priests and the Pharisees "to take counsel how to put him to death."[26]

Chapter 12 ties up the ends from the point of

view of Jesus' public ministry. The Passover is at hand. Great crowds are about. They are stirred by the report of the raising of Lazarus. Jesus' entry into Jerusalem was a truly royal procession. The Pharisees even said to one another, "You see that you can do nothing, look, the world has gone after him."[27]

This climactic sign, intensely and stirringly dramatic, has fascinated men and women over the centuries and has had a particular appeal to poets in the nineteenth and twentieth centuries. The reason for this is partly the situation of Lazarus, being brought back from the rich, clear world of the Beyond and with those memories having to re-adjust to our poor, flat, space-time existence.

Robert Browning, at the turn of the present century possibly the most popular English poet, developed the case of Lazarus with characteristic ingenuity and psychological acumen in the medium-length poem entitled "An Epistle containing the Strange Medical Experience of Karshish, the Arab Physician." Karshish in this poem is writing his master and teacher in the art of medicine, Abib, to tell him of a curious medical experience he had on a recent trip to Jericho and on to Jerusalem by way of Bethany where he spent a night.

It was of course here that he encountered Lazarus. Though incredulous, he was yet so impressed that he felt obliged to write Abib.

Karshish supposes that

'T but a case of mania—subinduced
By epilepsy, at the turning point
Of trance prolonged unduly some three
days:
When by the exhibition of some drug
Or spell, exorcization, stroke of art
Unknown to me and which 't were well
to know
The evil thing outbreaking all at once
Left the man whole and sound of body
indeed,—
But flinging (so to speak) life's gates too
wide,
Making a clear house of it too suddenly.
. . . .

The just-returned and now established soul
Hath gotten now so thoroughly by heart
That henceforth she will read or these or
none.
And first—the man's own firm conviction
rests
That he was dead (in fact they buried him)
—That he was dead and then restored to
life
By a Nazarene physician of his tribe:
—Sayeth, the same bade "Rise" and he
did rise.
"Such cases are diurnal," thou will cry.
Not so this figment!—not, that such a
fume,

Instead of giving way to time and health,
Should eat itself into the life of life,
As saffron tingeth flesh, blood, bones and
all!
For see, how he takes up the after-life.
The man—it is one Lazarus a Jew,
Sanguine, proportioned, fifty years of age,
The body's habit wholly laudable,
As much, indeed, beyond the common
health
As he were made and put aside to show.
Think, could we penetrate by any drug
And bathe the wearied soul and worried
flesh,
And bring it clear and fair, by three days'
sleep!
Whence has the man the balm that bright-
ens all?
This grown man eyes the world now like
a child.

The poet goes on to write that the elders of the
tribe led Lazarus, obedient as a sheep to hear Karshish's inquisition and that

He listened not except I spoke to him,
He folded his two hands and let them talk,
Watching the flies that buzzed: and yet no
fool.

Browning then cites as an example a beggar in

middle life who suddenly finds a treasure but finds
it hard to take in the change and adjust his straitened
habits, starved tastes, and impoverished brain to "the
undreamed-of rapture at his hand." Karshish, the
speaker throughout, then proceeds:

> So her—we call the treasure knowledge,
> say
> Increased beyond the fleshly faculty—
> Heaven opened to a soul while yet on
> earth,
> Earth forced on a soul's use while seeing
> heaven:
> The man is witless of the size, the sum,
> The value in proportion of all things,
> Or whether it be little or be much.
> Discourse to him of prodigious armaments
> Assembled to besiege his city now,
> And of the passing of a mule with gourds—
> 'Tis one!

Then, towards the end, through Karshish
Browning gets to the nub of the matter and the heart
of St. John's Evangel. He could not interview the
Nazarene who had wrought this cure, for he had
perished in a tumult years ago, accused of wizardry
and rebellion, at the very time "the earthquake fell."
Karshish is sure "our patient Lazarus is stark mad"
and hesitates even to set down his explanation of what
happened. Still—

> 'T is well to keep back nothing of a case.

This man so cured regards the curer, then,
As—God forgive me! who but God
himself,
Creator and sustainer of the world,
That came and dwelt in flesh on it awhile!
—Sayeth that such an one was born and
lived,
Taught, healed the sick, broke bread at his
own house,
Then died, with Lazarus by, for aught I
know.

It is clear, first, that in a world where virtually
all people believed in a heaven beyond earth and "the
life of the world to come," this miracle was appropriate in the truest sense. Christ, the God-man, was
the lord of life and therefore also of death. The Deists,
who promoted reason more extravangantly than even
the Greeks, were certain about God, freedom, and
immortality. Bishop Butler in his *Analogy of Religion*,
refuting these rationalists not for what they believed
positively but for their denial of revealed religion,
is equally sure of immortality and makes it the first
doctrine of which he treats.

The prevailing culture of the advanced
twentieth-century world, steeped in and dominated
by the outlook of science, and bereft of a fixed and
clear vision of a world or worlds beyond the space-
time continuum, finds the raising of Lazarus as re-
counted by John as irrelevant as it is preposterous.

But that is not the end of the problem.

Contemporary science has gone beyond the characteristic world-view of nineteenth-century scientific rationalism, which was extremely dogmatic. A La Place could write, "With my telescope I have swept the heavens, and nowhere do I find God." The Soviet cosmonauts said much the same things when they came back from outer space. A Matthew Arnold could say, at the height of the Victorian era, reflecting the dogmatism of autonomous Newtonian Science: "Miracles don't happen."

This is no longer the outlook of science. The new physics, rotating around the realization of the revolution in the concept of the atom, which is no longer merely theoretical, has dropped the iron determinism of the older science. Today it sees indeterminism, a kind of freedom, though not that of an Aristotle or of classic Christianity, installed in the very heart of physical reality. The logical positivists are careful to say that they have no evidence one way or the other respecting mysticism or religion or even alleged miracles. They may be skeptical, but evidence is another matter.

From the point of view of Christian theology this is a clear gain. The new physics provides a truly open view of the universe, making at least not incredible the confident assertion of the Christ of St. John, "In my Father's house (domain) are many mansions." Or, as I have sometimes figuratively transliterated or transposed this, at burial services or elsewhere: "In my Father's universe there are many orders of being."

If this were all there were to the matter, it might be possible to reinstate, not only miracles in general but the raising of Lazarus, John's triumphant, climactic, superdramatic, overwhelming sign of the power of God, in the exercise of which the Son and the Father are one. The difficulty is not so much philosophical or theological as evidential. And the evidence emerges from the outlook unescapably provided by the historical and literary study of the Bible itself—a kind of science though certainly not an exact one.

The difficulty with the Johannine miracle is not inherent, though there are touches in the narrative as it stands that are artful and purposive, suggesting perhaps that the author is more concerned with Christology and the meaning of history than with history itself. It must be remembered, too, that John, who puts considerable weight throughout his Gospel on the propagation of the Faith or Evangelism, presents the sign of Lazarus' resurrection as exerting a tremendous effect on the Jews and considerably increasing both the actual followers of Jesus and the enthusiastic multitude that welcomed him on Palm Sunday when symbolically—humbly yet majestically—he entered Jerusalem as the Messiah or King of the Jews.

This is not entirely inconsistent with the Synoptic tradition, for in that version of Passiontide or

Holy Week Jesus enjoyed wide and strong support—so much so that he moved freely in and out of the Temple and for three days entered into free and vigorous debate with leaders of various Jewish factions. This support dwindled and at last fell away, according to all accounts, the reason being that Jesus' concept of the Messiah was spiritual not military and represented the embodiment of a Suffering Servant, not a second and greater David. As a result, the great mass of people, volatile like all mobs, grew lukewarm and the rulers of the Jews were able to turn them into a violent and aggressive rabble, shouting for the release of the brigand, Barabbas, instead of Jesus, and intimidating even the Roman governor and the Roman sentiment of justice.

Why then could not the history of the pre-passion and the passion periods have been as John records? Without claiming certainty as to what could or could not have happened, it is difficult to believe that an event as open and spectacular as the raising of Lazarus, according to John, could have been left out of the common tradition and remained entirely unknown to the traditions and sources drawn on by the Synoptists.

John, of course, did not invent the raising of the dead by Jesus. According to Matthew 11:5 and Luke 7:22 Jesus claimed to have raised the dead and there are specific instances of this, as in Mark 5:35-43 and Luke 7:11-17. In the Lazarus story John has done what he does all through his Gospel: taking the

Synoptic tradition and freely recasting it to serve his doctrinal and evangelical purpose. The truth of history to which the raising of Lazarus bears witness is that Jesus was crucified not for what he said or claimed but for what he did—for demonstrating by his mighty works that he was the anointed one, the Messiah of God foretold by the prophets and expected by the people. In short, Jesus was put to death not as a teacher or a religious genius or even as a prophet (though some prophets had met rejection and persecution), but as the Son of God claiming the authority of God.

It is possible that John derived some of the idea of his supreme sign from the Lucan parable of Dives and Lazarus.[28] The point of this rather radical story is that even if someone (Lazarus) were to return from the dead to warn the five brothers of Dives about the place of torment, they would not believe or repent. Abraham speaks in this story and it is directed to the Jews who will not repent. John turns the saying of Abraham into a story of a Lazarus who does return, but the Jews remain unconvinced and move on to bring about his crucifixion.

Once again we see that John in his narrative hones the issue to one of Christology—who Jesus is. This is the crucial consideration, both for Christians and for Jews. And it is the key to the Crucifixion.

If chapter 11 is the account of the climactic sign and its role as the specific cause of the Crucifixion, chapter 12 is transitional. It is both postcript (to chapter 11) and prelude (to the Passion). It brings together several related events: the anointing of Jesus, anticipating his death and burial; his triumphal entry into Jerusalem; the request of the Greeks to see Jesus; the parable of the grain of wheat; John's version of the agony in Gethsemane; Jesus' withdrawal into hiding; and a reflective epilogue to the public ministry.

The anointing brings together Mark's account (14:3-9), followed by Matthew (26:6-13), and Luke's differing narrative (7:36-50). John's version has some unique features, such as the identification of the woman who performs this gracious act with Mary of Bethany and the singling out of Judas as the protester over the waste. The latter is denounced by John as a thief. Where Mark makes the anointing over Jesus' head a preparation beforehand of his body for burial, John has Mary anoint Jesus' feet and wipe them with her hair. She apparently did not use the whole pound of pure nard, and Jesus said, after Judas' intervention, "Let her alone, let her keep it for the day of my burial." But at the time of the burial, neither Mary nor any of the women are mentioned. It is the prominent Jewish rulers, Joseph and Nicodemus, who reverently discharge this task, Nicodemus having provided the fantastic quotient of a hundred pounds of myrrh mixed with aloes to be bound with the body in linen cloths.[29] Then, John says, they laid Jesus to rest in a garden, in a tomb completely new. Truly this burial by two Jewish rul-

ers was the entombment of a king—the King of the
Jews, as Pilate insisted, and the Saviour of the world.

We come now to the section of the Gospel—
chapters 13-17—which may be entitled "The Revelation to the Disciples." Just as a piece of sustained
writing, this is unique in the literature of the Bible,
of all religion, and of the world. But it is much more
than a contribution to mysticism and spirituality,
though in these respects it moves close to the high
water mark of all time.

John is a theologian, and in the special instruction and communication that Jesus now imparts to
the friends and followers he must now leave behind,
there are important ideas and, one might say, doctrines.

1. The most novel and arresting is John's doctrine of the Holy Spirit. First of all, the Spirit is on
a level with the Son and the Father. He proceeds from
the Father [30] (John means from the eternal standpoint with the implication that the Father is fount
of Godhead, just as the Son is begotten) but will be
sent by the Son on his return to heaven, after his
work is accomplished, to take his place as Advocate
or Counselor to the disciples. Also, this *Alter Ego* of
the Son is the Spirit of Truth. He will continue the
work of revelation, guiding the Church (which is
assuredly in the mind of John) into the fullness and
completeness of Truth.

The iterative and reiterative style of the Evangelist, which has a method in it without doubt, comes

out in this original and fundamental teaching. It is developed in five distinct passages, the last of which follows immediately the fourth.[31]

It is unnecessary to analyze these passages in detail. It will suffice to list summarily some of the chief assertions and implications.

The Spirit is fully divine. He proceeds from God and is God. He is sent on his special mission to the Church by the Father and the Son together, that he may complete the revelation, or more precisely the apprehension and understanding of it in the Church. It is said repeatedly that he will bring to remembrance the things that Christ has said, that he will bear witness to him and that in leading into all truth he will not speak on his own authority, but will take "what is mine and declare it to you. All that the Father has is mine; therefore he will take what is mine and declare it to you."[32] Finally, the Spirit will have as his mission convincing the world of sin, of righteousness, and of judgment. Here, too, his spiritual action will continue that of the Son in the flesh. He is the Son's other Self.

2. It is evident that John is theologically responsible not only for the ultimately dogmatic view of the Son, fought out so bitterly at Nicea and during the next fifty years, but for the viewing of the Spirit as a distinct Divine Person. He is therefore the real founder, under divine inspiration, of the doctrine of the Trinity.

Had the Greek spirit and mentality in the

Church received no check, it is possible that the
Logos would have continued to swamp the Hebraic
tradition and concept of a Spirit of God and that the
Church would have ended in a binitarian view of
God. It is striking that at the Council of Nicea in
the original Nicene Creed the best the bishops there
assembled could do was to say, in the third place,
"And we believe in the Holy Spirit."

From the point of view of the thesis and main
interest of this book, the chief check to Hellenism
had indeed come in the repulse of Gnosticism. The
issue here was the Old Testament and the Creator-
Revealer God of the Jews. After this crisis was surmounted, the Greeks, dominant in the East and influential in the West, took up the Logos-concept,
introduced by John, in dead earnest and with greater
input from philosophy than from Scripture. The
result was Arius and the Arian controversy, which
threatened, a second time, to rend the Church.

Arius failed and the Nicene-Athanasian point
of view prevailed, again in large measure because
of St. John's Gospel. Both Arius and Athanasius ran-
sacked the New Testament in support of their views.
For example, Arius was able to cite St. Paul's phrases
in Colossians 1:15: "the image of the invisible God,
the first-born of all creation." John was a harder nut
to crack, and St. Athanasius showed in his *Orations
against the Arians* that the sheet-anchor of the *homoou-
sios* (the same being or substance) was St. John.

3. The Christological thrust, which is the fun

damental motif of John is in no way diminished in
the discourses to the disciples preceding the Passion,
rather it is sustained, enlarged, and strengthened.
In chapter 14 we have the comprehensive assertion,
"I am the way, the truth, and the life." Hard on
this comes the magisterial pronouncement, "He that
hath seen me hath seen the Father."

There is firm emphasis on the Son being in the
Father, and the Father in him, and their complete
unity. Yet he does not speak on his own authority;
"but the Father who dwells in me does his works."
This leads to the announcement that the disciples
will do even greater works than these, "because I
go to the Father." Therefore, "if you ask anything
in my name, I will do it."

In this context, also, we can understand the
seemingly contradictory statement, seized on by
Arius and the Arians, that "the Father is greater than
I." Athanasius explains this by saying that the reference is to the human nature of the Incarnate Son,
but this is clearly proleptic. The dogma of the two
natures is by then in the making. While there is a
basis for it, by implication, in John's Gospel, the
Evangelist certainly did not think in such definitive
and abstracted terms. For him the Father and the
Son are in one another, and are perfectly one, but
the Father is prior and the Son's will is the perfect
reflection of the Father's, as are his words.

It is notable that here in the fourteenth chapter, as in the High Priestly Prayer of 17, the unity

and mutual indwelling of the Father and the Son is not something exclusive, but is shared by those who love Jesus and keep his Commandments.

From the christological standpoint, finally, chapter 17 has a special importance. Here the Lord Jesus makes explicit his transcendent and eternal existence and life with the Father, "before the world was." Now shortly, as he has glorified the Father by accomplishing the work given him to do, the Father will with his own self glorify him "with the glory which I had with thee before the world was."[33] There seems to be here in the prayer anticipation both of the Passion and death still ahead and of the ineffable reunion of Father and Son in heaven. For a little further on in the Prayer Jesus says, "And now I am no more in the world, but they are in the world, and I am coming to thee."[34] Finally, as toward the end the Lord prays for the unity of those who believe and love and whom the Father loves even as he loves his Son, he adds the sublime petition of desire, that they "may be with me where I am, to behold my glory which thou hast given me in Thy love for me before the foundation of the world."[35]

4. A principal theme in the revelation to the disciples, as in that to the world, is eternal life. Now it is more intimate and more definitive. This concept, which is all-pervasive in the Gospel of John and is also not a simple idea but a truth drawing into itself numerous facets of value and vision, is a signal contribution to the theology of the New Testament

and to Christian thought and experience for all time. It would be hard to exaggerate its importance or the brilliance of John's inspiration in conceiving and elaborating this seminal idea.

Eternal life as set forth in this Gospel is rooted in the Son of God and the knowledge of who he is as well as what he has done and in the perfect identification of all this, on the one hand, with the Father's will and, on the other, with the continuing mission and work of the Spirit of Truth in all who believe in and love Jesus, the risen Christ and reigning Lord. Probably John had the Church in mind, but it was of the essence of his mystical genius and calculated reticence about Christian institutions that he left the truth as it is in Jesus open to all attracted comers. It is this breadth along with the vital inherent appeal of the expansive concept of eternal life that has made John "the spiritual Gospel"[36] and the universal Gospel, with the widest outreach, probably, despite elements of narrowness in it, of any biblical book.

As is clear from all that has been said in the present work, John's Gospel is the bridge from Jewish particularism over to cosmopolitan universalism. To put the point more sharply, this Christian prophet, thinker, and mystic has moved out of Judaism, rooted in times and seasons and places, into the world of eternal truth, grace, and life. He has broken, as Paul had not been able to, out of the shell of Jewish eschatology with its literal scheme of spectacular pictured events into immediate spiritual fulfillment linked with the timeless reality of Infinite and Eternal Being.

John does not, it is true, completely burn the received eschatological bridges of the Jewish scheme. Here and there in his Gospel are patches of the older outlook of the Church. Examples that come to mind are 5:25-28, 6:39-40, and 11:23-24. But the deepest meaning of chapter 11, and indeed of all that has to do with Resurrection, is in vv. 25-26, immediately following Martha's conventional reference to "the resurrection at the last day." "Jesus said unto her, I am the resurrection, and the life: he that believeth in me, though he were dead, yet shall he live; and whosoever liveth and believeth in me shall never die."

With this one might compare such a comprehensive declaration as that of 6:47-51 in the great eucharistic discourse:

> Truly, truly I say to you, he who believes
> has eternal life. I am the bread of life. Your
> fathers ate manna in the wilderness, and
> they died. This is the bread which comes
> down from heaven, that a man may eat
> of it and not die. I am the living bread
> which came down from heaven; if any man
> eats of this bread, he will live forever; and
> the bread which I shall give for the life of
> the world is my flesh.[37]

And with this symbolic, mystical pronouncement goes the specifically eucharistic utterance, "Whoever eats my flesh and drinks my blood dwells continually in me and I dwell in him. As the living Father sent me, and I live because of the Father, so he who eats me shall live because of me. This is the bread which came down from heaven . . . whoever eats this bread shall live for ever."[38]

Two other points. One concerns the present or NOW reality of eternal life. This is both implied and expressed continuously in all John's writing—in 1 John as well as throughout the Gospel. In 17:3 we read: "And this is eternal life, that they know thee the only true God, and Jesus Christ whom thou hast sent." Beside this we may set the incomparable word of 10:10. "The thief comes only to steal, to kill, to destroy; I have come that men may have life and have it in all its fullness." (NEB)

The teaching about eternal life from this perspective is to be integrated with the unique and reiteratedly emphatic doctrine of light and darkness. This is the special Johannine view of what might be called immanental judgment. We judge ourselves and make our own eternal destiny by the choice we make between the Light, shining with such splendor in Christ, and the darkness and destruction of the way of Satan and Death. There are, of course, eschatological overtones in all this, but the decisive beginning and first fruits are in this life.

The present reality of life in its richness and fullness is underwritten and dramatically exemplified in the allegory or Johannine-type parable of the vine and the branches in chapter 15. All of this side of John fits in, as does the special teaching about the coming of the Comforter or Advocate, the Spirit of Truth, with what Professor C. H. Dodd has taught the modern Church to call and think of as "realized eschatology."

At the same time—and this is the other final point under the heading, Eternal Life—there is in this Gospel near the beginning of the Revelation to the Disciples a luminous assurance about the situation on the other side of the Veil, in the world beyond this temporal order. "In my Father's domain are many mansions" or as in the RSV: "In my Father's house are many rooms."[39] Perhaps we could say with an eye toward the new physics and its inclination to view the world as ultimately consisting of light and electricity: "In my Father's universe there are many orders of being."

This is part of Jesus' assurance to his disciples, when their hearts are troubled because he must leave them to lay down his life. In the context is a reference to Peter and his impulsive desire to follow Jesus literally at once. "Lord, why cannot I follow you now? I will lay down my life for you." Jesus in effect replies, Will you now? and says, as in the Synoptic tradition: "Truly, truly, I say to you, the cock will not crow, till you have denied me three times."[40]

Then, very quickly, Thomas is brought into the picture, and after him Philip.[41] No others, except that the Beloved Disciple, Peter, and Judas have just been mentioned.

5. Finally, there is what I regard as the supreme expression of John's inspired genius in bringing out the meaning of Christ and as the pinnacle of the revelation of the divine selfhood. I refer to the extraordinary, but incandescent, revolutionary and very thrilling doctrine of the true glory. And note that this sublime development, though it goes beyond anything the Jew could stomach any more than the Greek, is rooted linguistically and symbolically in the Old Testament vision of Yahweh. The Shekinah or glory of the Divine in the time and under the leadership of Moses was expressed in physical and localized terms, but also in the experience at and on the mountain of God, of the numinous or holy. The element of dread is strong.

> And it came to pass on the third day in the morning, that there were thunders and lightnings, and a thick cloud upon the mount, and the voice of the trumpet exceeding loud; so that all the people that was in the camp trembled.
>
> And Moses brought forth the people out of the camp to meet with God; and they stood at the nether part of the mount.
>
> And Mount Sinai was altogether on a smoke, because the Lord descended upon it in fire; and the smoke thereof ascended

as the smoke of a furnace, and the whole
mount quaked greatly.[42]

The word "glory" is one of the distinctive words
of Holy Scripture in both Covenants. It is a fluid
term, scarcely definable with any precision, but it
signifies an emanation of the divine presence symbolized by light and expressed in a sense, at once physical and mental, of the Sacred. It conveys the notion
of an Infinite Splendor. The verb "glorify" is dependent on the noun and asserts the action of creation or adding to, augmenting, the divine glory.

What does John do with this term, symbol, and
idea? He identifies it with love in characteristic action,
which is sacrifice. Love sacrificing for another is the
true glory, and this is the ultimate meaning of
Christ's Incarnation, Life and Death.

In a special way it is the reason for the Cross—
for the crucifixion of the Son and Word of God, who
is fully divine and one in being with the Father. John
really means it: he is expressing Gospel truth when
he writes, "God so loved the world that he sent his
only Son,"[43] and again, in the First Epistle, "God
is Love; and he that dwelleth in love dwelleth in God,
and God in him."[44]

With this in mind, and trying above all to pierce
the mists of distracting and benumbing familiarity
with such startling notions as glory, love, and sacrifice connected inseparably with the Divine, we are
ready to see what John sees as Jesus goes to the cross.

The key is that John sees Golgotha, the Place of the Skull, where the Son of God was executed, not as a scene of humiliation, not really as tragedy, but as the ultimate glory. Jesus goes to the cross as a king to his crowning. Far from being undone, as he is lifted up by the soldiers of Rome to a criminal's cross, it is in this way that the monarch of all ascends his throne.

The first scene in the last act but one of the extraordinary drama narrated by John is in chapter 13. It is the Last Supper, which the Evangelist turns into an enacted parable of Divine Majesty in voluntary servitude, ignoring the institution of the Eucharist. The Betrayal and the depth of Judas' depravity are highlighted, as is the special relation of the Beloved Disciple to the Lord. He lay on Jesus' breast, we are told. This expression of intimacy is clarified if we remember that in Greek and Roman times people reclined as they ate and drank at formal meals. And the custom sensibly, was of lying in twos head to head, not of a string of lone individuals with feet to head.

In the midst of the supper Jesus dips and hands a ''sop'' (a mark of special favor in the East) to Judas. Only the beloved Disciple and Peter realize the significance of this gesture. Judas receives the bread, then rises abruptly and goes out into the night. The hour of betrayal, arrest, sentencing, and death by crucifixion is at hand. The march of inexorable, linked events has begun. Looking ahead, Jesus sums up in words of light the meaning of what is to come.

There seems to be a connection between this luminous saying and Judas' departure. "When Judas had gone out," we read, "Jesus said, 'Now is the Son of man glorified, and God is glorified in him. God will also glorify him in himself; and he will glorify him now.'"[45]

It seems as if Jesus has in mind as he utters these words the mighty action that lies ahead. But, instead, a transitional sentence follows, opening up again the subject of Jesus' imminent departure from the disciples and the delivery to them of a new commandment, a law that shall be to his followers what the old Torah was to the Jews. Only this is a commandment to love one another, "as I have loved you." The Evangelist then works in Peter once more and the prediction that he will deny his Lord three times before the cock crows. Then without ceremony or introduction Jesus plunges into chapter 14 and the discourses through chapter 17 in which he develops what he has to reveal further and impress upon his disciples.

In chapter 17, as we have seen, Jesus returns to the theme and thesis of the true glory. But the text beginning "Now is the Son of man glorified" remains as an introduction to and summary of the Passion. One is tempted to view the Passion according to John as "the true glory" or "the triumph of Love" rather than "the Conflict of Light with Darkness," which is the entitlement of the Passion given both by Professor Hunter and by Archbishop William Temple in his *Readings in St. John's Gospel*.[46]

It is St. Luke who quotes Jesus as saying to the chief priests and captains of the temple and elders, "This is your hour, and the power of darkness."[47] His narrative of the Passion is the longest and the most sustained in intensity of the four accounts, though it is hardly as dramatic in climax as Matthew's Passion. I can find no reference to darkness in John's narrative or to a special conflict with Satan. No doubt both are implied, but John after rising to great dramatic heights in the dialogue of Jesus and Pilate, in which the majesty of the former is overwhelming and the drama etched with tremendous finesse, writes of the crucifixion without the crashing of cymbals. He has three sayings, as Luke does,[48] each of which is arresting and carries a symbolic as well as a literal meaning. But John is compelled by the basic framework of his thought to play down the agony and the human ordeal of the Cross.

It is the moment of the ultimate glory and the ascent to the highest throne of God. It is the victory that exalts the power of love and overcomes Satan, sin, and death, against which Christ the Lord set himself throughout his life as the Incarnate Son.

On the cross Jesus recognizes his Mother and exalts both her and the Beloved Disciple, who becomes henceforth her Son. In St. Mark the women who had accompanied Jesus from Galilee watch the crucifixion from afar; and there is no specific mention of Mary, the Lord's Mother. Alan Richardson suggests that St. John is thinking of theological significance, not of historical possiblity. He sees the Beloved Disciple as the type of the new family of God brought into existence by Christ's death. The unity of the Church, symbolized by the seamless robe, is pictured in the first word of Christ from the cross. His Mother is the second Eve, the mother of all who live in Christ. The Church is the womb of the new recreated humanity of the second Adam. "And from that hour the disciple took her to his own home:" that is, the lifting up of Christ on the cross is the hour of the Church's birth.[49]

Mark records a bystander offering Jesus a drink from a sponge full of vinegar, hoisted up to him on a reed. Luke says the soldiers did this. According to Mark (and Matthew), this happened after Jesus' despairing cry, Eloi! Eloi! (My God! My God!). It is not recorded that he took it. This reminded believers of the prophecy of Psalm 69:21: "In my thirst they gave me vinegar to drink."

John accepts this fulfillment of prophecy, but has Jesus calmly ask for the drink: "I thirst." Only instead of a long reed, the soaked sponge (with some wine) is put on hyssop, a small plant used at Passover for sprinkling over the lintels of the doors after being dipped in the blood of the Paschal lamb.[50] The symbolism becomes clear when one remembers that Christ is the door (John 10:9) and that he was crucified not on the Passover but on the Preparation.

Jesus received the wine, John says, and then said: "It is accomplished." The note is that of a triumphant cry: "He shall see the travail of his soul, and shall be satisfied."[51] He is content and happy that the ordeal is over and that he has accomplished the mission for which the Father sent him into the world.

Then Jesus bowed his head and gave up the ghost—a death almost, perhaps quite, as calm as that of Socrates when he drank the hemlock. But Jesus' stance in life and his bearing in dialogue with Pilate differentiate him decisively from the Greek sage. The passion that informed his life, career, and speech is suggested in his final word. But it is important to John that he die not like a slave or criminal writhing in agony, but majestically and in full command of himself.

When it is remembered that the Passion narrative was the earliest part of the tradition to receive in the Church a definite form and probably to be written up, a comparison of Mark, Matthew, Luke, and John is as fascinating as it is revealing. We are left, as is fitting, with a sense of unplumbed mystery. At the same time, we can see the mind and will of faith at work, moulding the portrait while maintaining the pattern of events with little change. Luke has drawn on the most sources and comes up with the most complex account. But equally with John though in a different direction, he is concerned with the portrait of the figure on the cross. The final act in John as in all the Gospels is the dawn, the rising from the tomb of the Lord Jesus and the communication to his friends and disciples of this liberating reality.

The dominating doctrine in the New Testament is the Resurrection. On this there is general agreement; about it there can be no doubt. St. Paul's assertion at the beginning of his Letter to the Romans is pivotal and seminal. In this document he goes beyond his usual writing custom and works in a short prefatory statement of the most fundamental sort prior to his customary greeting. This is the full, comprehensive statement, a summary really of early Christianity.

> From Paul, servant of Christ Jesus, apostle by a Divine calling, set apart for the Gospel of God. This Gospel God announced beforehand by the prophets in the sacred scriptures. It is about his Son, born at the human level of the seed of David, but at the spiritual level shown by the Holy Spirit to be the Son of God with power when he was raised from the dead, even Jesus Christ our Lord.[52]

Already in 1 Corinthians 15 Paul had repeated the tradition delivered to him respecting the appearance-manifestations of the risen Lord. After emphasizing that, according to the facts handed to him, Christ died for our sins, was buried, and on the third day was raised to life, the apostle goes on: "he was seen by Cephas, and thereafter by the Twelve. Then he was seen by more than five hundred brethren at once, of whom most remain to this day, but some have fallen asleep. Then he was seen of James, and thereafter by all the Apostles. Last of all, as to one untimely born, he was seen by me also."[53]

This, we must assume, was the teaching in the Jerusalem church at a very early point in time, certainly in the 30s. Paul's adding to this list Christ's appearance to him is especially noteworthy. This recital of tradition, remember, is the context of his great argument for the Resurrection, an important aspect of which is the concept of "a spiritual body," distinguished from "flesh and blood."

I mention this because for Paul the resurrection is foundational and in this he reflects the outlook of the New Testament in its entirety and of the Church ever since. But there are nuances in the traditions recorded in the New Testament, especially at the time of Dawn when the Gospels reach their climax on the further side of the Crucifixion.

Mark's account, so far as we have it, is terse and short. At the same time it affirms in an impressive manner the transforming event: "Do not be amazed; you seek Jesus of Nazareth, who was crucified. He has risen, he is not here; see the place where they laid him."[54] It is evident that John knew Mark and built on his narrative, whether using other traditional material or under prophetic inspiration with his creative theologian's purpose.

Joseph of Arimathea is solidly in place in Mark's account. He takes the body of Jesus, wraps it in a linen shroud, and places it in a tomb hewn out of rock, rolling a stone against the door of the tomb. Mary Magdalene and Mary the mother of Jesus saw where Jesus was laid, and the next morning, early, the Sabbath being past, Mary Magdalene with another Mary, the mother of James, and Salome, a third woman, came with spices to anoint the body of Jesus. It was thus that they discovered the stone rolled away, the body gone, and a young man in white sitting on the right side who addresses them.

Matthew follows Mark closely, but adds dramatic and apologetic touches, together with the appearance in Galilee to the eleven disciples, in accordance with the angel's direction to the women (given in Mark and in Matthew also). The narrative closes with the sweeping crescendo of the great commission, including the Trinitarian Baptismal Formula, and the promise to abide with his disciples to the end of the age.

It is St. Luke, the foremost historian of Christianity in the first ages but also an interpreter and therefore a theologian up to a point, who is the father of the doctrine of the Ascension as a specific, serial event. He alone gives the structure in time and delineated occurrence that was to inform the Creeds and the Christian Year.

It is clear from Paul's witness, the Gospels of
Mark and Matthew, and the Epistle to the Hebrews
that there was another and earlier tradition that made
no distinction between the Resurrection and the
Ascension. John has Jesus mention his ascension in
the account of his first appearance, which is to Mary
Magdalene in the garden. This may be an indication of the Fourth Evangelist's familiarity with Luke.
In the garden scene, however, Jesus merely tells
Mary not to cling to him, as he has not yet ascended
to the Father but to go to his brethren and tell them
that he is "now ascending to my Father and your
Father, my God and your God."[55]

That same evening Jesus appears to his disciples, shut in a closed room "for fear of the Jews,"
and after a brief commission breathes on them, thus
imparting the Holy Spirit, as he had promised, with
authority to forgive and retain sins. Since the Holy
Spirit could not be given until the Lord's return to
the Father, the Ascension has now taken place. It
is the final stage of the Son's glorificatin but is not
differentiated in any fundamental way from the
Resurrection. It is merely the final term of the Incarnate life and experience, but does not affect the
possibililty of the Resurrection-presence of Christ,
as is shown in the appearance to Thomas and the
involved narrative of chapter 21.

The point is that John has returned to the more
primitive, pre-Lucan tradition of the Resurrection
and Ascension as essentially one event in two aspects.

Also, John does not need the Resurrection as a proof of Jesus' divine sonship, in the manner of Paul in Romans. His whole Gospel is a declaration of Christ's divinity and oneness with the Father. He is glorified supremely in the sacrifice of love on the cross. As C. H. Dodd notes, "For John the crucifixion is so truly Christ's exaltation and glory that the resurrection can hardly have for him precisely the same significance it has for some other writers."[56].

Leaving aside the supplement of chapter 21, John seems to have two emphases in his treatment of the Resurrection. The first is his personalism; the second is theological, namely, imparting the Holy Spirit to the disciples, according to his reiterated promise and assurance.

The personalistic aspect of John's Resurrection narrative is notable. It involves the Beloved Disciple; Mary, a woman; and Thomas, a doubter. The main story is that of Mary and it is a gem. It exemplifies an insufficiently noted aspect of John the Evangelist: he is a gifted artist as well as a prophet and theologian.

The portrayal of Mary is delicately beautiful and the story perfect in its nuances and climax. It merits comparison as a work of art with Luke's "parable" of the Prodigal Son and account of the journey to Emmaus. The climax of the garden drama is Mary's realization that the figure she had mistaken as the gardener is really Jesus. She does not know this, even after he has asked her why she is weeping but only when he pronounces her name, "Mary"! She turns, eyes alight (we must assume) and face and whole body suffused with joy, and replies in Hebrew (really Aramaic), "Rabboni"! (Teacher).

I can never read this or think of Mary without recalling two great statues in Rock Creek Cemetery, Washington, D.C. One is very famous and constantly attracts visitors. It is the statue of a beautiful woman, a memorial to Mrs. Henry Adams, by St. Gaudens. Popularly called "Grief," it is really a marvelous portrayal of Vacancy, Nothingness, the icy imprint of Despair. It is thus a distinctively pagan memorial.

Not more than fifty yards from "Grief," concealed in the trees, is another statue commemorating another woman who lived long ago. It is by another famous sculptor, Borglum, and I think is a work of genius informed by Christian faith, hope, and love. It is a portrayal of Mary Magdalene, as she realizes that Jesus is alive and present and knows her name. With arms outstretched and eyes and face alight, she exclaims, "Rabboni"!

As a rector for ten years I buried many people in magnificent Rock Creek Cemetery, and one day after a burial I walked over to the St. Gaudens masterpiece, sat down before it and tried in meditation to decipher its meaning and message. Then rather idly I started walking away from it, still under its melancholy spell. Suddenly I came upon this erect image of a woman, every aspect and feature expressive of life, light, and joy, with the inscription "Rabboni."

It came to me with the force of a revelation: This is the difference that Christ made and makes!

So it is in John's story. In this narrative he includes the little story of the footrace between Peter and the Beloved Disciple. Mary herself had run breathlessly "to Simon Peter and the other disciple, whom Jesus loved, and said to them, 'They have taken the Lord out of the tomb, and we do not know where they have laid him!'"[57]

The two disciples—one easily imagines their concern—went off at a run, but the other disciple outran Peter and reached the tomb first. Stooping down, he looked in and saw the linen cloths lying there, but did not go in. Peter however did not hesitate. He went into the tomb, examining the cloths and the headcovering which was rolled up in a place by itself. Then the other disciple also went in, "and he saw and believed,"[58] a characteristic Johannine phrase. Mary meanwhile stood outside weeping, and this led to her encounter with the risen Lord. Her word when she went to the disciples was, "I have seen the Lord."

The account of Thomas, eight days later, is equally vivid and has had wide and continuing influence. His dubiety is overcome and he makes the ultimate confession. "My Lord and my God!" It is followed by John's characteristic note: "Have you believed because you have seen me? Blessed are those who have not seen and yet believe."[59]

It is believed that this personalism and special attention to Mary, a woman, influenced the Gnostics who were to become so prominent in the next two generations. *The Gospel of Thomas* is regarded by Professor Robert M. Grant as "perhaps the most significant document among nearly fifty books discovered about 1947 at Nag Hammadi in Egypt."[60] There is a *Gospel of Philip* and a *Gospel of Truth*, the latter possibly by Valentinus and both showing familiarity with John's Gospel. Another Gnostic work, the *Apocryphon of John*, is believed to be early second century in origin. Women appear important in Gnostic literature. Much is made of Mary Magdalene and her relation to Jesus.

C. K. Barrett has wisely observed that, although the Gnostic speculators at first seized on John's Gospel, seeing superficial contact with their own work, the main body of the Church gradually came to perceive that "his work was in fact the strongest possible reply to the Gnostic challenge; that he had beaten the Gnostics with their own weapons and vindicated the permanent validity of the primitive Gospel."[61]

There is finally chapter 21, variously referred to in Johannine literature as Appendix, Postscript, Epilogue, and Envoi or Envoy. This section seems to be in some sense an afterthought or supplement, for it follows the definite conclusion of 20: 30-31: "Now Jesus did many other signs in the presence of the disciples, which are not written in this book;

but these are written that you may believe that Jesus is the Christ, the Son of God, and that believing you may have life in his name.''

The appended or supplementary section is of evident, indispensable importance. The only question is whether it is the Evangelist's addition, much as in—John 5, the writer seems to back up a bit and start over; or whether we have to do with a new hand and a final, distinct redactor.

A. M. Hunter states succinctly the first view. ''There is no manuscript evidence'' for chapter 21 being by another hand, ''nor does a study of the style compel such a conclusion. We may therefore hold that it comes from the same hand as wrote chapters 1-20.'' He adds a suggestive and original consideration. ''A Gospel, as we know, does not end simply with an appearance, or appearances, of the risen Lord. It always includes his commissioning of his disciples for their future work. John 21 is such a commission.'' Envoy (a sending on one's way), he concludes, is a better word than appendix for this last chapter.[62]

Raymond E. Brown leans to the view that chapter 21 is redactional. While holding to the position that the rest of the Gospel is not anti-Petrine even though the Beloved Disciple had a more profound understanding of Jesus, Brown notes that the final chapter goes out of its way to underline the pastoral role of Peter and to emphasize the Johannine criterion of loving Jesus. ''Since no similar pastoral function is given to the Beloved Disciple, we may be hearing a symbolic description of the structural difference between two types of churches....In the redactional chapter 21 we may have a more moderate voice persuading the Johannine Christians that the pastoral authority practiced in the Apostolic churches and in 'the church catholic' was instituted by Jesus.''[63]

It is worth noting also that this epilogue or envoy reminds the Church and all Christians that the leading disciple who had denied his Lord three times had been forgiven, reinstated, and especially commissioned. We hardly remember this, but it is a fact that the Synoptic Gospels contain no specific record of Peter's forgiveness and reinstatement.

The scene is Galilee. May it not be that John realized after his first conclusion that he had said nothing about the risen Lord's appearance in Galilee, ignoring Mark 16:7 and possibly Matthew 28:16[ff] where incidentally we read that ''some doubted'' and are reminded of Thomas? At any rate the reader is transported to the Sea of Tiberias and seven disciples are mentioned, including for the first time the sons of Zebedee and two unnamed disciples. Then comes a subtle Johannine touch. Peter says, ''I am going fishing,'' thus launching Jesus' appearance, the big catch of fish, and the eucharistic breakfast, before the catechizing of Peter and his threefold commissioning by Jesus.

In addition, two matters involving tradition and

history are explicated. After commanding him for the third time to "feed my sheep," Jesus says to Peter, "Truly, truly, I say to you, when you were young you girded yourself and walked where you would; but when you are old, you will stretch out your hands, and another will gird you and carry you where you do not wish to go."[64] (This he said to show by what death he was to glorify God.)

As it is practically certain that Peter's death had occurred long before this work was written, we have here first-class historical evidence in support of the manner as well as the fact of his martydom.

The other matter concerns "the disciple whom Jesus loved, who had lain close to his breast at the supper." Peter turns toward him and says to Jesus, "Lord, what about this man?" (That is, what about his end?) Jesus replies, "If it is my will that he remain until I come, what is that to you? Follow me!" The Evangelist then goes on to explain that a current rumor in the Church based on this saying was that the Beloved Disciple would survive till Christ's Second Advent. As, we must assume, the Beloved Disciple, too, had died before the writing of the Gospel, verse 23 was written to remove any misunderstanding.

Involved here, also, is the reality in the Church of two eschatologies that to some extent lie side by side in the Johannine writings and represent deep tension caused by the passage of the decades without the Parousia. The conclusion of *Revelation* shows the intensity of Christian expectation in Asia and we cannot rule out some connection between the eloquent Apocalypse and the Johannine circle in Ephesus. With Revelation 22:20 and John 21:22, one may compare 1 John 2:28.

The Evangelist's explanation in 21:23 as to what Jesus did not say is directed to assuage the tension and distress occasioned by the delay in the Lord's coming. And it must not be forgotten that the thrust of John's Gospel as a whole is toward a "transmuted" or "realized" eschatology.

This is the direction alike of his doctrine of the coming of another Comforter or Advocate, the Spirit of Truth, who will guide the Church into all the Truth, and of the concept of eternal life as both present possession and future fruition in the larger life of an eternal order.

Finally we have in verse 24, a kind of certified statement that, it has been suggested, might have been written by the elders of Ephesus, assuring the readers of this Gospel that it has been written, or caused to be written (cf. 19:19), by the Beloved Disciple, and that they know his testimony is true. With this spare but firm declaration, we shall do well to compare the eloquent proclamation with which the First Epistle of John begins. This stirring word could almost be taken as summarizing the meaning of the Gospel of John.

It was there from the beginning; we have
heard it; we have seen it with our own

eyes; we looked upon it, and felt it with
our own hands; and it is of this we tell.
Our theme is the word of life. This life
was made visible; we have seen it and bear
our testimony; we here declare to you the
eternal life which dwelt with the Father
and was made visible to us. What we have
seen and heard we declare to you, so that
you and we together may share in a common life, that life which we share with the
Father and his Son Jesus Christ. And we
write that the joy of us all may be complete.[65]

1. From an original translation of the Prologue of John's Gospel by the author.
2. 2 *Cor.* iii. 7-13; iv. 6
3. Possibly the earliest Gnostic teacher of whom history gives
us some definite information. He was active c. A.D. 100 in the
area of Ephesus and seems to have propounded a Docetic view
of Christ. The Alogi charged that he was the author of both
John's Gospel and the Apocalypse. This sect (c. 170-180) also
opposed the Montanists.
4. Irenaeus took this literally, possibly because the Gnostics had
made so much of the age of thirty, according to Luke iii : 20.
This was the basis of the thirty aeons in the Divine Pleroma.
5. viii : 56-59
6. The "I am" without a predicate in vs. 58 would have suggested the name of God in the Greek Bible. Thus Ex. iii : 14,
Deut. xxii. : 39, and Isai. xliii : 10. This expression in Greek
occurs five times in John vi : 20, viii: 24,28, xiii : 19; and
xviii: 6. The NEB in Three of these translates: *I am what I am.*
7. The style followed, I believe, in the oldest codices we possess.
8. *H.E.* iii : 39. Aristion according to *Roman Martyrology* was

one of 72 disciples of Christ. The authority in this record appears to be Papias.

9. iv: 21-24
10. iii : 16-17
11. *Ency. Brit.*, 11th, Ed., Art. John, Gospel of St.
12. *Op. cit.*, I, p. 97
13. *The Community of the Beloved Disciple*, pp. 33-34. Also 31-32.
14. xiv: 8-9
15. *The Shape of the Liturgy*, p. 50. cf. pp 54n, 88-89.
16. *The Gospel According to Luke* (1965), p. 190.
17. Rev. xiii : 8. Av & Rv. This is a literal translation, but most modern scholars seem to think that "from the foundation of the world" goes with the names written in the book of the Lamb that was slain rather than with the Lamb slain. Cf. RV margin, SRV & NEB. The Lamb is a powerful concept and image in Revelation, being used as a title some thirty times. It first appears in v : 6.
18. x : 42-45
19. xxxii : 26-27. Italics supplied.
20. See *supra*, p.424, Footnotes 37 & 38.
21. ix : 38 RV
22. ix : 39-41 RV
23. I The Coming of Christ
    II The Revelation to the World
    III The Revelation to the Disciples
    IV The Conflict of Light with Darkness
    V The Dawn
    VI Envoy
24. x: 30
25. x : 33
26. xi : 53
27. xii : 19
28. Luke xvi: 19-31
29. xix : 38-42 The Roman pound referred to here weighed about 12 of our ounces.

30. xv : 26
31. The five references are xiv : 16-7, 26; xv : 26-27; xvi : 6-11, 12-15.
32. xvi : 15
33. vv : 4-5
34. vs. 11. RSV
35. vs. 24 RSV
36. Clement of Alex., c. 180
37. SRV
38. vv : 56-58. NEB
39. xiv : 1-2
40. xiii : 36-38
41. xiv : 5-8
42. Exodus xix : 16-18. cf. 2 *Cor.* iii : 7-18
43. John iii : 16
44. I John iv.
45. xiii : 31-32 (omitting the intrusive clause absent in many early and good mss.
46. Temple's structuring is a Prologue, Five Acts, and an Epilogue. The Acts are entitled: The Lord Introduced to Various Types of Men; The Lord in Controversy; The Lord among His Disciples; The Conflict of Light with Darkness; and The Dawn.
47. xxii : 53
48. Luke's first saying is absent in some good mss.
49. *Op. cit.*, pp. 202-203
50. Exodus xii : 22. See NEB on John xix : 29 for a different reading.
51. Isaish liii : 11.
52. Romans i : 1-4. A direct translation influenced in sentence arrangement by NEB.
53. vv : 3-8. A direct, literal translation.
54. xvi : 6.
55. xx : 17 NEB
56. *The Interpretation of the Fourth Gospel*, p. 438
57. xx : 2

58. v : 8
59. vv : 28-29
60. *Op. cit*, p. 326
61. *Op. cit.*, p. 114
62. *Op. cit.*, p. 191
63. *Op. cit.*, p. 162
64. vv : 18-19
65. i : 1-4 NEB

A Summary Note

The presentation of John the Incarnationist given at length above goes deeply into the Gospel associated with the name of John. While it was not my intention to get into detail in commenting on the Gospel, I realize that I have given the reader in the above essay a commentary in broad strokes as well as a theological summation.

To deal with John and the Johannine problem is to wade in deep water and to feel at times that one almost goes under. Yet there is nothing else associated with Holy Scripture that is more gloriously exciting and worthwhile.

Because the literature on this Gospel is so voluminous and the views taken of it so many and various, it may be of value to draw up in a short, detached note my outlook on John and the Johannine problem and what I have tried to do in treating him as a theologian.

As a youth, religiously inclined and probably unusually serious and devout, I had a great love for the Gospel of John. When I first hit the higher criticism of this book, at the Episcopal Theological School (now Episcopal Divinity School) in Cambridge, Massachusetts, I was quite upset. I believe, on looking back, that for a long time I was in a kind of limbo with regard to John, viewed in the light of modern critical scholarship. At Cambridge I took a course on the Greek text under Dr. William Henry Paine Hatch, a dear friend but a scholar more on the German than on the British model. At Oxford, in England, I did a massive thesis for the doctorate on the doctrine of the Trinity. Though I recognized and registered in this work the importance of John's introduction of the Logos as a concept and basic category, I was not able to feel existentially the meaning of this Gospel for the Trinity and for the Christian vision and the Christian life.

Looking back now over more than fifty years since I first wrestled with this whole issue, I judge that it was the existential sense and experience that was lacking and that was slow in taking hold of and really grasping me. Today—and the long essay I am presenting on John will verify the judgment—I feel grasped and compelled to a unique degree by what John undertook and achieved in his Gospel. I feel again, but more strongly and maturely, the love that I had for this book as a youth. I understand, perhaps have been influenced by Archbishop William Temple's feeling for St. John. In the preface of the first volume of *Reading in St. John's Gospel* (which he sent me as the volumes came off the press), he wrote:

"For as long as I can remember I had more love for St. John's Gospel than for any other book."

In my case the situation is more complex than it was for William Ebor. et Cantuar. He came in the English tradition of Westcott, followed to a great extent by J. H. Bernard, Scott Holland, E. C. Hoskyns, and Charles Raven among others. As an Oxford philosophy don reading theology, he was never exposed severely to critical scholarship in biblical matters. He once told me this himself. Thus he was able to his own satisfaction to see the Gospel according to John as essentially an historical record, shaped to be sure in some degree by time and ripe reflection on the part of the Beloved Disciple, John the Son of Zebedee, but still basically factual.

My fundamental conviction and starting point is quite different. I see the author of the Fourth Gospel, possibly but not certainly John the Elder spoken of by Papias in the present tense after mentioning John the Apostle, as first and foremost a theologian. He was a mystical rather than a systematic theologian and he inherited a tradition rooted, it may well be, in a Christian community whose hero was the Beloved Disciple. In any case I accept the historicity of this special disciple, who came from Jerusalem rather than Galilee and who was of the ruling high-priestly cast that produced Annas and Caiaphas. The reason for this is John 18:15-16. I am also intrigued by the statement of Polycrates, bishop of Ephesus, c. A.D. 190, that John, who lay on our Lord's breast, was a priest who wore the *petalon*.[1] This bishop was a Quartodeciman who got into a dispute with Victor of Rome over the date of Easter. (The Quartodeciman believed this feast should always coincide with Nisan 14, the first day of Passover.)

The overriding Christian concern in the apostolic and subapostolic periods was Christology: who Jesus Christ was and his meaning for the life of man. Paul, apostle to the Gentiles and the first theologian of the Church, is the most striking exemplar of this concern. It explains the comparative lateness of the Gospels and the fact that the faith-interest in them is extremely pronounced. They are written from "faith to faith." In the Gospel of John (his name sticks and is appropriate, just as is Matthew's) this motif is explicit and undisguised. "Now Jesus did many other signs in the presence of the disciples, which are not written in this book; but these are written that you may believe that Jesus is the Christ, the Son of God, and that believing you may have life in his name."[2]

John not only states this motive; it is exemplified throughout the Gospel in evangelical emphasis and concern not only for Jews but for Samaritans, Greeks, and "the world." John's is a universal Gospel as well as "the spiritual Gospel." There is no doubt that his book can be read at two levels: one designed for the intelligent, spiritually minded, seeking Graeco-Gentile; the other for the instructed, com-

mitted Christian churchman or churchwoman. The
latter will grasp at once the church background, even
though church and sacraments are never explicitly
mentioned.

This two-level aspect of John's Gospel explains
its popularity in all ages with the people who might
be called "Spirituals," persons aspiring to find truth
and reality for living, but unanchored or indefinite
and flexible from an ecclesiastical standpoint. The
earliest clear instance of this is the Gnostics, who
emerge in the first half of the second century as a
species of God-seekers: some would say, in the light
of the Nag Hammadi discoveries, as the first generation in the Christian era of existentialists. The Gnostics seem to have had an early affinity for John as
well as Paul; and this could be the reason why the
First Epistle of John was written. In time it was seen,
as we have emphasized above, that John wrote to
vindicate and extend the central Christian tradition,
not to undermine it.

John's position and purpose as a Christian
thinker can be seen by reading simply the first chapter
of his Gospel and setting it alongside the opening section or sections of the other three Gospels. This chapter opens with the immortal Prologue, which is an
index conceptually of what is to follow as narrative
and discourse interspersed. The Prologue among
other important things introduces John the Baptizer,
who is at once and at length made the uncompromising exponent of the Evangelist's Christological posi-

tion. Then, after calling five disciples—a quite
arbitrary number apparently, with one never named
—Nathaniel is intriguingly introduced and made a
spokesman for the Johannine Christology.

Throughout, the gospel is designed, structured,
and developed to present Christ as fully divine, perfectly one with the Father, and the Savior of the
world. *Kai Theos en ho Logos.* "And the Word was
fully divine."[3] "No one has ever seen God, but God
only-begotten who is in the bosom of the Father, he
has disclosed him."[4] "God sent not his Son into the
world to condemn the world, but that the world
through him might be saved."[5]

John, to be sure, brings his prologue to a climax by the stupendous affirmation of 1:14: "So the
Word became flesh; he came to dwell among us, and
we saw his glory, such glory as befits the Father's
only Son, full of grace and truth."[6] He is completely
serious about the humanity of Jesus; there is no question of a docetic unreality. He has introduced what
is to be another Gospel, a narrative account of the
man Christ Jesus who frequently refers to himself
as the Son of man. He eats and drinks, walks and
talks, grows thirsty after a long walk, knows love and
compassion, weeps on one occasion, and takes part
in angry disputations, though it is not clear that he
himself becomes angry. He does demand, "Which
of you convicteth me of sin? If I say truth, why do
ye not believe me?"[7]

Jesus' ministry follows a rough pattern, not unlike the Synoptic sketch, except that the movements are more rapid and the chronology more elaborated in an enlarged time scale. He is in and out of Jerusalem, and much attention is paid to successive Jewish feasts. The dominant framework up to the Passion seems to be the Seven Signs, all miracles more or less paralleling Synoptic occurrences except for the first Sign, the turning of water into wine at the Cana wedding.

The Passion in John is like yet very unlike the other three Passion narratives. It is the drama, not of a victim in any sense, but of a sovereign perfect in majesty who is on top of the situation at every point. Instead of being judged, it seems that he, the Christ, the King of the Jews, is rendering judgment —even on the proud Roman, Pilate. Christ goes to the cross, willingly, almost proudly, fully cognizant of the glory of the sacrifice he is offering in the name and for the sake of Love, the perfect love that he shares with the Father and which is the reason for his coming into the world. He dies, but there is no indication that it is a difficult or a torturous death. He is buried but even here there is a royal note. Nicodemus, a ruler of the Jews, joins Joseph in performing this sacred rite, bringing as his tribute and gift a hundred Roman pounds of myrrh and aloes mixed.[8]

John like the other evangelists has written of a human being, the man Christ Jesus. But there is an overriding purpose in all that he has set down and in the way he has set it down. He never forgets that he is writing about one who is the incarnation of God.

Jesus was a human being; he was flesh and blood. But he was so much more. He was very God of very God. His origin was in heaven, or rather he had no origin. He was in the beginning, the personal Word going forth from the Father, the Father in him as he was in the Father. He came down from heaven to become man and to rescue and save man. At all times and in all ways, he faced man not as another man, but from the divine side, as the Son sent by the Father whose words were in effect those of the Father, as God in man.

In short—and this is the crux—John was a theologian. He was a mystical theologian, perhaps a prophet-theologian on the model of Deutero-Isaiah; but he was a theologian who used the unique literary genre of the Gospel as the vehicle of theological writing. With consummate artistry he uses the Gospel form, with the tradition that has come to him through the Beloved Disciple or otherwise and the examples of Mark and Luke, which he has read though he may not have had them before him as he wrote, as a way of driving home with living power the being and mission of Jesus the Christ, the Son of God.

I believe that John is at the apex of the New Testament and probably of Christian literature for all time. In a sense it is impossible to go beyond him. The Evangelist of *the Word*—he has, under God, given us a *final word*. But it is the word of a thinker, of a theologian who has pondered deeply on God and man, and on Christ the God-man who mysteriously came and continues to come as the God-in-man who is the Saviour of the world.

We need the other Gospels; we need Paul's letters, and the Epistle to the Hebrews; indeed, we need the New Testament in its fullness and we must have the Old Testament if we are to know the living God that the New Testament assumes. But it is in John's Gospel that we shall see most clearly and feel most powerfully the purpose of God in sending his Son down into our lost world, and we shall have the deepest insight into the meaning of the history that the Epistles and Gospels together narrate, even though John consciously transmutes the history as he sets it down.

The Christ of Christian faith is for me the composite figure yielded by the New Testament as a whole. There is nothing comparable to this figure in beauty and appeal. It is small wonder that the Gnostics desired this Saviour, and sought to annex him for their pantheon, even as they rejected the background whence he arose.

From the point of view of imagery, the contribution of Revelation or the Apocalypse to the vision of the Christ is very great. Paul, Apollos, and the Synoptic Evangelists all contribute indispensably. But I believe that John as a thinker is the clearest and most acute, and that without him Christ would not have become the hinge of history and the supreme influence in continuing civilization. I had reached this conclusion about John the theologian independently in my pilgrimage, but I was happy to learn that Professor C. K. Barrett had in 1952 described the Evangelist who wrote John 1-20 as "a bolder thinker (than John the son of Zebedee who had written the Apocalypse), and one more widely read both in Judaism and Hellenism" and as "perhaps the greatest theologian in the history of the Chruch."[9]

It is this conviction respecting John the Evangelist, reached before reading Barrett, that led to the writing of the present book.

1. A word used in the Septuagint of Exod. 28:36 for the gold plate (rosette in NEB) fastened in front of the high priest's mitre.
2. John 20:30-31.
3. Ibid., 1:1.
4. Ibid., 1:18. Following Eberhard Nestle's Greek text, R.V. Margin, and William Temple.
5. Ibid., 3:17.
6. Ibid., 1:14 (NEB).
7. Ibid., 8:46 (RV).
8. Ibid., 19:39. A Roman pound was about twelve ounces.
9. Barrett, *Gospel According to St. John*, p. 114.

Chapter Eight
The Crucified God

Nothing in history is more remarkable, even fantastic, than the story of the Cross. For Roman justice, often rough but real as an intent and a sentiment, crucifixion was the accepted mode of capital punishment. Only Roman citizens—a privileged class in the empire—were exempt from this cruel and barbarous form of punishment. As a Roman citizen, Paul could not be crucified, and was martyred, we believe, under Nero by beheading.

There is no actual record of Paul's death, but he appealed to Caesar and to Caesar in Rome he had to go. We know that he got to Rome and lived under light confinement for a period of at least two years. We are certain that nothing was heard of him after the Neronian persecution, so undoubtedly he died a martyr's death in Rome under Nero.

Peter was not a Roman citizen, and for this reason he met the same fate as his Master a generation earlier. The tradition of Peter's crucifixion is a strong one, and it involves an especially painful though mercifully short form of crucifixion. According to tradition, Peter asked to be nailed to the cross with his head down, since he had denied the Lord and was therefore unworthy to die in the same manner as Jesus.

Death by torture is a terrible thing, and the human being naturally quails before it. A great Anglican churchman, architect of the First Prayer Book to whom every Episcopalian in whatever land is deeply indebted, Thomas Cranmer, Archbishop of Canterbury and godfather to Elizabeth I, was sentenced to die by burning in the reign of Mary Tudor, known to history as "Bloody Mary." Cranmer, who as a person was curiously reminiscent of Peter the Apostle, knew that the penalty for heresy was burning. In his weakness, dreading such a sentence, he gave up disputation with his theological accusers, some imported from Cambridge. The trial was held at Oxford in St. Mary's University Church. He ceased to argue and accepted the humiliation and dishonesty of total recantation. He renounced the Protestant faith by which he had lived and written, and accepted anew the Pope and Roman Catholicism.

But then he found out that his theological judges had been playing with him, like a cat with a mouse. There was no chance of his escaping the penalty of burning. Accordingly, he made what reparation he could: he boldly recanted his recantation. And then when he was carried down to the flames, he put out his right hand and said: "This shall burn first, for it signed the recantation." Thus Cranmer, like Peter a very human man of God not naturally courageous, died a good death, joining the host of true heroes in all ages.

We know that Peter was crucified, for in the Gospel of John in chapter 21, often called an appendix or epilogue, the risen Christ says to Peter after his three-fold commissioning as Shepherd of the sheep: "And further, I tell you this in very truth: when you were young you fastened your belt about you and walked where you chose; but when you are old you will stretch out your arms and a stranger will bind you fast, and carry you where you have no wish to go."[1]

At the time of Jesus' death, then, the cross was a sign of shame and ignominy. There was nothing holy or exalted about it. When Peter and Paul and other apostles began to preach about a crucified Saviour, it was a wonder and a paradox most curious. St. Paul was not just talking, he was speaking out of white-hot experience when he said, writing for the first time to the Christians at Corinth, a Greek city:

> The word of the cross to those who are perishing is foolishness, but to us who are being saved it is the power of God . . . .

> Where is the wise man? Where is the scribe? Where is the debater of this age? Has not God made foolish the wisdom of the world? . . . .

> For Jews demand signs and Greeks seek wisdom, but we preach Christ crucified, a

stumbling-block to Jews, and folly to Gentiles, but to those who are called, both Jews
and Greeks, Christ the power of God and
the wisdom of God.[2]

The crucial concept for Paul and all the first
Christians was the Messiah of Israel—the vicegerent
of God who would be raised up and come as a second and greater David to deliver the people of God
from bondage and establish them in a mighty earthly
kingdom, embracing many and perhaps ultimately
all peoples. Here many prophecies about a Messiah
come in.

This was the Messiah whom the Jewish people
generally predominantly expected. This is why we
find in the first three or Synoptic Gospels many references to David and the son of David. It explains the
first line and the first page of the New Testament.
It is no accident that the Gospel according to Matthew, the most Jewish, in flavor and awareness, of
the Gospels, begins as follows:

The book of the genealogy[3] of Jesus Christ,
the son of David, the son of Abraham.

The genealogy is then traced out through[4]
generations. Only then does the Evangelist proceed
to narrate the miraculous birth of Jesus Christ.

The Davidic Messiah does not seem to interest
Paul. He mentions David in connection with Christ
only once, in Romans where he speaks of him as
descended from David according to the flesh but

designated Son of God with power, according to the
Holy Spirit, by his resurrection from the dead. It is
also most striking that John excises all references to
David in his account of the triumphal entry into
Jerusalem and that the only reference to David in his
Gospel is in 7:42. It is the last day of the Feast of
Tabernacles and Jesus cries aloud that he is the foun-
tain of living waters. This causes people to speculate
as to his being a prophet or the Messiah. A third party
says, ''Surely the Messiah is not to come from
Galilee? Does not Scripture say that the Messiah is
to be of the family of David, from David's village of
Bethlehem? Thus he caused a split among the
people.''[4]

The explanation of Paul and of his Christ-
mysticism begins with his confrontation by the living
risen Christ on the Damascus Road. There was, as
it happened, a messianic and eschatological category
waiting and ready for use by him in his need to think
out the meaning of Jesus the Christ, crucified and
risen. This was the figure of a heavenly Son of man
in the Book of Daniel and the Ethiopic Book of
Enoch.

There were thus two views of the future existing side by side in the Jewish world in the time of
Jesus and Paul. The Zealot party represented one in
an extreme form—the Davidic dream. In Schweitzer's view Jesus lived entirely in the Son of man
eschatology of the Books of Daniel and Enoch.[5]
Whatever be the full truth about Jesus' view of him-

self, there can be no doubt that Paul worked out an amalgamation of Jesus as he knew him in the Church and personally with the heavenly Son of man, conceived as a kind of superangel in a special relation of sonship to God the Father.

This Christ or Messiah, known in the Church as Lord and Son of God, had out of his great love come down to earth to die for the sinful and needy race of men. Paul could never get over the emotion, the answering response of grateful love, that this realization of Christ's death on the cross aroused in him. This, I believe, was the deepest motivating factor in Paul's Christianity. It was the power, too, behind his apostleship. It gave him the drive and energy, the tenacity and tenderness, that are possibly unique in human biography.

But Paul recognized the difficulty, the scandal, the seeming absurdity of the cross. That God's man, his chosen one, the heir of heaven existing "in the form of God," should have been tried and executed, crucified, as a criminal! This was not easy to accept, to believe, to preach.

Nevertheless, Paul preached Christ crucified and Christ risen from the dead. And the word of the Gospel met with encouraging success, especially in the wide world of the Gentiles—in the cities rimming the Mediterranean Sea, cities under Roman rule but Greek and cosmopolitan in culture. It was a religious time as we have seen earlier in this book. It was one of the great salvation ages. Everywhere people were looking and seeking; and faiths were rampant. It was an era of "gods many and lords many."[6]

The future of Christianity, in the providence of God, lay not with the Jews of Palestine, not even with the Israel of the Dispersion, but with the pluralistic world of the Roman Empire. To this the New Testament bears cumulative witness, culminating in the Gospel of John. In the second century this trend became so pronounced that it came dangerously near getting out of hand. Graeco-Gentiles, emancipating themselves from the tutelage of the Law and the Prophets and the recognition of preparatory revelation in the Old Covenant, threatened to swamp the Church.

This crisis, occasioned by the rise of the Gnostics and their spiritual blood-brothers, the Marcionites, represents one of the most fascinating and instructive chapters of Church history, and one of the least understood, because of the paucity of evidence. This period is the *saeculum obscurum*.

It is because of this coincidence of obscurity and intense fascination that the present work was conceived and has been carried through. We are now at the point of attempting to bring into focus the Christological and theological development which is unique to Christianity and which imparted to it the appeal that proved irresistible.

Paul gives us the earliest transcript of Christian history. This fact and the character of his concentration as believer and thinker bear witness to the power

of the Passion of Christ and of his Resurrection, despite the scandal of crucifixion. Paul's constant emphasis on the Spirit, also, is a testimony to the
pneumatic and ecstatic form of Christianity in its first
period.

Soon other, more comprehensive documents of
the Church appeared. The first ones drew on individual and corporate memory—a definition of tradition. They may have been based, as Luke suggests,
and later Papias, on earlier written sources of some
sort. In the first three Gospels we get some biographical information and a great deal of Jesus' teachings,
along with extended accounts both of his Passion and
of his post-Resurrection appearances.

Paradoxically and unexpectedly, we do not encounter a Christology higher than Paul's, though we
do perceive a continuing and progressive centrality
in Christological emphasis. Jesus as Son of God and
Lord sums up the thrust and trend.

This is confirmed by the Acts, covering a wide
gambit, and by Hebrews and Revelation. Hebrews,
written we have guessed by Apollos the Platonist, is
more static and less historical in outlook than Paul.
There is in the lone epistle nothing comparable to the
eschatological-historical sweep of the Apostle in Romans 8 and 1 Corinthians 15. At the same time, in
Hebrews things of time, including the human experience and sufferings of Jesus, are made contributory
to eternal reality. It is by what he experienced in the
flesh that Jesus is fitted to be a perfect High Priest

in the heavens and our Advocate and strong Intercessor at the right hand of God. Moreover, it is by
his shed blood on the Cross that Jesus won forgiveness of our sins and was able to be the Mediator of
a new and eternal Covenant.[7]

At the same time the Christology of this Epistle
is very elevated. In contrast to the prophets, the Son
has spoken definitively in this final age. He is the
express image of the Father, bearing the stamp of his
hypostasis (substance or being). Through him God
created the world, and it is sustained by him. As son
and heir of the universe, he is above all angels and
is the recipient of their worship. However, the Son
appears to have been brought forth in time and is
called "the first-born,"[8] It is only at this point that
Hebrews seems not to have gone as far as John in
his prologue, nor is Christ called specifically God.
Revelation, in which for the most part, the heavenly
Christ is presented under the image of the Lamb,
reflects a very high Christology. The Lamb is worshipped as divine and is at all times beside the One
on the throne. In this "methaphorical theology,[9]
however, the question of the suffering of God is not
raised, nor is there ideational discussion of the relation of the Lamb and the Father. There is the implication of history in Revelation, as in all apocalyptic
writing, and the Lamb is finally all-conquering. It
could be said of the Lamb as Paul says of Christ,
"For he must reign until he has put all enemies under
his feet."[10]

All through this book I have stressed the primacy or ultimacy of John from a Christological and therefore a theological standpoint. Indeed, the growing conviction over a long life that this mystical disciple-theologian faced the final issues raised by the question, What think ye of Christ? is one of the chief reasons for this work, *The First Theologians*.

John's conclusion, that in Christ Jesus we have to do with God personally—not at one or two removes or by proxy—is the end of the road. You cannot carry thought any further. You can focus on the problems raised by the deity of Christ. The ante-Nicene church did this from the point of view of the divine side. The post-Nicene church wrestled with the problem of his humanity.

It cannot be said that the theologians and bishops of the Church were completely successful in their long, arduous effort of thought. The great monument of this Herculean mental and spiritual enterprise is the Chalcedonian Formula of A.D. 451, now happily printed in the 1979 Book of Common Prayer at the head of the section entitled *Historical Documents of the Church*

It has been suggested that the Chalcedonian Confession does not so much solve the problem as state it comprehensively. The mystery remains and it is inevitable that this should be so. If the nature and personhood of the human being is mysterious, and it is deeply so, how much more helpless are our finite minds in the presence of the infinite mystery of the Being of God!

The effort to penetrate these mysteries and to relate, with philosophical and psychological precision, divine and human natures within the personal unity of a figure who appeared in history, walked and talked among men, lived and died, lay ahead in the future. It would be the fruit of the spread of Christianity widely and deeply in the Gentile world and the rise of a professional, intellectual class of priests trained in the schools of philosophy and able to use the basic terms and concepts evolved by "the master of those who know," Aristotle, and his teacher, Plato.

To this extent Harnack was correct in speaking of the Hellenization of the Gospel. The dogmatic structure of theology was the work of the Greek Christian mind working with the categories of Greek thought, essentially philosophical. But where Harnack went wrong was in his own presupposition, undoubtedly unconscious, a part of the furniture of his mind, as it were, that the Gospel was the teaching of Jesus, recorded in the Synoptic Gospels, about God and man and ethical spirituality and eternal life.

Schweitzer was right in exposing the fallacy of the rationalistic quest of the historical Jesus and insisting, if too narrowly, on the eschatological character of the Christian faith from the beginning, including Jesus its founder and Paul its so-called second founder. The Roman Catholic Modernists, Alfred Loisy and George Tyrrell, shrewdly latched on to this scholarly development and attempted to utilize it apologetically. They saw it as vindicating Catholicism rather than Protestantism via Newman's doctrine of development and as providing a shield behind which Catholic biblical and theological scholarship could be brought into the modern world. These brilliant seers were premature, but they were true prophets of a future day.

The New Testament, as has been emphasized throughout this book, is the mirror of the Church in the first ages, including "the beginning of the Gospel of Jesus Christ, the Son of God."[11] We have been peering, with some attempt at thoroughness into this mirror. What we observe is the church moving intuitively, from a subjective standpoint, and progressively, under the guidance of the Spirit of Truth (the doctrine of John which provides or at least proposes an objective criterion) to positions that will be givens for more systematic, authentic theologizing.

These positions will remain normative. In a sense the Church produced the Scriptures but if the Creed has the right order in confessing the Holy Spirit, the Holy Catholic church, the production involved trial and error, discussion and argument, with final canonical decision. The result was, as the universal Church of the conciliar period fully recognized, a Spirit-directed, authoritative book of the New Covenant which was foundational for reading, teaching, and theologizing or reaching for clear understanding.

"All scripture is inspired by God and profitable

for teaching," writes the Apostle of the subapostolic period in 2 Timothy.[12] Article XX of the Thirty-nine Articles supplies an acute and needed norm for interpreting Scripture.[13] The instructed scribe will take account of it in its totality and avoid an interpretation that is one-sided and repugnant to the general sense.

At the same time there is a basic trend or thrust in the New Testament as well as in the Old. Development is a reality. From this point of view John's Gospel is of decisive importance.

We have spoken of this Evangelist as "John the Incarnationist." He is clear that there was a man named Jesus. There was a Figure in history with a history. He chooses the unique literary genre thrown up by the Christian movement as the vehicle of this theology. He writes a Gospel.

John is firmly anti-Docetic and anti-Gnostic in the face of Hellenizing extremes that have begun to make their appearance in the Ephesian milieu of intersecting religious circles and even in the Church. he is going to apply the realistic phrase *sarx* or flesh in affirming the humanity of the Son of God. He will frequently quote him as using of himself the familiar phrase, "the Son of man." In his entire Gospel he will never use the noun "knowledge," though the verb "to know" will be employed in some form numerous times. Similarly he will speak constantly of believing, but never of faith.

Even so, John begins his Gospel at the opposite pole from the human aspect. He starts out with divinity and daringly associates the creation with the One who comes in the Gospel as Saviour. To gauge properly the audacity and originality of this Evangelist, and to take a reading of his mind as a theologian, it is well to compare his opening words with the introductory portions of the other three Gospels. We have just noted Mark's first sentence, which is followed by the abrupt introduction of John the Baptizer and his Baptism of Jesus in the Jordan River. Matthew begins with the genealogy of Jesus Christ, linking him with David and Abraham. This is introductory to an account of Jesus' birth. Luke, the most literary of New Testament writers, has a personal preface, then plunges at once into birth narratives: the birth of John the Baptizer and the birth of Jesus, with a strong accent on Mary the Virgin.

John's leap from these previous starts is prodigious and is a fair measure of the bold distinctiveness of what is to come in his Gospel. He dares to begin even as the Hebrew Scriptures begin, both in phrase and in accent on creation. Assured of attention by his opening words, he moves to forge a linkage between the creation and the history of revelation and redemption which he is about to unfold in startling detail, centered of course on Jesus Christ, the Lord of the Church. (But the word ''church'' never appears in the Gospel, and ''kingdom'' is used very sparingly.)

One motive for this linkage with creation

through the creative reason and word (the Logos) was the desire of John at the outset to distance himself unequivocally from the outlook and world-view of the Gnostics. For them the world is material and therefore evil; it is impossible that the true and highest God could be the Creator. John, on the contrary, identifies himself and his Gospel with the God who, as he viewed what he had made, is insistently portrayed as seeing everything, including man and woman, as "very good."

The late Bishop Stephen Neill used a diagrammatic scheme that brings out vividly and usefully the verbal relationships between the opening words respectively of the two books. This is his parallel arrangement:[14]

> Genesis
> In the beginning
> God created
> And God said
> Let there be light
> John
> In the beginning
> All the things made
> was the word
> the light was the life of

John is anti-Gnostic. This is a motif of the Gospel, though this is not expressed as explicitly as it is in the First Epistle of John. The Evangelist is also anti-John the Baptizer, not in any personal way, but

in order to refute and make short work of the followers of John who made him the head of a cult in
opposition to the Church and the Church's Lord.
This Gospel also appears to be anti-Jewish; there is
at times a vigorous polemic in it, sometimes against
the Pharisees but usually against "the Jews." Yet
this cannot be anti-Semitic, in the common use of
that phrase today, for John speaks of many Jews that
believed and followed Christ. Much is made of
Nathaniel, "an Israelite without guile," and the
Beloved Disciple, and all the other disciples are Jews.
To the woman of Samaria at the well of Jacob, Jesus
says without qualification that "salvation is from the
Jews."

Two things are reflected in this Gospel in the
anti-Jewish connection. One is the hostility that has
evidently developed between the Synagogue and the
Church. "A parting of the ways" has come for the
two faiths and their respective adherents and the
mutual antagonism comes out in the conversations
reported between Jesus and "the Jews" and between
the latter and those who believe in Jesus.

But there is a deeper issue and one that goes
to the heart of John's concern and the central purpose of his Gospel. Beginning with the opening verse
of the Prologue, reasserted in the climactic affirmation of the Incarnation in verse 14 and the related
declaration of verse 18,[15] and driven home with many
variations all through the work, is the conviction that
Christ is fully divine. He is both Lord and God. He

is perfectly one with the Father, not only mystically and spiritually, but metaphysically. The words that he says, the works that he does, are the Father's words and works. No one has ever seen God, but he who sees the Son sees the Father also.

This unity of will, love, and being carries through the entire life and career of the Incarnate Son. It is not affected by the crucifixion and death of Jesus. Indeed, the intent and meaning of the Cross is that it is a divine sacrifice, the ultimate expression of the divine love. It is not until this event that the divine glory is fully revealed and made known to all men for all time. "Now is the Son of man gloried and God is glorified in him. God will also glorify him in himself; and he will glorify him now."[16]

This remarkable and to me most thrilling statement is followed by his giving his disciples "a new commandment": "love one another; as I have loved you, so you are to love one another."[17] Then after inserting three chapters of farewell discourse (somewhat illogically but logic seems of little import in such a work as this Gospel), the same theme is taken up again in the incredible High Priestly Prayer of chapter 17. Here Jesus is indeed glorified and all devout Christians with him. All, in all ages, have felt that here John's Gospel rises to its supreme height.

> After these words Jesus looked up to heaven and said: 'Father, the hour has come. Glorify thy Son, that the Son may

glorify thee. For Thou hast made him
sovereign over all mankind, to give eternal life to all whom thou hast given him.
This is eternal life: to know thee who alone
art truly God, and Jesus Christ whom thou
hast sent.
'I have glorified thee on earth by complet-
ing the work which thou gavest me to do;
and now, Father glorify me in thy own
presence with the glory which I had with
thee before the world began.'[18]

These are the words that John in the Spirit gives
the Son of God as he goes to betrayal, arrest, arraignment, torture, and nailing on a cross. They are intended as history, as part of the transmuted history
of the life and death of the man Christ Jesus who
was God incarnate. The whole story is viewed as of
one piece, like the seamless robe for which the Roman soldiers drew lots. There is no transfiguration
on the mount as there is no searing agony in a lonely
garden and no dreadful, despairing cry as of a soul
forsaken and suffering the torments of the damned
for sinners. Instead, the whole Gospel is of a tran-
figured Son trailing clouds of glory and bringing the
perfect love of Heaven down to sinful earth—the love
that the Son had with the Father before the world
was, and still has, for there can be no breaking of
that Divine communion.

The one touch of human realism, of the breaking through of pain and after that of relief mingled

with satisfaction and even a note of triumph, is on the cross when Jesus asks for a drink. "I am thirsty," he says. When someone presumably a soldier, filled a sponge with sour wine (the usual drink of the soldiers), put it on a javelin and handed it up to his mouth,[19] he received it, then said, "It is accomplished" and, bowing his head, gave up his spirit.

A final feature of the Passion according to John was that it was unnecessary to hasten his death by breaking his legs, as frequently happened. Thus Psalm 34 was fulfilled: "Not a bone of him shall be broken." Then a soldier thrust his spear into Jesus' side, making sure that he was dead, and "there came out blood and water."[20] Thus in John's profound way, we get the symbolism of the healing waters of baptism and the life-giving blood of the Eucharist, flowing out of the side of the crucified God. These meanings would be evident to the faithful as they read, but not to uninitiated readers.

Such was "the Passion of my God," as Ignatius, bishop of Antioch, would express it in A.D. 108, writing to the Roman Christians while he is waiting in their city for martyrdom and desires nothing to interfere with this crowning moment of his life.[21] It is not certain that Ignatius knew John's writings, though the two have a good deal in common except on the subject of church order and the threefold hierarchical ministry.

Ignatius certainly knew Paul, who had a less advanced Christology and who clearly states at the beginning of the Epistle to the Romans that it is by the Resurrection that Christ was designated the Son of God with power according to the Spirit of holiness. The Passion and Death of Christ are central also in Paul's Christianity, though it is the fact and not any particular description or account that he emphasizes.

There are four accounts of the Passion. Mark's is the earliest. It is direct, succinct, and relatively short. He gives as the only word from the Cross the awful cry of dereliction and says that Jesus uttered a loud cry just as he breathed his last. The crucifixion, he tells us, began at the third hour (9:00 A.M.) and lasted six hours. From the sixth until the ninth hour (when Jesus cried with a loud voice, "Eloi, Eloi"), "there was darkness over the whole land." This, along with the impact of the whole scene and the Person crucified, are what presumably caused the centurion (the officer in charge) to say, "Truly this man was the Son of God."[22]

Mark also states that the curtain of the temple was torn in two, from top to bottom. At the beginning, when the principals reach "Skull Place," he tells us that the soldiers offered Jesus drugged wine to drink, but he declined it.

Matthew follows Mark closely, except for adding that at Jesus' death there was a strong earthquake that caused rocks to split and many tombs of saints to open, so that their bodies were raised as they appeared to many after Jesus' resurrection.

Luke principally adds the account of the repentant thief and omits the cry of dereliction, substituting three "words" from the Cross. Except for the lamentation of the women, like a chorus in classic drama, the general effect of Luke is a toning down of the terror and strangeness of the scene. He alters the comment of the centurion, making him "praise God" and say, "Certainly this man was innocent!"[23]

John's account, as we have seen, is independent and different in what Jesus says from the cross. Also, it is surely notable that Jesus was able to bear his own cross to "Skull Place" and that all physical accompaniments that in the Synoptic accounts add so dramatically to the terror and the tragedy are excised. John's sketch is devoid of all suggestion of "the pathetic fallacy" favored of poets and tragedians of all times. As far as he is concerned, Nature smiles upon what is happening; she is in sympathy with the God of nature in the mighty act of love that he is performing.

In a word, John's approach to the event of Good Friday is one of understatement, of *meiosis* as the Greeks would say, rather than of building up the terror and pity of the human drama. The reason, I believe, for this is his controlling theological conviction that, in the Passion as in the Life, God is the ultimate subject and actor. It is God in the person of the Incarnate Word who is crucified, giving his life for the life of the world and making the supreme sacrifice so that men may know the greatness of his love and believe and love in turn.

This is the true and final glory. It is also the distinctive and absolute mark of Christianity as a religion, transcending both Hebraism and Hellenism, the two traditions from which Christianity drew and continues to draw.

"A crucified God" was a contradiction both to Jews and to Greeks, but it proved to be the power of God and the wisdom of God in universal and all-conquering appeal as the decades, centuries, and ages passed. Today, as much as ever, perhaps more than ever, only a nail-torn God can succor a suffering, disillusioned, and very uncertain humanity.

Here in life's chaos make no foolish boast
    That there is any God omnipotent
    Seated serenely in the firmament,
And looking down on men as on a host
Of grasshoppers blown on a windy coast,
    Damned by disasters, maimed by mortal ill,
    Yet who could end it with one blast of Will.
This God is all a man-created ghost.

But there is a God who struggles with All,
And sounds across the worlds his danger-call.
    He is the builder of roads, the breaker of bars,
The One forever hurling back the Curse —

The nail-torn Christus pressing toward
the stars,
The Hero of the battling universe.

Edwin Markham, long remembered and universally hailed for his poem *The Man with the Hoe*,
reflects in this sonnet entitled ''The Nail-torn God''
a mood and judgment that have been prominent in
a period of world wars, dropping of atom bombs,
the Jewish holocaust, and insensate slaughter and
cruelty on a scale without precedent. Army chap-
lains, parish priests, plain people, and even theologians turned away from abstractions such as
Divine Impassibility to a suffering God.

A conspicuous example was G. A. Studdert-
Kennedy, the most famous padre of the British Army
in World War I. Known as ''Woodbine Willie'' by
the troops to whom he passed out cigarettes and gifted
as preacher and poet, he exerted a wide influence
on a whole generation. His book of poems, *The
Sorrows of God* became a classic. Such different but
representative men as H.R.L. ''Dick'' Sheppard,
Charles Raven, and William Temple were deeply
affected by Studdert-Kennedy.

It was my privilege to hear and meet him in
Indianapolis, just after Christmas 1923. He was one
of the featured speakers at the Student Volunteer
Convention. (Twelve years later William Temple
addressed a similar gathering.) I do not remember
the details nor all of the conversation, but I encountered Studdert-Kennedy somewhere in a hall and we

talked in front of a window. In the clear light which thus came in, I could see him well. I have never got over the impression his eyes made on me. They seemed to be deep wells of sadness, responding to and marked by the sorrows of God. I should add that the impression he left on a very green and impressionable lad of 18 was of a very human and understanding person. Three years later, I met Charles Raven, handsome, magnetic, and articulate; and I remember that one of the subjects we discussed was Studdert-Kennedy, his personality and influence.

The church in the third century condemned the heresy of Sabellius for, among other things, its "Patripassionism"—that the Father suffered. Despite the Cross and the dogma of the deity of Christ, orthodox Christianity accepted and has ever held to the impassibility of God. In my theological salad days, as a young professor, I was wont to champion this doctrine. From a logical point of view, there is a good deal to be said for it. How could God die? How could he for that matter, know hunger or thirst, affection or pain? In a word, if he is changeless in his eternal, transcendent perfection, how would it be possible for him to experience suffering, as human beings universally must experience it?

I considered that the classical doctrine of the two natures of Christ was sound and that, although their union in one persona and hypostasis was an ineffable mystery, strictly incomprehensible, the distinction of natures was the clue to the conjunction of passion and impassion or impassibility in the being of the Incarnate Word. I went further and tried to transpose the *enhypostasia* of Leontius of Byzantium (c.A.D. 610) into a unipersonal frame comprehending layers of consciousness. Ultimately, the human consciousness might rise to the realization of its ultimate oneness in and with the divine consciousness, as Jesus in John remembered the glory he had had with the Father before the world was.

The details are unimportant, even if I could be sure I remembered them accurately. They do illustrate the problem, and the impossibility of any clear grasp by our minds of the being of God. The divine impassibility does stand for a truth. Was it Karl Barth who once said, You cannot get God by shouting man with a loud voice?

God is other, transcendent, essentially unchanging and unchangeable, eternal, and, in some sense, infinite. This truth must be conserved in all our thinking. But so must other truths: God's goodness and his love, his relation to what we recognize as the highest values of human persons—sacrifice, servanthood, forgiveness, understanding: in a word, agape, which we learn from Christ who is one with the Father.

The logic and ultimate bent of impassibility can be seen perfectly in Aristotle: a God so perfect in reason and interior perfection that he is fulfilled in eternal self-contemplation and does not know or need to know that there is a world, though the world is moved by its *eros* for him. The same problem exists for Plato, though he knew a great deal about love, as the Symposium shows, and was concerned about improvement and realizing justice and goodness in human affairs. William Temple, in an early book called *Plato and Christianity* (1916), concluded that with regard to two fundamental problems, the character of God and the destiny of man, "Plato comes curiously near the Christian position." Even in the Republic, he goes on, justice is changed from "anything like a selfish claim of rights into an unselfish rendering of service." But the one thing Plato falls short in is his entire failure to appreciate the excellence of sacrifice. Love goes beyond justice even at its noblest, for "love finds sacrifice its most natural expression and does not stop to balance up the good abandoned and the good secured, for it knows that in itself, active in sacrifice as it is, it has a value greater than either."[24]

What, however, of the God of Judaism? He is the living God, anthropomorphically conceived in many respects, and very different from the impassible, abstractly removed and transcendent pure Being, in which the Greek tradition ended. Yet the Cross was a stumbling-block for the Jew, even in relation to his Messiah; and though love is evidently an attribute of the God of Israel, there is no evidence indicating the ability of Judaism to say, God is Love, in the manner of a Christ-centered Christianity.

The Law has something to do with this. The

God of Judaism remains a God of the Law. Exclusivity of Jewish consciousness and identity is another factor. Love by its very nature must overleap all boundaries; it must reach out to all nations and races—indeed to all creation—the animal world as well as the human.

Interpretation of the Old Testament would come in here. The early Christians had this library of books for their Bible as much as the Jews; the first Christian apologetic is argument from and over the Law, the Prophets, and such writings as the Psalms and Job. Jesus himself was nourished on the Old Testament Scriptures and drew much of his teaching and—we are bound to believe —a great deal of the inspiration for his recasting and reconstruction of the meaning of Messiahhood from the scriptures of his people. Without the Servant Songs of Deutero-Isaiah there could not have been a Jesus Christ.

One must add that the general form and content of the God-concept taken over and adhered to by the early Christians was, naturally and inevitably, that of the Old Testament at the highest stage of its development. There is little independent thought about God in the New Testament, save as Christology comes in together with the powerful pneumatism or Spirit-centered consciousness of the first Christian age. Gradually there is modification, as we can see in Paul, Hebrews, 1 Peter, and the Johannine writings, including Revelation. But the modification is mainly toward a plural manifestatión of God and a trinity of *personae*, expressive of the sense of God's purposeful activity, out of his Love, for the redemption of the world and the salvation of all men.

This brings us back to the scandal and the power of the Cross and the role of the crucifixion of Christ. Inseparable from this—and from his role in the Christian cultus or worship as Lord and Saviour, Lamb and Son—is Christology, the question of the meaning of Christ and of the identity of the bringer of such meaning and reality.

Thus we are brought to the pivotal role of John and the answer—inevitable as we look at the story backwards—he gave to the mystery of the nature and person of Christ. Only God could do what Christ did! Only God could be what Christ was!

Thomas was right in his spontaneous utterance when he had felt the nailprints on the Lord's hands and put his hand in his side. All Thomas could say—and it was everything—was: "My Lord and my God!"

There is a stanza in Charles Wesley's great Advent Hymn, *"Lo! he comes with clouds descending,"* which reminds one of Thomas and never fails to move and excite me in a peculiar way. It is the third stanza, as given in The Hymnal of 1940 (Episcopal):

> Those dear tokens of his passion
> Still his dazzling body bears,
> Cause of endless exultation
> To his ransomed worshippers:

> With what rapture
> Gaze we on those glorious scars!

Comparing the American version of this hymn with that of the English *Songs of Praise*, I find several variations. I suspect that the English version is nearer the original, and I find one change that is theologically significant. In the first stanza, the American version of the last line reads: "Christ the Lord returns to reign." The English original, as I surmise, is Johannine, forges a link with Thomas in John, and is more powerful if slightly startling. The stanza entire reads (I presume as Charles Wesley wrote it):

> Lo! he comes with clouds descending,
>> *Once for favoured sinners slain;*
> Thousand thousand saints attending
>> Swell the triumph of his train:
>>> Alleluya!
> *God appears, on earth to reign.*[25]

God, in order to appear, whether at the end of history or at a great moment of *Kairos* (the fullness of time or a juncture of history big with possibilities and crucial for the future), had to elect and form a man. Nor is this too singular, for was not man created in the image and likeness of God?

Thus the Incarnation required man as well as God. This was well understood by John, as it was not by the Gnostics and Marcion, with their repudiation of creation, matter, flesh, and a Dediurge or Creator God who was truly Divine. John did not understand just how such a miracle could be, how God could take manhood or how a man could be God. But he is clear on the facts, as he saw and felt them; and he never deviates from asserting the flesh-and-blood reality of Christ. Indeed, in the eucharistic discourse of Chapter 6, the reality of this aspect of the Son of God is by implication heavily underscored. Similarly, there is no compromise on the passion and death of this strange God-man. Just as in the other Gospels, they are described, stage by stage, event by event, up to the end—the taking down of the Lord's body and its burial on the eve of the Sabbath.

The point, however, that John is most concerned to push and that it has been the foremost purpose of his Gospel to drive home is that God is personally present in Jesus both to act and to be acted upon, to offer the ultimate sacrifice and to receive the worst the misguided and evil men could inflict upon him. In this sense we can say that God carried the cross, that he accepted the scorn and indignities heaped upon him, and that he—the God of the universe—was crucified.

There is a very striking passage in Archbishop Temple's great book in which he makes this point explicit, which it is the distinction of John to be clear about and to emphasize. Temple, of course, sees the Fourth Evangelist as concerned with literal history all the way and so is concerned to harmonize all the records. I cannot follow my great mentor in this view of John, but the important thesis of the Evangelist is not affected.

Temple is dealing with the obvious discrepancy over the bearing of the physical, heavy wooden cross along the dusty roads and up the hill to Skull Place. John says simply that "bearing the cross for himself he went forth to the place of a Skull, which is called in Hebrew Golgotha, where they crucified him and with him two others on this side and on that, and in the midst Jesus." Temple writes, "The Lord goes forth *bearing the cross for himself.* Later he would sink under its weight and they would make Simon of Cyrene bear it after Him (St. Mark 15:21)."

The Archbishop then goes on, most thoughtfully: "He bore it for Himself; when we turn to the spiritual load which it represents, we know that none other can bear this; only God can bear it. And even for Him it seems too great. We must ever keep in mind two thoughts—God the Creator of the universe, which came into being at His word; God the Redeemer staggering beneath a load that crushes him as he goes from Jerusalem to Calvary: so far harder it is to redeem men from selfishness to love than to create the wheeling system of the stars."[26]

In a similar manner we recognize and can only take with the utmost seriousness the material on the human side of the Jesus in the earlier Gospels. There is the richness of his teaching in parables drawn from the countryside and household economy of his background. There is the concern for the sick and the demon-possessed who thronged him, as they still do

proven spiritual healers and some unproven and even
questionable. There is his refusal to let even this concern distract him from his vocation to preach as at
hand the Kingdom of God. Above all, there is the
issue of his messianic call, consciousness, and vocation. Much of this is in hints and by implication.

Of particular importance is the Temptation by
the Devil as narrated by Matthew and by Luke. This
Temptation account has been hailed by the Russian
Dostoevsky as one of the most penetrating and revealing creations in all literature and philosophy. It
is from any point of view an astonishing story. Its
whole point and special Christian value is its bearing on the messiahship of Jesus. What it gears into
is the kind of Messiah he was to be. As we have seen,
the current popular hope and expectation was of a
new and greater David, endowed with supernatural
power, who would not only free Israel but be instrumental in establishing a world-wide kingdom of God.

When John the Baptizer preached the Kingdom
of God and called people to repentance and baptism,
this was what they had in mind. Jesus was John's
cousin, he was of the House of David, and he allowed himself to be baptized, having in this connection a remarkable religious experience connected with
messiahship and sonship. He went into the desert
to brood over this and to think things out. It was then
that Satan made his bid and that Jesus rejected the
dream of worldly power in favor of a kingdom of a
very different sort. Of this kingdom he began to

preach and teach.

> Now after John was arrested, Jesus came
> into Galilee, preaching the Gospel of God,
> and saying, "The time is fulfilled, and the
> Kingdom of God is at hand; repent, and
> believe the Gospel."[27]

We see this with hindsight and from the Christian point of view. But if we could imagine ourselves as contemporaries of Jesus—as Jews and followers of him—how different would our outlook be. The land was teeming with discontent. The Zealots were a strong party. It was not hard to stir up the people. And the kingdom Jesus preached could have different meanings. There is evidence that he did create a vast stir. No doubt the word that he was of the house of David spread, and crowds flocked to hear him. We read of his feeding 5,000 and 4,000 people, and that they wanted to make him king.[28] He had to run away, to cross over the Lake of Galilee, and eventually to leave Galilee, to get away from the people who wanted to enthrone him as king of Israel.

Moreover, there is evidence that in the wider area of the Middle East there was much unrest. The eminent German historian Theodor Mommsen (1817-1903), who in his time knew more about Roman history and the Roman Empire than any other living person, believed that the whole Semitic world, and not merely Judea, was ripe for revolt against Rome.[29] As it was, the Jews rose against the

Romans in A.D. 66 and it took the ablest legions
of Rome four years to subdue this revolt.

The destruction of Jerusalem and the Temple
had a profound effect on both Jews and Christians.
The Jews, however, came back and sixty years later
renewed their war against Rome. This struggle lasted
three years (132-135), and some idea of its magnitude and of the size of the Jewish population alone
may be gauged from the fact that in this revolt,
according to the historian, Dio Cassius, no fewer than
580,000 Jews were slain.

Where the Jews failed, their brother Semites,
the Arabs, succeeded. A simple, unlettered visionary
named Muhammad[30] (569-632) started a desert
movement based on a simple monotheistic creed. In
a generation it had become a powerful political force
and in a century had made itself an empire on a world
scale, stretching from the Indus (in Northwest India)
to the Atlantic. Taking Spain, the Arabs continued
their advance into France but in 732, at Tours, were
hurled back by the Franks under Charles Martel,
"the Hammer of God." It was a close call for Christianity and the Christian civilization yet to be.

The point is that Jesus was a person and a leader
far more gifted than Muhammad. His greatness was
recognized by his disciples and by thousands of his
countrymen who were ready to follow him. Much
of the populace was with him, and he needed only
to say the word to have had a civilian force that could
have overthrown the corrupt ruling class in Jerusalem

and engulfed the Jewish nation and quite possibly the entire Semitic world in flames.

In other words, as Theodore Wedel put it, "There might actually have been born a kind of Jesus-form of Islam six hundred years before Mohammed."[31] This did not happen, for reasons that are spelled out in various ways by numerous observers and writers whom we encounter in the New Testament. The best short commentary on why it did not happen, and on the contrast between Jesus and all other messiahs, is the tenth chapter of John: the parable or allegory of the Good Shepherd.

There is a searing verse in this chapter where Jesus is recorded as saying, "All that ever came before me are thieves and robbers." This verse used to trouble me, as it has troubled many readers of St. John. It need not. The key came to me one day at the Virginia Theological Seminary in the Hitler era, after I had visited Germany in August 1939, following the World Conference of Christian Youth in Amsterdam. In that whirlwind three-week, investigative tour, talking with scores of both ordinary and highly placed Germans, I could not help being impressed with the high morale and abounding general prosperity. To my surprise, too, I found a people in no way cowed or afraid or unwilling to speak their minds. There was no war fever in Germany. The people believed that war would not come. The Fuhrer wills peace, they would say. Even the Danzig question (a city 96 percent German) would not warrant going to war.

It seemed to me, as I left Germany on August 21, that any rational mind or any person who cared about what he had achieved would think twice before he wantonly risked it all in a vast gamble. Hitler had of course thought twice. That is why two days later the news came over BBC at 6:00 p.m. that Hitler had signed a nonaggression pact with Stalin. A week later, just before I arrived in New York, he had unleashed the dogs of war and taken his gamble. He had invaded Poland.

It was against this background that John (10:8) one day leaped up at me from off the page. I realized that Jesus was not talking about teachers, prophets, seers, sages, poets—the great and good of earth—but of messiahs, professed shepherds, rulers who claimed to be lovers of their people. They key was in the word "came" or "come"—in Scripture a messianic word. Nor was the meaning of this stern, seemingly harsh saying confined to pretender-messiahs before Christ. The same, sorry, weary story of political man had continued and in our twentieth century had erupted in a rash of secular messiahs trumpeting secular salvation to the guileless sheeplike masses of their people.

Shortly afterwards, I preached a sermon on this verse and it became a favorite text. Jesus was the good Shepherd, the one who loved his sheep and called them each by name, and was willing to lay down his life for his sheep. He did lay it down. He saw that this was the one thing men could never forget.

But this action was not simply that of a good man, of a well-meaning but mistaken idealist. It was not the tragic fate of a man who was a great religious genius. This is the view of Jesus that a good many people took, up into the second century: the Ebionites, for instance. It was a view widely held in the Enlightenment and since. In our time Middleton Murry wrote a book entitled *Jesus, Man of Genius.* This has been the earmark traditionally of the Unitarian movement. Samuel Taylor Coleridge, the poet, who was for a period a Unitarian minister, being later converted to orthodox Anglicanism, used to say that word "Unitarian" was a misnomer since orthodox Trinitarians believed in the unity of God as much as anyone. The real mark of Unitarianism, he said, was *Psilanthropism* or the view that Jesus was a mere man.

The doctrine of the New Testament is quite different. It is the story of the rising tide of belief that Jesus is Lord. Far from being just another rabbi or even a prophet, he faces men and women from the side of God. He came as a Saviour, as his name Jesus or in Hebrew, Joshua, means. "You shall call his name Jesus, for he will save his people from their sins."[32] "For the Son of man came to seek and to save that which is lost."[33] "For the Son of man also came not to be served, but to serve, and to give his life as a ransom for many."[34] "I have come that men may have life, and may have it in all its fullness."[35]

Clearly this was more than a humam being, though he was that. You cannot worship a mere man, and no man can speak with absolute spiritual authority or assume the prerogatives of divinity. So the early Christians used various names and titles as Christ or Messiah, Lord, Son of God, only-begotten Son, Logos or Word, probably God only-begotten,[36] and "I am."

There are four "I am" passages in John. Three are in chapter 8, which might well be called the "I am" Chapter; the fourth is in 13:19.

The Greek in every case is *ego eimi,* simply "I am." In the case of 8:58, the climactic verse "Before Abraham was, I am," there is no question about the translation or the reference to Exodus 3:14. This verse reads: "And God said to Moses, I AM THAT I AM:[37] and he said, Thus shalt thou say unto the children of Israel, I AM that sent me unto you." (AV)

The other three Johannine verses (8:24, 28, 13:19) have troubled translators. It seems clear that they represent a not too-cryptic allusion to the seminal Exodus verse and the sacred name. The NEB translators abandoned the unclear "I am he" for "I am what I am."[38]

I have emphasized that "I AM" title, since it is perhaps the most unambiguous ascription of deity to Christ in the New Testament. And it would appear to have been intended to leave no doubt in the

minds of either Christians or Jews as to who the
Incarnate One was.

Martin Luther, whose five-hundredth anniver-
sary was celebrated in 1983, was thinking in a manner closely analogous to that of the Evangelist (whom
incidentally he revered above all others), when he
wrote the second stanza of the great Reformation Bat-
tle Hymn, *Ein feste Burg ist unser Gott*. Here it is in
English verse (the German is even stronger):

> Did we in our own strength confide
>   Our striving would be losing;
> Were not the right man on our side,
>   The man of God's own choosing:
> Dost ask who that may be?
>   Christ Jesus, it is he;
> Lord Sabaoth his Name,
> From age to age the same,
>   and he must win the battle.[39]

It is notable in this hymn, as it is in the Gospel
of John, that the man Christ Jesus is in the center
of the picture, in no way displaced by the confession that he is in the fullest sense God. This is the
point at which the New Testament leaves its construction of history and its witness. This is, has ever
been, and will ever be the foundation of the faith and
doctrine of the Christian Church. Understanding
how such a thing can be, and working out the details of as much of the mystery as can be known or
even guessed at by reverent speculation, is another

matter. We are required to confess the faith, not necessarily to understand it in any scientific sense.

Included, as a vital part of the Christian Gospel and the faith of the Church, is recognition of "the Crucified God." This is not a put-down of man, for it is he who had fallen and was unable of himself to save himself. The rescue of humanity, involving both a full revelation and a mighty action, had to be undertaken by the Lord God himself.

In carrying out his plan, it was necessary for God to withhold at first the divine device on which he had hit. If man was really to be reached, the stratagem of surprise had to be employed. To convince man and turn him round, and at the same time leave him free, continuing the providence of noncoercion, was not a light enterprise. In the Epistle to the Ephesians the most Catholic and one of the most mature writings of the New Covenant, the Apostle gives us an inkling of God's secret will and purpose.

> In Christ he chose us before the world was founded, to be dedicated, to be without blemish in his sight, to be full of love; and he destined us—such was his will and pleasure—to be accepted as his sons through Jesus Christ, in order that the glory of his gracious gift, so graciously bestowed on us in his Beloved, might redound to his praise. For in Christ our release is secured and our sins are forgiven through the shedding of his blood. Therein

lies the richness of God's free grace lavished upon us, imparting full wisdom and insight. He had made known to us his hidden purpose—such was his will and pleasure beforehand in Christ—to be put into effect when the time was ripe: namely, that the universe, all in heaven and on earth, might be brought into a unity in Christ.[40]

Even so, the full measure of the secret plan had not yet been disclosed. He who appeared first as a follower of John the Baptizer, then as a teacher and healer extraordinary, and last as a ''pretender'' to the throne of David, hailed by the populace as the king of Israel, had at the critical moment weakly thrown in the towel and given himself up to the infuriated and frightened rulers of his people. They had promptly arranged for his execution by Pilate under Roman law.

All had missed one thing—the divinity dwelling *incognito* in this remarkable yet disappointing son of David. This crucified ''king'' was no mere man, but a divine being in human guise, a God concealed as a man, the creator of all worlds masquerading as a creature.

The stupendous reversal, the recognition of who Jesus really was, did not happen all at once. It could not without overpowering people and destroying their freedom and accountability. The Resurrection was the first sign of reversal and true recognition, but it was limited to chosen disciples and witnesses. It, of course, put the cross of shame in an entirely new light. It gave the friends of Jesus a very different slant on the things he had talked about and had tried to teach them.

Out of the recognition that the Kingdom had indeed come, though not in the form or manner of popular expectation, the Church was born. In the outpouring of the Spirit on Pentecost, the second powerful sign, the Apostles and the gathered assembly of believers in Jerusalem were endued with supernatural energy and enthusiasm. Filled with trust and grateful love and charged with the mandate of the risen Lord to preach the Gospel to all nations and to baptize those who believed, the Apostles could not remain in Jerusalem or even in Judea, but went out further and further with the message of Christ the Lord and of the New Covenant sealed in his blood.

Slowly, steadily, increasingly, ever conscious of the present, guiding Spirit of truth, the recognition of what it all meant grew. We can see much of this in the mirrors provided by the New Testament. The predominance of Christology is the evidence of growing recognition and enlightenment. God the Holy Spirit was leading the church into ever deeper experience and insight.

The climax was the penetration by the church of the Divine Incognito—that God had personally visited his people—that I AM in the person of the

Eternal Word had not only assumed human form and flesh but out of his Infinite Love had given himself up to the Passion and death described in the annals called Gospels. The plot of this mystery play was thus finally disclosed. The climax was the Crucifixion followed by the Resurrection. The denouement was the realization that it was really God whom men had crucified.

What did it mean when Christians realized that God was personally involved in the Passion and death of Christ—that the glory of this sacrifice was his glory, as the love which had prompted it was his love? The answer, I think, is in the First Epistle of John. In this letter, which is really a meditation—a devotion and celebration—the sort of thing a very holy man who had once been the opposite, Dean John Donne, wrote, but in a simpler and more unselfconscious vein—in 1 John we have the final reflective word of the New Testament.

We have its theology—in words of one syllable —blended with its ethic. We have set forth its meaning for the nature of God and the life of man. We also have the unique differential of Christian theism from that of both Jews and Greeks. And the reason is "the Crucified God" of John's Gospel.

To pick out of the first Johannine Epistle one nugget of purest gold, the Evangelist (or his close associate) is exhorting his readers in the spirit of "the new commandment" given by the Lord to his disciples on the night before his Passion. He writes at length on this, noting that everyone who loves is a child of God and knows God, whereas "the unloving know nothing of God." For, he says for the first time, "God is love." Dwelling now on God's love and its relation to us as shown by the imparting to us of his spirit, the writer goes on to a kind of sacred peroration:

> God is love; and he who dwells in love dwells in God, and God in him. This is for us the perfection of love, to have confidence on the day of judgment, and this we can have, because even in this world we are as he is. There is no room for fear in love; perfect love banishes fear. For fear has to do with punishment, and he who fears is not made perfect in love. We love because he loved us first...And this commandment we have from Christ himself, that he who loves God must love his brother also.[41]

Robert Browning, a very Victorian poet in some ways, was profoundly interested in Christianity and particularly in its doctrine of divine love. He was William Temple's favorite poet from Rugby schoolboy days. Undoubtedly he was a strong influence on the great archbishop. In two poems Browning explored the faith of John and of the New Testament against the background of an age that still believed but was beginning to be troubled by doubt, as witness Matthew Arnold and even Alfred Lord Tennyson.

We have already referred to "An Epistle of Karshish," occasioned by an Arab physician's encounter with the resurrected Lazarus in Bethany, near
Jerusalem. At the end of his letter to Abib, his medical teacher and mentor, Karshish in spite of himself breaks out:

> The very God! think, Abib; dost thou
> think?
> So, the All-Great, mere the All-Loving,
> too—
> So, through the thunder comes a human
> voice
> Saying, "O heart I made, a heart beats
> here!
> Face, my hands fashioned, see it in myself!
> Thou hast no power, nor mayst conceive
> of mine.
> But love I gave thee, with myself to love,
> And thou must love me who have died for
> thee!"
> The madman saith He said so: it is strange.

A Death in the Desert is a longer and more involved
work, recording an imaginary last scene in the life
of St. John, accepting him as the Beloved Disciple
who lived to a great age and wrote the works tradition assigns to him. Browning gives him a foreknowledge of the age of philosophic doubt that had
come upon the modern world and made the Apos-

tle his mouthpiece in answering its doubts. The interest of the poem for us lies in the concluding lines
of a disciple who witnessed John's death and helped
bury him and in a postscript that heightens the historical effect by bringing in Cerinthus and his opposed
views. These Browning seems to have based on Tertullian's now abandoned personification of "Ebion"
and the assertion that he was the pupil of Cerinthus.

These are the concluding lines of the witness
to John's death:

> Believe ye will not see him any more
> About the world with his divine regard!
> For all was as I say, and now the man
> Lies as he lay once, breast to breast with
> God.

The postscript that introduces Cerinthus, standing by, contrasts his supposedly Ebionite views[42] with
John's conception of life as love and the joy and freedom many souls have found and are continuing to
find:

> Hundreds of souls, each holding by
> Christ's word
> That he will grow incorporate with all,
> With me as Pamphylax, with him as John,
> Groom for each bride! Can a mere man
> do this?
> Yet Christ saith, this he lived and died to
> do.

Call Christ then the illimitable God.
Or lost!
    But 'twas Cerinthus that is lost.

Poetry can take us a certain distance. Indeed, it is the towering metaphysician, Professor A.N. Whitehead, who has called God "the poet of the world," with tender patience leading it by his vision of truth, beauty, and goodness." Whitehead writes further: "What is done in the world is transformed into a reality in heaven, and the reality in heaven passes back into the world. By reason of this reciprocal relation, the love in the world passes into the love in heaven, and floods back into the world. In this sense God is the great companion—the fellow-sufferer who understands."[43]

It would be rash to suggest that I understand at all fully Whitehead's idea of God. It is also doubtful that whatever it means, it is reconcilable with the biblical doctrine of a living Creator God, who as a matter of fact Whitehead has perceptively described as the rationalization of a tribal deity. It is the image of this God, the God of Abraham, Isaac, and Jacob, and the Father-God of Jesus and the New Testament, which enables us to short-circuit the dogma of Divine Impassibility and at the same time hold to the truth of the Eternity and the Essential Identity and Unchangeableness of God. In our human experience we know something of suffering that ennobles us and leads not to personal disintegration but to deeper maturity. If God is truly and essentially love, suffering cannot be foreign to his being and experience.

There is a prayer of Soren Kierkegaard, the probing Christian and religious genius, who has taught the whole Christian Church to think of the Divine *Incognito* in Jesus, which seems to me a helpful commentary on the subject of passibility and impassibility. It is the prayer he used before an address on "The Unchangeableness of God," delivered in the Church of the Citadel on May 18, 1851.

PRAYER

O Thou who art unchangeable, whom nothing changes! thou who art unchangeable in love, precisely for our welfare not submitting to any change: may we too will our welfare, submitting ourselves to the discipline of Thy unchangeableness, so that we may in unconditional obedience, find our rest and remain at rest in Thy unchangeableness. Not art Thou like a man; if he is to preserve only some degree of constancy he must not permit himself too much to be moved nor by too many things. Thou on the contrary art moved, and moved in infinite love, by all things. Even that which we human beings call an insignificant trifle, and pass by unmoved, the need of a sparrow, even this moves Thee; and what we so often scarcely notice, a human sigh, this moves Thee, O Infinite

Love! But nothing changes Thee, O Thou who art unchangeable! O Thou who in infinite love dost submit to be moved, may this our prayer also move Thee to add Thy blessing, in order that there may be wrought such a change in him who prays as to bring him into conformity with Thy unchangeable will, Thou who art unchangeable!

In conclusion, I wish to share with those friends who are good enough to stay with me to the end of this book—or enterprising enough to turn prematurely to its conclusion—an image and symbol of the Trinity drawn from the longleaf pines of the North Carolina sandhills. There are large, tall trees indigenous to a restricted area that is actually a geological freak. I have seen pine cones as long as nine inches. The land is as sandy as the seashore and the hills are sizable sand dunes. Wells are commonly reached by drilling through as much as 85 feet of sand, yet it is 125 miles to the ocean at the nearest point.

Half a mile from our retirement home alongside the fifteenth hole of a golf course three trees stand out, an arresting sylvan trinity. Ten years ago they caught my attention, and have steadily nourished my meditation on the Christian doctrine of the Triune God. The condition of one of these trees struck me immediately and has caused me to see and feel the reality of "the Crucified God" in a manner and

to a degree previously unknown and not a possibility
for me.

As is well known, the artists of the Christian
East developed a tradition in the portrayal of the
Blessed Trinity different from that adopted as more
or less standard in the West, probably during the
Renaissance. The notation of this fact over many
years and reflection on it prepared me for the impact of the ''sylvan trinity.''

In the West, a typical portrayal of the Trinity
will involve God the Father (a venerable, ancient,
bearded figure) supporting on his lap or in some other
posture Christ on the cross with the Holy Spirit in
the form of a dove going down from the beard of
the Father to touch (light on) the head of the Son.

The Eastern, Byzantine tradition of artistic portrayal is quite different. One surmises that the Cap-
padocian Fathers may have influenced it. The usual
symbol in that part of Christendom is three identical
human figures, vital and young rather than old—
mature would be the word—with the middle figure
identified by a cross, attached or worn in some
manner.

The three trees are sufficiently isolated to stand
out. They are sturdy, with large trunks and abundant, spreading foliage. Two are tall, but the third
has at some time been truncated and its upward
growth has been stunted. If one looks closely, too,
the effect of the central beheading of the tree at some
point in time can be seen. Arms or shoulders on

either side have grown up and out, and the growth is luxuriant, but this tree bears the everlasting mark of a grievous wound.

This luxuriant, generally normal, but stunted tree symbolizes for me "the Crucified God." The tree in the middle, normal and central, stands for God the Father. The third tree is as large and as tall as the one in the middle, and like it except that on its free side it has spread out more luxuriantly all the way up. I call it God the Holy Spirit and quote the wisdom of Solomon: "The Spirit of the Lord filleth the world."[44]

I came upon this trinity of trees suddenly one day and was immediately taken with the symbolism it seemed to convey with propriety and yet originality, especially in the case of the truncated member. Every material symbol is of course limited, and this one might not have continued to have so much meaning if I had not discovered three-quarters of a mile away a curious but most suggestive production of nature also involving three longleaf pines, but this time intertwined most curiously. Closer together and more slender, more a part of a woods, two of the three would have stood normal beside one another, attracting no particular attention, but for the fact that the third leaned like the Tower of Pisa and had grown organically into the other two, at different levels, becoming temporarily one with them but then continuing its independent growth and stature.

Thus one has in this unusual trinitarian symbol a perfect exemplification of what the Greek Fathers called *perichoresis* (literally "going round about") and the Latin Fathers circumincessio ("mutually pervading") or circuminsessio ("mutually resting in or continuing one another"). Interpenetration and coinherence are probably as good English equivalents as any, and mutual indwelling is the most useful way of pointing to or in some mannner describing the reality of the relations of the three Divine Persons who are yet of the same Being or Substance.

The mystical relation that John the Evangelist constantly refers to and sees as the fundamental underlying unity behind distinction of the Father and the Son is well symbolized by "mutual indwelling." Nor can this be conceived of as an exclusive communion or formation, for the Spirit proceeds from the Father and is especially sent as the *Alter Ego* of the departed Son. And beyond this, Jesus in John makes it clear that his disciples are to share in this ultimate communion that is the expression of love. The High Priestly Prayer brings this out explicitly: "Holy Father, protect by the power of thy name those whom thou hast given me, that they may be one, as we are one."[45] And again: "And the glory which thou hast given to me I have given to them, that they may be one as we are one—I in them and thou in me, that they may be perfected into one, that the world may come to recognise that thou didst send me and didst love them as thou didst love me."[46]

All this is in no way to suggest that through symbols thrown up by nature or mystical relationships expressed in the language of love and personal oneness, we solve the problem of conceiving of the Holy and Blessed Trinity. We do not have the mentality to do this. I have wrestled for more than half a century with this doctrine and there was a time—a number of years ago now—when I probably had as much information joined to far-reaching speculation about the Trinity as any person in the English-speaking world. I have lived, however, to realize the abiding truth of St. Augustine's frank admission that one writes about the Trinity not in order to say anything, but in order not to keep silent.

The saint for all his modesty did manage to write at length and to say a great deal of immense suggestiveness and value. For me the great thing that has happened is that the Trinity has become an operational concept: it is a necessity if I am to put together the great lines of biblical experience and thought, including the synthesis of *personae*—fundamental personal manifestations and relationships—which comes to a head in the Gospel of John.

This has given me a sense of liberation and deep satisfaction. The Trinity, instead of being primarily a conceptual arithmetical puzzle or a rarefied scholastic abstraction and technicality, has come to be a living reality, the appropriate and stimulating expression of authentic Christian experience and thought.

Nor do I mean to imply that this metamorphosis of outlook happened all at once. Indeed at Oxford, in the ponderous, immensely ambitious tome I produced, which ran to 550 foolscap pages with about a third of the whole given up to single-spaced footnotes a la Harnack, I attempted to sketch out a scheme of cosmological as well as spiritually operative functions in interpreting the "economic Trinity." Then in the book *The Trinity and Christian Devotion,* commissioned and entitled by William Cantuar, soon after he became Primate of All England (though his Lent series had been begun at York and was initiated by A.D. Lindsay, the Master of Balliol, with his arresting volume, *The Two Moralities),* I made a considerable break with the central ontological conclusion of the Oxford dissertation. So the existential process of which I am speaking was a stretched-out affair.

As I put down my pen, I think of a statement by an Oxford theologian, the Rev. Principal Nathaniel Micklem, which over the years has influenced me both doctrinally and devotionally. It is this:

> Therefore the whole Christian "story" is epitomized in the triumphant declaration of the believing Church that Father, Son, and Holy Ghost together are worshipped and glorified, one God blessed for ever. Nor can any man deny this confession and accept the "story" which is the Gospel, the Christian revelation.[47]

Accordingly, I find myself often saying and praying, not as a substitute for the conventional *Gloria Patri* but as a helpful variant, this form of words:

> Glory to the Father and to the Son and to
> the Holy Spirit, one God, blessed for ever
> and ever. Amen.

1. John 21:18 (NEB).
2. 1:18,20,22-24.
3. RV margin, SRV. The AV read "generation"; the NEB reads "table of descent."
4. John 7:41-43 (NEB).
5. Schweitzer, *Mysticism of Paul the Apostle,* p. 79.
6. 1 Cor. 8:5.
7. Heb. 9:12,15,22; 10:19.
8. Ibid., 1:6, also 5:5.
9. Cf. the recently published *Metaphorical Theology* by Sallie McFague (Fortress Press).
10. 1 Cor. 15:25.
11. Mark 1:1.
12. 2 Tim. 3:16.
13. Quoted supra., Chapter 4, p.181.
14. Neill, *Jesus Through Many Eyes,* p.144.
15. The original reading of this verse may well be: "No one has ever seen God; God only-begotten who is in the bosom of the Father, he has disclosed him."
16. John 13:31-32. A composite translation; cf. RV and NEB note.
17. Ibid., 13:34 (NEB).
18. Ibid., 17:1-5 (NEB).
19. Ibid., 19:29 (NEB, see note).
20. Ibid., 19:34.
21. Ignatius, Ad. Rom. vi. 3.
22. Mark 15:39.

23. Luke 23:47.
24. Temple, *Plato and Christianity* (1916), pp.87, 91.
25. Italics mine, showing original of altered lines.
26. Temple, *Readings,* vol. II, p. 365.
27. Mark 1:14.
28. It is John who specifically records this.
29. My attention was called to this historian by the late Dr. T.O. Wedel, who in his little classic *The Drama of the Bible* throws out the idea of a possible earlier parallel with Islam had Jesus consented to be a warrior-Messiah.
30. I was tutored in the spelling of the Prophet's (Messenger's) name in 1955 by Sir Muhammad Zafrulla Khan of Pakistan, an eminent and devout Muslim layman as well as a prominent statesman and international jurist.
31. Wedel, *Drama of Bible*, p. 67.
32. Matt. 1:21.
33. Luke 19:10.
34. Mark 10:45.
35. John 10:10 (NEB).
36. 1:18.
37. Cf. NEB: "God answered, 'I AM; that is who I am.' "
38.   Cf. Moffat's rendering "who I am" in all three instances. He seems, however, to have muddled badly 8:58.
39. Mit unser Macht ist nichts gethan,
Wir sind gar bald verloren;
Es streit fur uns der rechte mann,
Den Gott hat selbs erkoren.
   Fragst du, wer der ist?
Er heisst Jhesus Christ,
Der Herr Zebaoth,
Und ist kein ander Gott,
Das Felt mus er behalten.
40. Eph. 1:4-10 (NEB).
41. 1 John 4:16-19,21 (NEB and RSV).
42. "It will probably always remain an open question whether

his fundamentally Ebionite sympathies inclined him to accept Jewish rather than Gnostic additions.'' John Murray, *A Dictionary of Christian Biography and Literature,* (London, S.V. ''Cerinthus.'' 1911).

43. Whitehead, *Process and Reality,* pp.490, 497.

44. 1:7.

45. John 17:11 (NEB).

46. Ibid., vv. 22-23. William Temple's translation: *Readings,* vol. II, p. 326.

47. Nathaniel Micklem, *What Is the Faith?* p. 133.